NORMAN NICHOLSON
THE WHISPERING POET

BY THE SAME AUTHOR

Non-Fiction

Margaret Cavendish: A Glorious Fame
Christina Rossetti: Learning not to be First
A Passionate Sisterhood: the Sisters, Wives and Daughters of the Lake Poets
Catherine Cookson: The Biography
Seeking Catherine Cookson's Da
Katherine Mansfield: The Story-Teller
Margaret Forster: A Life in Books
The Lives of Others (an anthology of life-writing)

Fiction

The Sun's Companion
Three and Other Stories

Poetry

Unwritten Lives
Not Saying Goodbye at Gate 21

NORMAN NICHOLSON

THE WHISPERING POET

KATHLEEN JONES

The Book Mill

© Kathleen Jones 2013

The Book Mill
www.thebookmill.com

Book design and typesetting
by Neil Ferber, The Book Mill
printed and bound in Great Britain by
CPI Antony Rowe, Chippenham and Eastbourne
A CIP record for this book is available from the British Library

ISBN 978 0 9574332 4 3

The right of Kathleen Jones
to be identified as author of this work
has been asserted in accordance with
the Copyright, Designs and Patents Act 1988

The Book Mill is an imprint of
Ferber Jones Ltd
Bongate Mill
Appleby
CA16 6UR

'To know fully even one field or one land is a lifetime's experience. In the world of poetic experience it is depth that counts, not width.'

>Patrick Kavanagh,
>*'The Parish & the Universe', 1967*

CONTENTS

Acknowledgements	8
Introduction	11
Part 1: Iron in the Blood	**17**
Chapter One	19
Chapter Two	30
Chapter Three	39
Chapter Four	46
Chapter Five	53
Part 2: Flower and Stone	**65**
Chapter Six	67
Chapter Seven	76
Chapter Eight	90
Chapter Nine	102
Part 3: Provincial Pleasures	**115**
Chapter Ten	117
Chapter Eleven	130
Chapter Twelve	141
Chapter Thirteen	151
Part 4: Giving it Wigan	**167**
Chapter Fourteen	169
Chapter Fifteen	182
Chapter Sixteen	194
Chapter Seventeen	207
Chapter Eighteen	217

Postscript	228
End Notes	235
Bibliography	248
Index	250

ACKNOWLEDGEMENTS

Particular thanks must go to the Trustees of the Norman Nicholson Literary Estate for asking me to write this biography and giving me a great deal of help and support along the way. Norman's cousin, Doreen Cornthwaite, has been a wonderful source of information and I couldn't have written this without her. Thanks also to the John Rylands Library in Manchester, to Fran Baker for her meticulous cataloguing and to her and the staff for their endless patience in dealing with my requests. Material at the JRL is reproduced by courtesy of the University Librarian and Director, The John Rylands Library, The University of Manchester. Permission to quote from Norman's writing has been generously granted by the Hunt family who hold the copyright to all Norman's work, both published and unpublished, including letters. Norman's agents, David Higham Associates, particularly Georgia Glover, have been very helpful and sympathetic, and I owe much to Peggy Troll, Antoinette Fawcett and the Norman Nicholson Society. Chris Wadsworth has also been very generous with information relating to Percy Kelly's friendship with Norman Nicholson, and images and quotations from Percy's letters to Norman are reproduced with her permission. A.L. Rowse' letter to Norman is copyright The Estate of A.L. Rowse. Reproduced with the kind permisson of Johnson & Alcock Ltd. The poem 'Night in Martindale' and quotations from the letters and prose of Kathleen Raine are reproduced by kind permission of the Literary Estate of Kathleen Raine.

Thanks are also due to Lord Bragg, Professor Alan Beattie, Dr Ian Davidson, Dr David Cooper and Neil Curry for sharing their thoughts and expertise with me; to Philip Gardner for permission to quote from his study of Norman Nicholson; to Anna Hopewell, Professor Kate Wilson, and the family of Yvonne Gardner, Sarah and James Ross, and Liz Simpson, for allowing me to quote from private letters and reproduce family photographs. Many other people talked to me about their memories of Norman, including Mike Smith, (aka Brindley Hallam Dennis), Rev. George Bracegirdle, Chris and Sylvia Pilling, Martin Byfield, Maurice Payne, Jean Clarke, Margaret Spencer, Henry Slater, Margaret and Peter Lewis, Hunter Davies and Margaret Forster.

I am very grateful to Grevel Lindop and Mick North who took the time to read the manuscript as I wrote it and make valuable and detailed comments. Any errors are my own. I must particularly thank Neil Ferber for his encouragement, advice and tolerance throughout the research and writing of this biography, and for his technical expertise in designing the finished book, including the cover.

There are several individuals I have not been able to trace and I would be delighted to hear from any copyright holder who has not been contacted.

INTRODUCTION

The Whispering Poet

There was often a moment in Norman Nicholson's poetry readings – a moment of supreme theatre – when he would lower the timbre of his husky, baritone voice, point his finger at a random member of the audience, and say, 'You,' swivelling round to aim the finger at someone else, 'or You'. Then he would say, in a whisper that filled the room;

Wait! Wait!
Come closer;
I've something to tell.

The lines are from his poem The Whisperer, an account of his twenty months in a sanatorium where he was forbidden to raise his voice above a whisper in order to protect his tubercular vocal chords. Few who heard his spell-binding performances knew how close he had come to having no voice at all. And when, at the end of his life, a tracheotomy reduced him once more to a whisper, one of his last and most poignant notes to a friend was, 'They have taken away my voice'.

But his voice on the printed page can never be silenced. His poetry, rhythmical, colloquial, glittering with oral devices, is written to be performed – the Nordic vowels and consonants rattle in the mouth like stones, to be hurled towards the back of the auditorium, 'like iron quoits', in the manner known locally as 'giving it Wigan' – a colloquial phrase (originating in Rugby League) that is synonymous with total commitment.

Norman was proud to 'give it Wigan' to the end. He published seven collections of poetry between 1944 and 1985, four plays, two novels, one biography, and seven other prose works, edited innumerable editions of other writers' works, reviewed for the broadsheets, made regular radio and television appearances and was the subject of a South Bank Show special, introduced by Melvyn Bragg. He was awarded the Queen's Gold Medal for poetry, the OBE and is still the most famous Lakeland poet after Wordsworth.

But strange things happen after a poet dies. If they are young and the circumstances are controversial it can boost their reputations into the stratosphere; but if they fade into quiet old age, their reputations often fade with them. Norman had the added problem that he had spent his entire life in Millom – almost as far as you can get from the recognised artistic and literary centres of England. Even in his own day he was accused of being a recluse and would remark drily – 'What they really mean is that I haven't been seen much in London'.[1] He was branded as a provincial, which, according to Doctor Johnson, was simply another word for 'rude and unpolished'. It was a label Norman Nicholson claimed to relish, believing that the provincial person, rather than the metropolitan, had a better handle on things than his urban counterpart. But there was always an uneasy defensive element in his responses. And in his poetry there were echoes of regret for some of the choices he had made.

Norman had several relationships with women. The first was a young Jewish woman, four years older than himself, during his time in the sanatorium and the years just afterwards. She introduced him to classical music, encouraged him to write and sent off his first work to magazines. In the late nineteen thirties and early forties he was engaged to a young teacher from Kent, called Enrica Garnier, and dedicated his first collection of poetry to her, but found it impossible to leave his parents and the secure life they provided for him in Millom in order to marry her. Enrica was devastated when he broke off their engagement and she never married anyone else. Some close friends found it difficult to forgive him. In the early nineteen forties he was also in love with the poet Kathleen Raine, and the brief relationship between the two produced some uncharacteristically erotic love poetry. Kathleen moved on, though they remained friends. Then, in 1956, at the age of forty two, Norman married Yvonne Gardner, who was teaching at a school in Millom, and they were together until she died of cancer in 1982.

Norman corresponded regularly with some of his contemporaries, finding minds sympathetic to his own northern slant of thought. He became friends with Ted Hughes, David Wright, Anne Ridler, Sid Chaplin, and Charles Causley. He was never in tune with academia and had notable spats with A.L. Rowse, George Barker and Philip Larkin. Norman was a victim of establishment snobbery and even the Poet Laureate John Betjeman, who eventually recommended him for the Queen's Gold Medal, privately classed him as an 'untechniqued poet' one of those 'silly fools' who 'like to see themselves in the *Daily Herald*'.[2]

His poetry, centred in the natural world and man's place in it, can often be classified as 'Eco-poetry'. Norman was 'fervently green' before the phrase had ever been coined.[3] Dr Philip Gardner, who wrote the first full-length study of his work, wrote that 'the connection of man with nature, and of man with man in past and present dimensions – are central to a proper understanding of Norman Nicholson's poetry'.[4]

As early as the nineteen fifties, Norman felt strongly that the National Trust should preserve 'examples of landscape created and shaped by industry and then deserted'. They should choose factories, coal mines, quarries, lead-workings and iron foundries; landscapes like Millom. 'They give a glimpse beyond the scale of history; they set man in the greater perspective of biology and geology, of the pre-historic and post-historic processes of nature'.[5] They were examples, not just of ruin, exploitation and decay, but of renaissance. The planet could and would survive whatever man did to it.

Norman's early brush with death made him conscious of the mutability at the heart of everything, that even the mountain rock we stand on shifts and erodes and eventually finds its way to the sea as grains of sand. There is a natural cycle of entropy, of which we are part. This seems to be the message he wants us to hear. In Rising Five, he plays on the small boy's wish to seem older than he is, and the ending is bleak.

> The new buds push the old leaves from the bough.
> We drop our youth behind us like a boy
> Throwing away his toffee-wrappers. We never see the flower,
> But only the fruit in the flower; never the fruit,
> But only the rot in the fruit. We look for the marriage bed
> In the baby's cradle, we look for the grave in the bed:
>   not living,
> But rising dead.[6]

Norman Nicholson was a writer of place, and the industrial fringe of the Lake District was his chosen spot, featuring in his poetry and the two novels he wrote in the nineteen forties. But his prose writings address a much more international audience. He wrote books on the history and topography of the Lake District, a biography of William Cowper, a critical study of H.G. Wells, edited the Camden Classics' edition of Emily Brontë's *Wuthering Heights* and anthologies of religious verse. And it was a Canadian scholar and poet who wrote the first academic analysis of Norman's poetry.[7]

He was proud to be known as a 'regional' writer – a phrase often used by critics in a pejorative way. It was defined in 1955 in the *Dictionary of World Literary Terms* as 'the tendency of some writers to set their works in a particular locality, presented in some detail, as affecting the lives and fortunes of the inhabitants', though not, by inference, the wider world. But Thomas Hardy is, by this definition, a regional author, and no one would argue that Hardy's work is not universally relevant. Norman Nicholson hated the literary snobbery of these classifications. He wrote in the *Times Literary Supplement* about the inconsistency of labelling some poets 'regional' in order to dismiss them as 'minor', while failing to include others, like Hardy, in order to exalt their work above the others. 'To refuse to call a poet "regional" when he so obviously is, is to fail to understand part of what he is saying; to insist on the "universal" aspect of his work at the expense of the local is to show that we have missed something of that which makes him universal'.[8] But it is in the context of the Lake District, like Wordsworth, that Norman Nicholson seems destined to have his work contained.

Any poet writing in Cumbria has somehow to come to terms with the monumental bulk of Wordsworth towering behind them. Norman chose to lock horns with him at a very early age. Although he acknowledged Wordsworth's place as one of the greatest writers in European literary history, his own, private, opinion of the bard was that his work was very uneven – 'he is quite capable of hiding his loveliest lines in among a lot of rubbish'.[9] And Norman criticised Wordsworth for fudging the truth in order to romanticise the landscape, particularly in the Duddon Valley sonnets, where the river, already altered by man's early activity, is described as being 'remote from every taint of sordid industry'.

Norman Nicholson detested the 'cult of the picturesque'. His chosen space was in the edgelands between the Lake District and the sea. He is the celebrant, not of the emotions aroused by landscape, but of man's relationship with the land, above and below ground, documenting man's capacity to produce industrial holocausts, exploring geology and its consequences. Norman had great admiration for the poet William

THE WHISPERING POET

Cowper. He wrote a biography of Cowper and praised him for 'showing the English country scene more as it really was and less as it was imagined to be'. Cowper's was not a landscape 'of mountains, torrents and romantic wildness' but of a more commonplace reality. Cowper 'celebrated the usual, the everyday, the humdrum',[10] and this is where Norman chose to place himself, turning his back on the mountains and torrents that formed the north eastern horizon, to focus on everyday life in Millom.

PART ONE

IRON IN THE BLOOD

1914 – 1936

'…the ore out of the rock; the iron out of the ore; and the houses, the streets, the churches, the schools, very nearly the children themselves, out of the iron'.

Norman Nicholson, 'The Wheel of Fire', 1952

Chapter One

Most people have heard of the Lake District, at the northern edge of England, in what is now the county of Cumbria,[1] facing out across the sea to Ireland. Many people internationally have heard of Keswick and Grasmere, small towns that have a long association with the Romantic poets, Wordsworth, Coleridge and Southey. Tourists know Ambleside and Windermere and other beauty spots among the hills and lakes left behind by the last ice age, forming a miniature Switzerland with breath-taking views. Walkers and climbers know its peaks and the tracks that Wainwright mapped. But few have heard of Millom, where the author and poet Norman Nicholson spent his life, and few ever visit the industrial coastal fringe.

The landscape of West Cumbria isn't one to lift and gladden the heart like the rest of the Lake District, though it has its own bleak beauty. It's a weary landscape, one that has been used and abused by mankind over a long period. It used to be lined with shipyards and docklands, coal-mines, iron-ore workings and factories – but most of them are now closed, leaving behind a scarred location and a tidemark of poverty. Of the industries that remain, the uneasy bulk of the Sellafield Nuclear processing plant dominates the countryside fifteen miles north of Millom, and the gigantic sheds that service the United Kingdom's nuclear submarine fleet can be seen across the bay at Barrow. Not a landscape, you would think, to nurture a poet ... but poetry thrives in unlikely places.

It seems to take forever to get to Millom from the motorway that skirts the eastern edge of the Lake District. Going reluctantly west, the narrow road curves around the fells, wriggles around estuaries, dips through the Duddon valley and then, over the shoulder of the hill, the sea suddenly glints silver against the sky. And there, on a peninsula jutting out in the

---

1 Cumbria was formed from Cumberland and Westmorland and part of Lancashire in 1974

lee of the dark, lowering mass of a hill called Black Combe, a huddle of buildings and a church spire come into view. This is Millom.

Once the town was dominated by slag heaps and a gigantic iron-ore smelting works, but these are long gone – a casualty of the de-industrialisation of Britain. On the Dismantling of Millom Ironworks is one of Norman Nicholson's most powerful poems. It describes what the event meant for him and other members of the community.

> They shovelled my childhood
> On to a rubbish heap. Here my father's father,
> Foreman of the back furnace, unsluiced the metal lava
> To slop in fiery gutters across the foundry floor
> And boil round the workmen's boots;

As the poem suggests, Norman Nicholson's family had a close relationship with the ironworks. Iron ore was discovered at Hodbarrow, on the peninsula, in 1860 and by 1867 Millom ironworks had begun production. There was an influx of miners and ironworkers into the area from as far afield as Devon, Cornwall and Ireland. Millom, previously a village, became a small town. The Nicholsons were a local family, probably of Viking origin, whose genetic networks had spread into a family tree too large and complex to map. Norman wrote of 'all the uncles and great uncles scattered about farms and parklands from Kendal to Morecambe Bay'.[1] Although Norman had a tendency to think back through the paternal line, there were also aunts and great aunts, as well as cousins and second cousins of both sexes, connected either by blood or by marriage, scattered throughout the old counties of Cumberland, Westmorland and Lancashire.

Norman's paternal grandfather, Richard Nicholson, came from nearby Cartmel, a farmer's son who came to the ironworks to earn better money. He was an intelligent man whose skills were highly valued by his employers. After a period as foreman, he was offered the job of Works Manager but turned it down because – so the family were told – he feared that his numerical skills weren't up to it. The truth was that (like many working class people in rural England) he had had little education and was ashamed of it. He married an Irish gamekeeper's daughter from Dallam Tower, across the bay at Milnthorpe, Maria Brennan, a girl who had been in service at Dallam and who was completely illiterate. But, despite her lack of education, Maria was a spirited woman. A family story, and one of

CHAPTER ONE

Norman's poems (The Seventeenth of the Name) recorded how, crossing the Duddon sands, travelling to join her husband at Millom, Maria had had her first sight of the industrial wasteland that was being created, 'the tubas and trombones of the ironworks, blaring into the sky',[2] and shouted to the carter, 'Turn the horse back!' But the sea was already flooding in across the estuary and there was no way back for her at all.

In his poetry Norman imagined her nostalgia for pastoral scenes where cattle stood hock deep in tides of meadow flowers and sheep lay slumped 'like grey bolsters' under the trees in summer heat.[3] Instead, in one of the cramped terraced houses newly built to accommodate the ironworkers, with views only of other streets and the slag heap from the works, the couple had fourteen sons, three of whom died at birth or in infancy. Two others died as young men. Norman's grandmother rarely left Millom and when she died in 1928 the local paper recorded (with some incredulity) that she had never been on a train.

Several of Norman's paternal uncles worked either in the mines or at the smelting works. The eldest son, Bill, was a blacksmith there, and the youngest, Arnold, worked in the foundry. A middle son, Jack, was killed in an accident at the mine, leaving a pregnant widow. More than one of Norman's cousins were ironworkers. Three generations of the Nicholson family earned their money from iron and the rest earned a living from servicing the industry. The visual collision between idyllic scenery and industrial wasteland was at the heart of Norman Nicholson's life and work.

Norman Cornthwaite Nicholson was born in a small terraced house in Millom, number 14, St George's Terrace, where his father, Joseph, ran a Gentleman's Outfitters in the front room of the ground floor. Apart from a spell in a sanatorium as a teenager, Nicholson spent his life in its narrow compass and would have died there but for an emergency admission to the local hospital after an acute illness.

The southern Lake District that encloses Millom is an area of outstanding natural beauty – wild and bleak, with an ancient history. The neighbouring Furness Peninsula has some of the earliest settlements identified in the British Isles. People have been living and working here since the end of the ice age and many different waves of settlers and invaders have left their marks on the landscape. The fells are crossed by drove roads that have been used for hundreds, if not thousands, of years. There are medieval fortified farmhouses built to withstand Scottish marauders, Norman castles, Viking crosses, 9th century Norse churches, and Roman forts. Before the Romans arrived, ancient people erected standing stones and circles and decorated them with cup and ring marks. One of the most interesting complexes of stones is perched on the brow of a hill overlooking Millom and one of the biggest stone circles in Britain is within walking distance at Swinside. And under it all, the ancient rock is seamed with minerals and precious ores dating back to the birth of the planet – where 'cliffs of coal/Slant like shale' and 'veins are stained with the blood of the ore'.[4]

Norman Nicholson had a strong sense of connection to that pre-historic landscape. Every child in the community, he wrote, 'is joined by an umbilical cord, stretching back through the ooze to the shelled, creeping creatures of the warm lagoons'.[5] Time for Nicholson was not linear – the past and the present were there in every moment of his life, in everything he saw and touched. His childhood, his youth, were 'built into the everyday life of today, into the bricks of the house where I live and the walls of the room where I am writing ...' When he talked about his early life, memory and imagination fused to produce their own narrative truth. 'I cannot separate what I think I saw from what I know I must have seen.'[6]

His mother's family, the Cornthwaites, had also come to Millom in the 'Iron Rush', and their name, too, goes back to the Viking settlement in the 9th century. Cornthwaite in Norse means 'the clearing of the corn'. Norman was always conscious of the Norse dialect that named the features of the landscape around him '*tveit* and *dal* and *fell*' and that his 'umpteenth great grandfather' had 'scratched those words on the rocks,/naming the Cymric cwms in a Norse tongue.' The Cornthwaites were farmers and tradesmen. Grandfather George was a farmer's son from Boretree Stile Farm near Ulverston. He came to Millom with two of his brothers and became a butcher, selling meat to the ironworkers and making a good living from it. George Cornthwaite married a young woman from Keswick, and he and his wife Eliza were comfortable enough to employ a maid when the children were young and had the money to give their children an education.

Norman's Cornthwaite grandfather was dead by the time Norman was born, but his widow Eliza still lived in a cottage next to the abattoir, with her eldest daughter Lizzie who remained unmarried well into her thirties and worked as a draper's assistant. In 1916 Lizzie married a man who owned a horse-drawn lorry and ran a carter's business and Eliza continued to live with them after their marriage. Lizzie had two brothers, William Cornthwaite who worked as a butcher and lived in Millom with his wife and two children, and George Cornthwaite junior, who had moved south

CHAPTER ONE

and ran a butcher's shop in Preston. Edith, Norman's mother, was the younger daughter and she had trained as a dressmaker before her marriage to Joe Nicholson in 1905.

Norman Nicholson claimed that he couldn't remember his mother at all. At five years and two months old, barely recovered from influenza, he was taken down to the living room, behind the shop, where his grandmother told him that his mother 'had gone to live with the angels'. Apart from an incident where he cried inconsolably when he saw the stained glass angels in the windows of St George's Church, he said that he couldn't remember anything of what he had felt and for the rest of his life, told people that his early childhood was a blank. 'My mother,' he wrote later, 'has been cut out of the picture as if with a pair of scissors.'[7] When pressed about this in an interview he explained that 'the child did not want to be hurt, so it just forgot'.[8] There are very few family photographs, but among Norman's own, is one of a very pretty young woman, who may be his mother, though no-one is certain.

The entire family had fallen victim to the Spanish Flu epidemic that swept through Europe after the First World War, encouraged by dirt and poor nutrition in the trenches, and spread to other countries across the world by returning troops. Norman and his father were ill, but both survived; his mother developed broncho-pneumonia and died on March 11th 1919, aged only thirty nine. It was the second major tragedy for the Cornthwaite family – Edith's older brother William had died only ten days earlier and had been interred in St George's churchyard, only yards from where 'Edith Maud Mary, beloved wife of Joseph Nicholson', was laid to rest beside her infant son Harold – the Nicholson's first child who had died more than a decade earlier.

The Nicholsons had been married in 1905 but their first baby didn't arrive until 1907. Harold was born in June and died six months later, from enteritis and convulsions, just before Christmas. Infant mortality was extremely high in the first decades of the twentieth century and, without antibiotics, babies often died of minor ailments, as well as all the childhood diseases we now immunise against. It was a tragedy his parents never really recovered from. The whole of Norman's early life was over-shadowed by the emotional fall-out of bereavement – not only his mother's death but that of his infant brother, seven years before he himself was born. Norman remarked that one of the only things he could remember about his childhood was that there had been about his mother a sadness, a regret, which he later connected with the death of the baby. Whether he remembered this, or deduced it from things he was told afterwards, isn't clear. Edie, as she was known in the family, didn't have children easily. Norman wasn't born until 1914 and was a sickly baby. His parents feared that he too, would succumb to one of the childhood diseases that still claimed two lives out of every ten children.

Even before the death of his mother, Norman was wrapped in the proverbial cotton wool. 'I was lagged in layers of clothing like a water pipe protected from frost… I was not encouraged to play with other children; I was not allowed out into the street; I was cosseted, comforted and protected, and I grew up, as I could hardly help growing up, pale, timid, dependent, self-absorbed and rather girlish'. But Norman claimed that he didn't regret not growing up to be 'rough, tough and untidy … like an ordinary boy'.[9]

After his mother died, Norman's Cornthwaite grandmother, Eliza, stayed on in the house to look after both him and his father. Joseph Nicholson had a shop to run and no time to care for a small boy still weak from the influenza and not yet in school. In Norman's memoir of his early life, *Wednesday Early Closing*, he describes Eliza as 'Mrs Noah', a short, round figure, dressed in black, with a face 'creased like a shrunk potato',[10] who was perpetually cleaning and baking. Although she lived with the Nicholsons for three years, taught Norman to read, and took him on outings to see his other relatives, there's little affection in the way he writes about her as being 'unceasingly active, like a tense, irritable, continually fidgety, broody hen'.[11] She was very particular in matters of morals, cleanliness and good manners, and Victorian in her attitudes. Norman thought that she had little understanding of small boys and a tendency to complain to his father when he misbehaved, rather than deal with it herself. He preferred the direct, if sometimes rough, approach of his Nicholson grandmother who would 'skelp him on the backside' when necessary, but keep the reasons to herself.

Number 14, St George's Terrace, was a crowded place – three floors with two tiny rooms on each one with an extension into the yard at the back. On the ground floor, the dividing wall between the hallway and sitting room at the front had been removed and the space was occupied by the shop. Access to the living quarters was through the shop. The room behind it became a living-dining room, with a big black range for cooking and heating, and a door opened into a small yard with a 'back kitchen' or scullery in the extension, a wash house and an outside lavatory. Upstairs, the front bedroom served as a sitting room, the other bedroom

CHAPTER ONE

was occupied by Eliza Cornthwaite, and Norman and his father slept in the small bedroom built out over the back kitchen extension. There were two small, cold attic rooms in the roof space used for storage.

Although Norman portrayed himself at times as a 'motherless boy' that others felt sorry for, his childhood seems to have been a happy, secure one. He may have been an only child, but he grew up surrounded by relatives who felt they had a duty to take care of him. He was part of a tribe. When he was taken to buy a pair of new shoes by his grandmother, it was his Uncle Jim Nicholson – his favourite uncle – who measured his feet and made sure he had the right size. Jim managed the boot and shoe department of the Co-op and Norman's Uncle Tom worked in the same department as a cobbler. Uncle Bill, a blacksmith at the ironworks, forged him a hoop and iron crook to run around the lanes with and bought him sweets on Saturday nights. Lizzie Cornthwaite's husband took Norman with him on the cart whenever he could, and there were frequent walks to visit his Great Uncle Tom Cornthwaite, who worked in the brewery at the nearby village of Kirksanton.

The influenza and the aftermath of his mother's death, delayed Norman's entry into school by at least one term. There were only two schools in Millom – the nearest, Lapstone Road, was also the roughest, and so it had been determined that Norman should go to Holborn Hill – about three hundred yards from the end of his street in the other direction, up the hill towards the original village that had expanded to become the town of Millom. At the age of five Norman was a shy, timid child, who wet his trousers at school because he was too afraid to ask to go to the toilet during lessons. That fear was one of Norman's earliest memories. Although Norman claimed to have little sense of smell, he also remembered the characteristic school odour; 'airless, humid, fungoid, an attar of unwashed clothes, unwashed hair, sweat, spittle and mucus, adulterated with chalk-dust, stale ink and fumes from the coke stove'.[12]

His contemporaries were children he'd grown up among; 'boys of an iron time in an iron town. Born into war rations and bred on the dole, they lived in a world where poverty seemed too natural to complain about'.[13] It was clothes that made the class distinctions. The children who wore ill-fitting clothes bought by charity fund-raising – clogs and collarless shirts – had parents who were out of work. Norman observed boys whose big toes were 'squirting through their boots'.[14] Others, the children of the low-income workers, had clothes that were hand-me-downs, hand-made, hand-knitted, but clean and patched. Those boys whose parents were tradesmen, sported Eton collars and smart jumpers, bow-ties and new shoes. Norman, whose father was in the clothing trade, went to school in clothes from the shop, and he hated the fact that everyone knew it. He was a walking advertisement for his father's trade.

Three years after his mother's death, Norman's world was turned upside down. His father took him for a walk through the fields and explained that he was going to get married again, that Grandma Cornthwaite was leaving and they would be going to live with Grandma Nicholson over the winter months until the wedding. Joe Nicholson had agonised over this announcement for weeks and later admitted to Norman that it had been 'worse than proposing'.

Norman was too young to have seen it coming. Rosetta Sobey, usually known as Rose, was a woman in her early thirties, one of the generation of women whose hopes of marriage had evaporated in the slaughter of the First World War. She managed the music shop in St George's Terrace, next door to the Nicholson's house. Norman had been going in and out of the shop for some time, drawn by the music. Rose would sit at one of the pianos and play during the day and she had made a name for herself by playing for local concerts and as an accompanist. She fascinated Norman, who thought her 'young, lively, laughing, welcoming'.[15] And without his being aware of it, she fascinated his forty-five year old father too. Eliza Cornthwaite wasn't amused by the developing relationship. She thought Rose Sobie was 'flighty', the spoiled daughter of doting parents, who had 'never had to do a hand's turn' in the house in her life. There was friction between the two women. Once, when Norman repeated a fairly innocent comment that Rose had made about his grandmother, Grandma Cornthwaite had been so angry, his father had to intervene and dragged Norman next door to apologise to Rose for repeating her comments. It left him with a sense of injustice. 'I had no feeling of guilt. I had said nothing I should not have said, and, anyway, I could not understand why my father thought that it had anything to do with him.'[16]

Standing beside his father in the field looking out over the town, the penny suddenly dropped and Norman was delighted. His grandmother was not. Rose Sobey's name was not to be mentioned in the house. Eliza Cornthwaite was faced with finding somewhere to live and someone to support her at a time when there was no welfare state or pension system. Since the death of her eldest son William, there had been another widow

CHAPTER ONE

and two children to be provided for out of the family business and there can have been little to spare for Eliza. Her daughter Lizzie was not exactly enthusiastic about having her mother back, but sharing a house with Rose and Joe was not an option. Eliza didn't wait for the wedding, she left as soon as the engagement was announced. As an adult, Norman acknowledged that she must have felt cast off and unwanted.

Since it was unthinkable for a man with a business to run to also look after a house and a small boy, Joe and Norman went to stay with his Nicholson grandmother. Maria's husband, Richard Nicholson, had died before Norman's parents were married, so she lived a couple of streets away at 157 Albert Street with her four remaining bachelor sons, Bill, Tom, Bob and Arnold and her sister's illegitimate daughter Annie Brennan, to whom Maria had given a home.[17] It was a small house, about the same size as Norman's own, so there was little room for the extra guests. Annie slept with Maria, three of the brothers shared the double bed in the front bedroom and the other slept in the attic with Norman and his father. There was a parlour, but it was hardly ever used and had become a shrine to Norman's uncle Jack – a well-known Millom cricketer and footballer – whose back had been broken in a fall of haematite underground at Hodbarrow. He was the second of Maria's sons to die in young adulthood – another boy, Richard, who was believed to have been epileptic and had never been able to work, died from a seizure. The 1911 census recorded that she had only nine sons living out of the original fourteen.

Maria, Norman's Nicholson grandmother, was not, by reputation, a sympathetic figure. She had had a hard life and it had made her hard. Norman's description of her, as she appeared in a family photograph, is very accurate. She is sitting in a chair with two of her grandchildren beside her;

> 'her back straighter than the back of the chair, her black skirts barrelled round legs splayed wide apart. One hand, clenched in emphasis, is pressed on one knee, and she glares steadily at the photographer, as if daring him to take the picture at all. Her grey hair is raked back from her forehead tight as a skull cap. Her large ears angle out like chimney cowls, and her lips are snapped to, leaving the mouth not enough play, it would seem, to speak let alone to smile. She was tall, bony, square-chested, so masculine that most men looked effeminate beside her.'[18]

But despite the harsh description, Norman was fonder of her than his

Cornthwaite grandmother. Maria had a tongue like a lash, yet he wasn't afraid of her and could tell her things that would have shocked his maternal grandmother; 'She knew all about little boys. She knew what they did and how they talked'.[19]

By the time Norman knew her Maria was approaching eighty, and crippled, having fallen and broken her femur. She sat on the settle near the range in the kitchen and ran the household with the help of Annie Brennan. Maria's eldest son Bill had forged long handled kitchen implements for her and she could manipulate the saucepans and kettles over the fire and supervise the cooking. She could get around with a crutch, but rarely stirred out of the house. Only those close to her knew that she had a softer side to her nature and kept a caged linnet in the kitchen that she crooned to daily, and which would sing only for her.

Norman's two grandmothers had one thing in common; they both disapproved of Rose Sobey. They disliked her for her 'airs and graces' and her lack of domesticity. She was also a Methodist and they were both firmly Anglican. Grandma Nicholson made sly remarks to Norman about joining 'them Wezleens', having to be saved, 'becoming Cornish' and living on a diet of pasties. This was a dig at the Sobey family's south-western origins. They were 'off-comers' – a Cumbrian term for people who have moved there from somewhere else.

One of Norman's most memorable Christmas's was spent that winter at his Nicholson grandmother's house. He was teased for bringing his Christmas tree with him – an artificial affair made of wire and raffia with candleholders on the branches – but it was duly erected on the sideboard. When the gas pipe sprung a leak on Christmas Eve, the tree came into its own as a source of illumination, the candle light 'glissading along the bars of the bird cage and the knobs and grating of the big kitchen range'. Norman had hoped for books as a Christmas present, but his future stepmother came to the house with a box of crackers 'like huge, over-dressed dolls, decked out in tinsel and crêpe paper'. He hated crackers and was upset and disappointed not to have been given books. There was also a jolt of warning; 'that someone I admired so much should have so little understanding'.[20] The knowledge that his grandmother had also thought them a 'silly present and a waste of money', made Norman aware of what she really thought of Rose Sobey. The crackers were evidence of frivolity.[21]

Norman was less watched and feather-bedded in Maria Nicholson's house. It was a very masculine world, with uncles who wrestled on the

CHAPTER ONE

kitchen floor like boys, played cricket and football, and teased their nephew about having his nose in a book, convinced it was bad for his health. Norman's grandmother chided him gently about being so timid.

> 'You couldn't say *Boo* to a goose,' my grandmother said
> When I skittered howling in from the back street – my head
> With a bump the size of a conker from a stick that someone threw,
> Or my eyes rubbed red
> From fists stuffed in to plug the blubbing. 'Not *Boo* to a goose,' she said.
> But coddled me in the kitchen, gave me bread
> Spread with brown sugar ...[22]

Maria encouraged him to go out in the winter cold to play with the other children in the back lanes. She didn't seem particularly concerned about what he did, or the time he came home and Norman revelled in the freedom. During a particularly cold and snowy February he briefly became part of a gang, building a snow fort with solid ice walls, which was manned by the neighbouring girls and boys. He learned street games with rhyming couplets:

> Nebuchadnezzar the King of the Jews
> Sold his wife for a pair of shoes.

Even at that young age, Norman was very comfortable in female company and often deliberately sought it out. One of the older girls adopted him, teaching him a few words of French, showing him how to make 'transfers' – a northern word for tracing things out of books with a pencil and greaseproof paper. Norman realised later that he was yearning to be mothered; 'there was an ache in my feeling for her, which I could neither understand nor express'.[23] As a small child he was aware of the need, but it was only in later life that he could see clearly the link between the absence of a warm mother or sister-figure and the way he had attached himself to older girls and particularly female teachers. He wrote in his autobiography that, ' any reasonably kind woman teacher became a substitute for my dead mother'.[24]

Chapter Two

Norman was taken by his father to the jeweller's shop to buy his new stepmother a wedding present. He chose a bedroom clock with a brass surround which, fifty years later, he still had in the bedroom, part of the continuity of his life, where time past and time present existed in the same space.

He had hazy memories of the wedding – being measured for his sailor suit, collecting the rose for his father's buttonhole, repeating a vulgar expression he had heard his Uncle Jim's wife use about the wedding. This didn't go down well with the Methodist Sobey family. Rose, the child of elderly, conservative parents, seems to have been rather prudish. Sex, in her family was 'unreferred to, unread about, almost, by a kind of unspoken agreement, non-existent'.[1] The traditional nuptial hymn, 'The voice that breathed o'er Eden, that earliest wedding day', was not sung at the wedding, because it mentioned Adam and Eve, and Rose was heard to remark, 'Everybody knows what *they* were doing'. The wedding breakfast was tense with a 'chapel-like silence' and a feeling of 'us and them'. When someone gave the bride a naked baby doll at the reception – a traditional joke – to ripples of ribald laughter from the Nicholson clan – she was speechless with anger behind the polite smile. It didn't bode well for Joe Nicholson's chances of a happy relationship. They went off to London for their honeymoon, where Joe wanted to see Preston North End play in the cup final, and Norman stayed on with Maria Nicholson.[2]

He had now acquired yet another set of grandparents and become part of another, very different, tribe. The Sobeys were slightly better off than many of the Nicholsons. Rose's father had been a joiner at the Hodbarrow iron mine and, although he was over seventy and had an injured leg from an accident at work, he was still employed on light duties. Their terraced house had a bathroom and was furnished with many of the things that

CHAPTER TWO

James Sobey had made. Norman, in middle age, was proud of the fact that he still hung his clothes in his step-grandfather's wardrobe. The Sobeys had had children later in life, with a big gap between the older daughter Laura and her sister Rose. Consequently Rosie, as they called her, was their favourite and had been spoiled and cosseted, excused from helping with household chores and allowed to develop her musical talents.

Norman described the diminutive Mrs Sobey as 'a Beatrix Potter mouse-wife'. She was 'neat, bright, sleek' and may once have been a lady's maid in Devon before her marriage. Her pretentions, which were passed on to her daughter Rose, were definitely middle class. When Norman was first taken to visit them and shown round the house at 16 Wellington Street, the name, Wellington House, displayed in gold letters on the fanlight above the front door was the first indication, he wrote later, of a home that spoke 'of steady employment, careful housekeeping and not too many children'.[3] Even as a small child he was amused by Mrs Sobey's descriptions of each room – the entrance passage was called The Hall, a bedroom with a skylight was 'The Roof Garden', the yard at the back was 'The Garden', and an area glassed over by Mr Sobey to make a greenhouse was 'The Conservatory'.[4] Their parlour, where Rose's piano stood, was regularly used, unlike the working class parlours that Norman had known, which were cold and closed up, to be occupied only on festivals or opened for very special guests.

After the honeymoon, Norman moved back into his home above the shop in St George's Terrace with his father and Rose. It was decided that he would call her 'mother', to distinguish her from Edie, whom he had always called 'Mammy'. Lots of changes had taken place in the six months they had been living in Albert Street with Grandma Nicholson. The whole house had been re-decorated, a piano installed in the parlour, and the small back bedroom had been converted into a bathroom. No more trips across the yard in the rain, and no more washing in a tin bath in front of the kitchen range. But there were disadvantages too. With the loss of the back-bedroom that had been his since he was born, Norman found himself upstairs in one of the attics – in the room he would occupy for the rest of his life, even after marriage. It was, he wrote, 'a tiny, airless box'.[5] The room was shaped by the pitch of the roof, with limited space to stand up in. There was a small window in the dormer looking out northeast-wards across the rooftops of Millom towards the fells, through which he peered 'like a cave-dweller, half-way up a cliff'.[6] The room was cold in winter and hot in summer and the window didn't open to let in any fresh air, something Norman thought should have been regarded as essential. He told the story in his memoir of childhood, *Wednesday Early Closing*, with a tone of accusation. 'We had taken another step up the social ladder, and I had taken a step down towards chronic ill-health.'[7]

Rose had given up her job in the piano shop, as women were expected to do when they got married, in order to look after her new husband and step-son. Norman quickly began to realise the disadvantages of having a mother who had never learned housekeeping. In place of the big roast dinners, home-baked cakes and pies they had been used to, there were thin slices of bought ham from the grocers, and pasties, pies, iced buns and 'fancies' from the baker. Everything was bought ready-made. Norman later blamed this diet of shop-bought food for his poor health. 'She fed us on cake,' he complained to one relative.[8] There was a great deal of bread and butter eaten too – for breakfast, as a substitute for vegetables at lunch and on the menu again for tea. In his autobiography he wrote 'it did not occur to her that she was digging my grave with a bread-knife'.[9]

Rose had the fixed idea that shop-bought food was more wholesome than home-made, and would throw away gifts from family and friends, saying, 'You never know what's in it'! Rose tried, but she didn't like cooking, and she found house-work demeaning. 'It's the maid's day off,' she would say, only half-joking, when laying the table for guests, and couldn't bear to be caught by visitors in an apron. 'She hated cookery books,' Norman remembered, 'and magazines of household hints, and when she opened a tin or a packet of foodstuff, she hadn't the patience to read the printed instructions'.[10]

But Rose brought something very special into Norman's life; the poetry and musical rhythms of the Methodist chapel. Anyone who has ever listened to a northern Methodist choir singing the great Wesleyan anthem, And Can it Be, in parts that soar and plunge and vibrate with energy, creating a wall of sound, will know what Norman meant when he described the moment the congregation burst into song: 'suddenly the organ sang out, the best basses and contraltos of the Millom Mixed Voice Choir tromboned into four-part chording, and every member of the congregation opened wide his mouth, until the whole baffle-board of pews and panels boomed and echoed with all the fervour of Charles Wesley's thousand tongues'.[11] It was words and music as a physical and emotional experience – 'thumping, hand-slapping, heart-prodding tunes', that 'banged and bounced about the galleries, till the pillars shook and twanged'.[12]

Very often it was Rose sitting at the organ, playing the hymns she had

CHAPTER TWO

practised on the piano at home. Family gatherings usually ended with a sing-song. Norman believed that those old Wesleyan tunes, which had already been sung for more than a hundred years, had become the 'folk-songs of industrial northern England', and he pointed out that On Ilkley Moor Baht'at had started out as a setting for While Shepherds Watched Their Flocks.[13] 'Enough of Charles Wesley,' Norman wrote, began to 'hammer its way into my mind forever'. When he wrote his first poem, So in September, at the age of 10, he copied the 7,7,7,7 syllabic lines.

> Summer slowly sinks to rest,
> Of all the seasons, the best.[14]

Poetry was beginning to find a place in Norman's life. His teacher at Junior Bible Class, an elderly local grocer called Chris Walmsley, used to quote Pope's Essay on Man, and recite the poems of Edgar Allan Poe – many of which he knew by heart. One of Norman's most vivid memories was of walking home with Chris Walmsley after Bible Class, listening to him declaim the whole of Annabel Lee, caught up in 'the potent, sexy, heavy-seasoned, witch-brew of the words' that stayed in Norman's imagination for the rest of his life.[15]

And it wasn't just poetry. A visiting preacher at the Methodist chapel introduced Norman to John Bunyan's *Pilgrim's Progress*, by giving a (quickly forgotten) lecture on the book. But Norman was curious enough to find his father's copy on the bookshelf when he went home. The exalted prose didn't seem too difficult to a boy used to listening to the Bible being read in the King James' version, and he found the story interesting enough. But when he came to the part where Pilgrim witnesses the waking of the dead, he was arrested.

> 'This night, as I was in my sleep, I dreamed; and behold, the heavens grew exceeding black; also it thundered and lightened in most fearful wise, that it put me into an agony. So I looked up in my dream, and saw the clouds rack at an unusual rate; upon which I heard a great sound of a trumpet...'[16]

Norman was so affected by the power of the words that he began to tremble with fear. 'No words I have read since then have drilled so deeply into my mind'.[17]

Methodism also provided Norman with a lively social environment, because it wasn't just a religion, it was a way of life. The chapel, as Norman later wrote, wasn't just a place of worship, it was a place of entertainment; 'their ancestral home, their music hall, assembly room, meeting house, club and gossip-shop'.[18] Many northern children share the same memories of a Wesleyan childhood – of the concerts and festivals and anniversaries, quizzes, bring-and-buy sales, Bazaars, the Band of Hope, Bible-study groups, choir practises, Faith Teas, Harvest Suppers, Christmas parties and summer outings, youth-camps and even literature societies. For Norman, a shy child whose social horizons had been limited to the immediate family circle, 'the chapel seemed to me to be one of the happiest places in the town'.[19] He enjoyed 'the lovely scrimmage and mixing together of so many people of so many types and ages'.[20]

Norman kept an autograph book which contained entries from family members, childhood friends, school-teachers and the Methodist minister and his wife. Ada Brewer's entry – a quote from Robert Burns – gives a glimpse of the homely philosophies that Norman was being taught, grounded in a fierce, working class pride.

> What tho' on homely fare we dine
> Wear hodden-gray and a' that…
> The honest man tho' ne'er so poor
> Is King o' men for a' that.[21]

And a 'D. Nicholson' urged Norman to -

> Bite off more than you can chew,
>   then chew it.
> Aim for more than you can do,
>   then do it.
> Hitch your wagon to a star,
> Keep your seat and there you are.[22]

The life of the chapel was fundamental in developing, not just Norman's awareness of language and music, but also his sense of belonging to a community and it enhanced the feeling of being rooted in a particular place. 'No child has ever had a more comfortable feeling of belonging than I had in the Methodist schoolroom, or, indeed, anywhere in Millom'.[23] In Millom, there wasn't an alley or backyard, wall or shed that wasn't utterly familiar

CHAPTER TWO

and imbued by a strong sense of history. The street-lamps – still fuelled by gas – twinkled 'all the way through boyhood back into the beginnings of the town'.[24] Being the son of a local tradesman also brought with it status and recognition. Norman's father had always been a well-respected figure – in his youth Joe had been an athlete and had run the local gymnastic association. Norman was recognised everywhere as Joe's son. And his stepmother Rose was well-known for her musical abilities – no local concert was complete without her. Norman had a distinct local identity; 'for I was Joe Nicholson's lad in the streets, just as I was Rose Sobey's stepson at the chapel, recognised and greeted everywhere'.[25] That sense of belonging, the security of having a fully-formed identity, was vitally important to Norman and may be one of the reasons why he stayed in Millom.

Norman was a precocious reader and was also beginning to be commended for his writing skills. In 1924 the school took a group of boys to London to see the British Empire Exhibition at Wembley and Norman was among them. Afterwards, he wrote a long letter about it to the *West Cumberland Times* and it was published in the Children's Corner and also won first prize in the essay competition. He was one of a small group of boys given extra coaching to pass the scholarship exam necessary for the grammar school. Thanks to a gifted teacher, Walter Wilson, Norman was introduced to a much wider range of books than his age group would normally have read. At ten he won the *Pickwick Papers* as a school prize and began to consume the novels of Charles Dickens. Mr Wilson also recommended Victor Hugo and Norman read *Les Miserables*. Walter Wilson had obtained his own education the hard way – working as a pupil teacher in order to gain his teaching certificate and then continuing to study privately while he taught. When he was at Millom he studied for, and gained, a degree in biology. Norman was always grateful for his enthusiasm, and the help Walter gave him was acknowledged in a dedication at the beginning of Norman's book *Cumberland and Westmorland*, to 'Walter Wilson, Schoolmaster and Friend', published in 1949. The dedication was repeated in *Portrait of the Lakes*.

All the coaching paid off, Norman passed the preliminary exam in the autumn and was able to take the main scholarship exams in March. It was something he looked forward to; 'I thoroughly enjoyed exams. They were the sport at which I knew I could win'.[26] He was then put through a Viva Voce. He passed all of them. The only embarrassment was having to buy the uniform from his father's rival, Seth Slater, who was the only other tailor in town. Joe Nicholson had once been apprenticed there and his departure to open his own shop, in the same street, had generated some ill-feeling, but Slater's shop had the school uniform agency and the Nicholsons were forced to cross the threshold for the first time in years.

At twelve, now a grammar school student, Norman was about to begin forging a reputation for himself in Millom, not just as a promising scholar, but as a performer. Doing 'recitations' was always a part of the concerts and chapel entertainments that were organised. Under Rose's influence, Norman had grown into a more confident child with a good 'mezzo' voice and the capacity to learn poetry by heart. He performed in school and Sunday school concerts and people began to notice. One of the defining moments of his life came when he was asked to be the Chairman of a big children's concert that was being planned in Millom. The Chair was usually taken by a local dignitary, so it was revolutionary to offer it to a child. Norman was both pleased and proud and so confident that he could do it, he refused the speech that had been written out for him and insisted on doing it 'extempore'. The lively, sociable Rose had been gradually developing Norman's talents, giving him piano lessons, teaching him middle class manners, encouraging him to socialise. The boy who had not been able to say '*boo* to a goose', now felt able to get up on stage in front of a hall packed with adults and children and compere the show.

But the climax of the concert was a recitation by Norman himself; a performance of Rudyard Kipling's poem Big Steamers. Norman didn't just recite the poem, he acted it out, drawing the audience into the drama of it. There was tumultuous applause and Norman felt 'for the first time, the lovely, dangerous, electric power of verse to excite and communicate'. From that time on, 'the idea that I might be a poet was persistently in the back of my thoughts'.[27] But he was also aware that part of the excitement was being the centre of attention – he didn't want to be a lonely poet writing in a garret. Writing for himself was never going to be an option – 'I wanted an audience; I wanted to make people listen'.[28]

Rose coached Norman for the elocution class of the children's day at the Millom Musical Festival. Millom has always had a strong musical tradition, with choirs and an amateur operatic society. Thanks to Rose, both Norman and his father were involved; Joe was on the committee and Norman was still a member of the Holborn Hill Boys School choir. There was strong competition for the children's event, but Norman was the outright winner with a strongly dramatised performance – what he referred to as the 'blatant melodramatics' – of R.L. Stevenson's Christmas at Sea.[29]

The result was a flood of invitations for Norman to recite at local

CHAPTER TWO

events, but Rose had her own plan for his career. She searched through anthologies of recitation pieces and helped Norman to learn and perform a number of ambitious verse narratives. She also decided which events he would accept – he even took the lead in a children's operetta. There were so many occasions and so many prizes that Norman later found it difficult to remember them – they all merged into one. Rose was delighted with his success, but it was Norman's headmaster who put an end to it because he told Joe Nicholson that Norman needed to concentrate on his schoolwork in the evenings – studying had to come first. Rose protested, but Joe put his foot down.

Norman had been doing very well at school – one of the brightest and best of his year. In 1926 he had won a coveted George Moore Scholarship, worth £10 and then the following year he won a George Moore Exhibition, worth a £100, in competition with other children from the whole county. Now at fourteen he was coming up to the all important matriculation exam as part of an educational elite. At that time children could leave school at fourteen and most did. Norman had passed the scholarship exam for the grammar school and it was hoped that he would go on to university and a teaching career. He had left behind most of his peers who remained at Holborn Hill School until they left to begin work. Even those boys who passed the scholarship exam weren't guaranteed a place at the grammar school – it all depended on whether their parents could afford to send them. Before the Second World War, secondary education was a luxury and only the children of the better off benefited from it. Two of Norman's good friends at Holborn Hill School had suffered in this way. Now the poverty of the industrial depression affected one of his classmates at the grammar school. The boy didn't know as he sat the matriculation exam that his father had just been sacked from Hodbarrow mine a couple of weeks earlier. The man hadn't told his family and had pretended to go to the mine every day until after the exams were over because he didn't want to spoil his son's chances.

Many more people lost their jobs in Millom with every day that passed. Some men worked only one week in three. It was the cousin of another of Norman's Millom contemporaries who described the atmosphere, Montague Slater, whom Norman knew as 'Charlie', who later wrote two novels and the libretto for Britten's opera *Peter Grimes*, supposedly set on the east coast. But Norman insisted that it was a 'Millom opera', because Montague Slater had used his experience of Millom in the nineteen twenties;

'half the population rotting away in idleness, at the edge of the foetid tidal marshes ... broken boats mouldering in the salt mud, the almost worked-out mines, the men standing about in aimless clumps at the street corners and the churchyard gates. The scandal, the injustice, the waste, the muddle of it, made a deep mark on his soul.'[30]

This passed Norman by for most of his childhood. The poverty around him was so normal, so part of everyday life he took it for granted, 'like bad weather in winter',[31] partly because it didn't affect him or his family directly. His father's trade relied on the better paid middle-classes rather than the iron-workers who were being made redundant and, although there were some lean years, their way of life was unchanged. Joe Nicholson was a careful man, a man of meticulous accounting, who looked on 'bankruptcy as almost the same as adultery'.[32] He kept to regular routines; local people would set their clocks by him when he set out on his afternoon walk after lunch while Rose minded the shop. Every Sunday morning Joe walked – often with Norman – up the street to visit his brother Jim. The two were very close in age and also close in affection. After a short chat to Norman's aunt, they would all three walk out towards the sea, Norman running in front with the dog, his father and Uncle Jim, bowler-hatted and 'as solemn as sidesmen',[33] walking behind him at a steady pace, on a circular pathway, down Aaron's Lonning and up past Limestone Hill, always the same route that brought them back to the house in time for Sunday lunch. Joe liked the security of the known way, and he never took chances – his characteristic phrase was 'just to be on the safe side'. And there was something of Joe's careful genetic make-up in Norman too. A childhood story, which dated back to the First World War, at a time when his mother was still alive, told how the three year old Norman was asked, by his father, to give some of the money in his piggy bank to be converted into war bonds to support the war effort. Norman refused to let the money go.

Chapter Three

The Nicholson and Cornthwaite families were predominantly male. Norman had two male Cornthwaite cousins – children of his deceased Uncle William – and several male Nicholson cousins, though he was closest to his Uncle Jim's two boys. Rose had also brought him a new cousin – the son of her sister Laura. Passing the scholarship brought Norman into close contact with girls for the first time. The grammar school was co-educational, whereas his primary school, Holborn Hill, had been segregated. Norman recorded that the introduction of girls into the classroom, brought a kind of 'kitchen cosiness', a gentleness, 'something which had been missing from my sisterless life'.[1] Although he had several close friends among the boys, Norman was isolated from the majority by his dislike of sport and his interest in books. It made him an oddity even in his own family. Norman's father had been a gymnast and athlete; his uncle Jack had been a sporting legend, and the whole family followed the fortunes of various local football and cricket teams enthusiastically. Norman grew to like cricket, but his close friends at Holborn Hill and the Grammar School tended to be boys who shared his academic nature.

Albert, Norman's close companion at Holborn Hill, was the orphaned son of one of Rose Sobey's cousins. His mother too had died while he was a small child. Norman lost touch with Albert after his family moved away from Millom in his teens, but he later became an eminent psychologist. Another close friend, John 'Ted' Fisher, was the son of a local policeman, whose family were farmers in the Duddon valley. Norman described him as having 'a subtle mind that is capable of appreciating delicate shades of thought and art'.[2] Ted would go on to become a brilliant teacher and, years later, was responsible for sending the young Ted Hughes' work to Norman for an opinion.

Tom Morton was the son of the widowed Headmistress of the Girls'

School at Lapstone Road. He had often been bullied because of his bookishness. Norman and Tom spent their free time climbing the local peaks and cycling long distances through the southern lakes.

> 'We wandered through oak woods and fir woods, along rock-cluttered paths and the peaty floors of corries; we scrambled across screes, squelched through fell-side bogs. We crossed becks by natural stepping stones, slithered into the water and sat bare-foot on the bank, while our socks dried in the sun.'[3]

It was an idyllic time for Norman, and was also probably the healthiest time of his life. Ironically, without his knowledge, he might already have been incubating the TB bacilli. Doctors all recognised that, by the time symptoms appeared, the patient had probably had the disease for at least one or two years.

It wasn't surprising that several of Norman's school friends were girls. He always related easily to women and became close to two of the girls in his class, who continued to keep in touch even after they left Millom. Marjorie Thompson – 'a small, fair, pretty girl' who eventually married a professor and Bessie Satterthwaite, who married a clergyman and as Bessie Schiff became one of Norman's greatest friends in later life. At fourteen he also fell in love for the first time, with a girl he calls 'Maureen' in his autobiography. She was a year older than Norman and lived at Broughton-in-Furness, commuting to Millom every day by train. Norman always sat in the desk beside her or directly behind her in the classroom. It was a very intense relationship, even though (or perhaps because) they could only see each other at school. During the day they were so inseparable that the headmaster made a joke about making them walk arm-in-arm around the playground. Every evening Norman would walk her to the station after school and later, when the ten o'clock siren sounded the end of shift at the ironworks, they had a pact to think of each other before they went to sleep.

There was no sex in their relationship, according to Norman. Some cuddling, chaste kisses – 'my love for Maureen was a thing of antique poses and styles'.[4] Norman was a dreamy, romantic, old-fashioned boy, emotionally young for his age, and disturbed by the changes that were taking place in his body, which was displaying an awareness of facts he admitted he didn't understand. He was puzzled by Freudian dreams. 'I used to dream, over and over again, that I was falling down a mine-shaft or over a

CHAPTER THREE

cliff-edge or down flight after flight of long, steep, sharply-twisting stairs.'[5] Norman's sexual education consisted of a few (more or less accurate) facts related by his friend Albert, and a church leaflet passed on to him by his father. Although the entire school knew about his teenage love-affair, he was terrified his parents, particularly his step-mother, would find out about Maureen, without knowing why, and almost fainted when Rose questioned him about 'hanging around the railway station' after school.[6] Analysing it later, he said that he wanted to keep his two lives – school and home – separate. Rose was the dominant influence on Norman's life, and he was beginning to need a life of his own.

Since he went to the Grammar School, Norman had begun to see the inhabitants of his home town, and the friends of his childhood, differently. 'People I had looked up to as a boy now seemed old-fashioned, ungrammatical in speech and narrow in outlook'.[7] This included the Nicholsons. Norman's paternal grandmother Maria Nicholson, who died in 1928 when he was fourteen, had been completely illiterate. Education was taking Norman away from his family mentally, long before it threatened to remove him physically. He couldn't talk to them about the books he was reading, or the ideas that he was coming into contact with, 'or anything else that seemed to matter'.[8] From his father there was an admiring incomprehension, and unexpressed pride in his clever son. Rose, always practical, saw it as Norman's way out. He would go to university, get his degree, and take a teaching post elsewhere. She was aware of the limitations of the declining town, and had begun to think about moving away from Millom too, but Joe wouldn't hear of it.

Norman's attitude to the Methodist chapel was changing as well. His father Joe, who had gone regularly in the first years of his marriage, now attended less frequently. Joe was not particularly religious and had been brought up in the Church of England. Norman's eyes also began to turn to St George's, at the top of the road, where his mother and other relatives were buried and where he had been taken as a child. Since then he had sometimes attended Sunday School there, partly because his Uncle Jim was one of the teachers, but also because he liked it better than the chapel Sunday School. St George's was, he said, more organised, more disciplined, more serious, more suited to his own temperament. Now he began, with encouragement from his father, to think about changing his religious allegiances. There was a belief that if you were going to university, you stood more chance of getting a place if you had been confirmed – the establishment was always seen as overwhelmingly Anglican.

At the age of fourteen, Norman began to take instruction with a view to confirmation. He was struck, immediately, by the intellectual, rather than emotional, nature of the Anglican approach to Christian doctrine;

> 'At the Methodists, it had mainly been a matter of exhortation: "Do this; don't do that; accept the Lord Jesus Christ as your Saviour."... But now, religion was presented as a straightforward set of statements or propositions, like geography or geometry. Something you could really learn.'[9]

The beautiful language of the Book of Common Prayer was a big factor in capturing Norman's enthusiasm. It was 'the Flesh taking word ... both mysterious and taken for granted, both other-worldly and this-worldly'.[10] Becoming confirmed was a powerful emotional experience for Norman. During the intense period of prayer and study just beforehand he experienced a curious sensation of peace and stillness. All his anxieties seemed suddenly to be removed. 'The air clarified, leaving me, nevertheless, taut as a telephone wire. For a time, every part of me vibrated with an emotion more intense than anything I had felt before'.[11] But the sensation of ecstasy didn't last for long. He was outraged when Rose insisted he drink a hot cup of tea before his first communion, but a few weeks later even his church attendance had lapsed.

Norman passed his matriculation exams easily. At fifteen and a half, almost a year younger than the average age of the class (which was sixteen years and four months), Norman was top of the class in both English and Maths, earning a distinction in the latter. He knew that he was safely launched into the sixth form on track for university. His parents had arranged a holiday in Scarborough as a post-examination treat. A photograph taken on another holiday shows them together as an affectionate family group. Joe is smiling but stiffly upright, Rose smiling as if someone has just cracked a joke and Norman is clowning happily next to Rose. The holiday was a great success, except for a sudden down-turn in Norman's health. He went with his father to watch a long-drawn-out county cricket match on an oppressively hot day and fainted when he stood up to leave. Rose believed that it must have been something he had eaten; Norman had always been prone to stomach upsets – what he called 'bilious attacks'. But after a couple of days he was well again and no-one gave it any thought.

In Scarborough Norman had seen a review of Bernard Shaw's play *The Apple Cart* and become interested in Shaw and his Fabian politics. Back in

CHAPTER THREE

Millom it sparked a new political consciousness. When he looked at the town, after his return from the affluence of Scarborough, he saw things he hadn't noticed before because they had been so familiar. Now he looked with a new kind of awareness. Slag banks 'slobbered over acres of salt marsh and meadows', the land had prolapsed into worked-out mine shafts, almost swallowing one of the ore trains, and the sea threatened to break through the barriers and flood Hodbarrow. The once-busy harbour was rotting with disuse. 'All around there were signs of stagnation: huge heaps of unsold ore lay beside the shafts … and, at the Ironworks, the unsold pig-iron was stacked like enormous, dirty, grey bamboo huts.'[12]

Under the influence of socialism Norman also noticed the human wreckage. 'I saw the people of the town abandoned and seemingly forgotten … Hundreds of men stood about the street corners all day, as if waiting for a funeral'. The houses at the poorer end of town, close to the slag bank, 'were cracking and flaking from neglect and age'. Schools and other public buildings were dilapidated, institutions were in debt and the shops were barely managing to survive.[13]

Norman joined the Socialist party and when their local candidate was elected to Parliament, stood in the doorway with his parents to watch the Victory March. He was shocked by the sheer poverty of the marchers; 'women in appalling old coats and jumpers, carrying babies, wrapped in rags; children hopping along, with their toes burst out of split boots; old men, their faces little more than skin-covered skulls, pinched and black from years of work and worklessness.' At school, discussing the town's decline with his friends, they told each other 'this is what we have to get away from' and Matriculation seemed to them to be 'a Free Pass out of the town'.[14]

Norman loved the intensive study of the sixth form – the long hours of private study in the library, the discovery of new authors, new books, new ideas; 'we read, we discussed, we argued'.[15] But Norman's health had begun to deteriorate again. All winter he coughed with a cold he couldn't shake off. There were frequent 'bilious attacks' and on several more occasions he experienced the strange, fainting sensation he had felt at Scarborough; 'the room would seem to slide away from me, to become strangely distant, and I would feel, as it were, a wind rising up in my head, drowning the sound and sense of the world around me'.[16] Then, as consciousness returned, Norman would begin to shake and shiver violently. His father took him to the doctor, who recommended fresh air and more exercise.

In July his parents took him off on holiday again, this time to Harrogate, but Norman was too ill to enjoy it. He felt permanently hot and thirsty and had a sore throat that made him sound husky, 'croaking like a corncrake', as his father put it. Rose thought his voice was still breaking. In the days before the NHS, doctors were visited only as a last resort because they had to be paid for. No one wanted to pay unless it was absolutely necessary. But back in school in September, the headmaster insisted that Norman see the visiting School Medical Officer who came to the house to see the Nicholsons afterwards, and advised them that Norman would have to see a specialist and should be kept out of school from that moment on. Joe didn't wait for the appointment to come through, but took Norman back to the family doctor and then to see a specialist in Liverpool. Norman was x-rayed and the Nicholsons were warned what to expect.

When the doctor's report came it was not good news. Norman had tuberculosis of the lungs and throat and would need to go into a sanatorium. The diagnosis was terrifying for the family, though Norman had no sense of its significance. For many people TB was a death sentence. There was no cure, the only possible treatment was rest, good food and clean, fresh air. The doctor advised Joe not to let Norman go to the County Sanatorium in Cumberland, which didn't have a good reputation. He recommended a private TB hospital if they could afford it and suggested that they consider sending him 'down south'.[17]

Joe, having lost one son as a baby, and then his first wife from influenza, was quick to see the danger implied in the doctor's comments and didn't hesitate. It wasn't a question of money, what mattered was getting the best treatment for Norman. Rose had a cousin, known to Norman as Uncle Dick, who had settled in Bournemouth. His father was one of James Sobey's brothers who had originally come to Millom, but fallen out with the mine management and subsequently gone to Mexico where he had made a fortune. The son had then come back to England to live down south and, although not the millionaire he was sometimes rumoured to be, was very well off indeed. The cousins were consulted and recommended a sanatorium at Linford in Hampshire which had a very good reputation. If Norman was there, they could keep an eye on him.

There was considerable speculation in the family as to the source of Norman's tuberculosis – a disease associated with poverty and overcrowding. Joe blamed 'war bread' and rationing while he was still a baby, for his son's ill health; Norman thought it was the diet his step-mother had fed him. No-one seemed to consider the communal communion cups passed from infected lips to healthy ones. The Methodists were unique in

CHAPTER THREE

providing individual glasses for the communion wine. The capacity of the TB bacteria (present in saliva) to be passed on by shared cups and spoons had been known to doctors since before Norman was born. But when Norman was being prepared for confirmation, he had heard the Vicar pour scorn on the idea that anyone might catch some kind of infection from the communion cup. 'I ask you,' the man had said, 'could there possibly be any infection in the blood of Our Lord Jesus Christ?' It was this kind of ignorance that allowed diseases like TB to flourish in communities.

In the same way, few people questioned the safety of the milk they drank straight from the farms, unpasteurised, from untested cows riddled with TB. The Nicholsons got their milk from a farmer, tipped straight into a jug, still warm from the cow. Norman was also in close contact with other TB victims in Millom – both children and adults. In the year 1929, a thousand people a week were dying of TB in Britain; it was a modern plague that lasted until the introduction of antibiotics, the pasteurisation of milk and the compulsory testing of dairy herds. Better child nutrition, housing and other public health measures, introduced after the Second World War, also played a part in stamping it out.

So, Norman prepared to leave Millom for Linford. It would only be for three months or so, the doctors said. He would soon be on his feet again and back at school catching up with his contemporaries. Norman had no inkling that his life had just been brutally wrenched out of its trajectory and that he would never set foot on the pathway he had imagined for himself.

Chapter Four

Norman travelled down to Bournemouth by train with Rose, while Joe stayed in Millom to look after the shop. It was a journey Norman had done before, two years earlier, when he had come to Bournemouth for a summer holiday with his parents. This time they stayed overnight with Rose's cousins and then were taken to Linford in Dick Sobey's chauffeur-driven Daimler.

Linford was typical of many TB sanatoriums – a two storey manor house with large grounds, in the heart of the country. Linford was in the New Forest, on the slope of a hill surrounded by thirty six acres of meadow and garden, and fifteen hundred acres of woodland. Woods and forests were thought to be particularly beneficial to patients with lung infections. Woodland soil was believed to be 'antagonistic to pathogenic bacteria' and the air purer than any other except mountain and sea air. At a time when Britain's cities were fouled by industrial pollution and chimney smoke so strong it created lingering 'smogs' that brought life to a standstill and did immense damage to people's lungs, pure air for recovering TB patients was essential. It had also been noted that 'the psychic effect of beautiful woodland scenery' was beneficial to seriously ill patients. This was the thinking behind the establishment of Linford, which was at the cutting edge of TB treatment in England before the Second World War. It practised what was known as the 'Nordrach' treatment, which consisted of a Spartan regime – 'an absolutely open-air life, day and night, and in sunshine, fog, and rain; abundant diet; rest before meals; and exercise regulated by the bodily temperature'.[1]

Chalets were scattered all over the grounds of Linford, sheltered by trees and privet hedges. The room allotted to Norman was open to the elements;

'From my bed I faced the two, always-open, sliding-doors, half the

CHAPTER FOUR

width of the wall, that gave onto a little porch, screened by the privet. At my bed-side, and on the opposite side of the chalet, were glass windows, which I was allowed to close only in a storm, while only the fourth wall, behind my back was solid.'[2]

It was bitterly cold, but the room was warmed by an anthracite stove. The furniture was sparse – apart from the bed there was a wash-stand, an invalid's reclining chair, small table, and a chest of drawers.

Joe Nicholson may have realised the danger faced by his only child, but it wasn't until Rose arrived at Linford that she seemed to become aware that her stepson was seriously ill. They were met in reception by a nurse, who walked them down to Norman's chalet. She turned down the bed and told Norman to undress and get into it. According to Norman, Rose was astonished. '"He won't have to go to bed will he?" she almost wailed.'[3] The nurse was not sympathetic. Norman was running an extremely high temperature and his x-rays showed extensive infection. He was a high risk case.

A doctor came to examine him and explained the principles of Linford and emphasised the importance of co-operation with the strict regime. If Norman didn't follow the rules, then he would be letting everyone down. While his temperature was high he would have to be confined to bed, and – to protect his larynx – he was ordered to whisper.

Left alone in his wooden hut, Norman slept, ate, read, listened to the radio and looked at the small section of landscape he could view through the open door. He could see through the trees on the slope of the wild garden to the gorse bushes on the heath-land of the New Forest, where ponies and a herd of TB tested cows roamed. He didn't realise, on that first day, that it would be a year before he was allowed to walk along the paths that he could see between the trees.

It was an isolated existence for a boy barely seventeen years old. There were no other patients to share his room – patients were separated to prevent the spread of infection – and, until his temperature came down, he was barred from taking part in the communal activities at the main house. Nurses came and went, maids delivered food and hot water and emptied the commode. The weather swirled through the open doors and windows – some mornings when Norman woke he found his breath frozen on the pillow. Birds flew in and out and some of them were tame enough to steal food from his plate. Norman borrowed a bird handbook from the Sanatorium Library and began to learn to identify them. He learned to recognise the common species as well as rarer visitors. There were moments of enchantment; 'throughout May and June, I woke, night after night, as from one dream to another, to find the moonlight or the pre-dawn darkness freaked and shot through with the flashes and dim, low glimmerings of the nightingale's song'.[4] He read Gilbert White and Richard Jefferies. When he looked back, it was this period of observation at Linford that had shaped his vision of the world and man's place in it:

> 'As season followed season, I breathed in the dews, dawns, rains, frosts and sunshine of the Forest, feeling the sap and surge of it pulsing through my blood until it hardly seemed to matter whether I got well or not, for to share in, to be aware of that life of nature was itself a mode of living. I had not then read D.H. Lawrence, but his poems and early novels express much of what I felt – an almost ecstatic joy in the thrust and flux of life, in the renewal of the seasons and the renewal of generations and even in death as part of the cycle of renewal'.[5]

The enforced rest and seclusion left little to do but read and fortunately the Sanatorium had a big library, stocked with Victorian and Edwardian literature. Norman read everything – 'I had not the slightest feeling that what I read was in any way out of date'.[6] It was a diet of Hardy, Dickens, Wells, Bennett, Galsworthy and Shaw, as well as all the 19th century classics. He later said that Linford had been his university. What he lacked was someone to discuss it all with. He wrote long letters to his parents, and to his friends Ted and Tom. When he was allowed to have visits from other patients his life became more sociable and he played occasional games of chess, but conversation was restricted by the fact that he was still under orders to whisper. He had to use a policeman's whistle to gain attention and it wasn't always popular.

Norman's progress didn't live up to the doctors' initial optimism. The tuberculosis was deep-rooted and had been eating away at his lungs – particularly the left – for a long time. His temperature would go down briefly, only to rise again when the strict regime of rest was slackened. His weight also remained too low. Nine months later, Norman was still confined to bed, to the consternation of his father, who came to visit during the following summer, enquiring when Norman was coming home. Norman couldn't understand his father's reaction to the fact that he wasn't going back to Millom, at least for the foreseeable future. Staying in Linford wasn't a problem for Norman. 'It caused me no dismay … for by this time, the sanatorium had become my entire world. I could not see beyond its

CHAPTER FOUR

horizon. I could barely imagine the time when my life would have to be lived somewhere else.'[7] Because of the nature of the treatment, most TB patients stayed in sanatoriums for a long time and it wasn't unusual for them to become institutionalised. Joe Nicholson wanted his son home, healthy and whole, not just because he loved him, but because the fees were gradually draining his life-time's savings, put aside for his retirement – essential in the days before state pensions. Norman was blissfully unaware of the sacrifices that were being made to keep him there.

He was already envisaging a future that didn't include a return to Millom, because Linford was providing another kind of education – in class snobbery. Since the fees were high, the patients were mainly middle or upper class southerners. They spoke differently and Norman found himself adjusting his own accent to theirs. It was rather a shock when he had visitors from Millom and 'heard the sounds that came out of their mouths'.[8] He learned to be ashamed of his parents and his father's trade. Every week he was sent the *Millom Gazette* and one of the nurses noticed an advert for 'Jos Nicholson – Gents Outfitter' and teased him about it. Norman was so embarrassed that he made sure the *Millom Gazette* was destroyed as soon as he had read it. This new sensation of class distinction was difficult to come to terms with. Watching his parents walk up the path towards his chalet, he was 'embarrassed for their sake and ashamed of my embarrassment'.[9]

There were other visitors to Linford too – the Rev Walton, once curate at St George's during Norman's confirmation classes, was now a curate at Bournemouth, and he came to see Norman regularly. On one occasion he brought some of the younger boys from the grammar school who were visiting him. One of them was Henry Slater, a couple of years younger than Norman, who remembered him because he had a reputation for being very clever, and whose collapse into TB had been much talked about in Millom. Henry remembered being shocked at Norman's physical condition. There was general pessimism about the prospects of his recovery.

These 'intrusions' from a place Norman had left behind seemed unreal to him. Millom had become 'a part of the world to which nothing in me now wanted to belong'.[10] It resulted in a period of profound depression. Norman couldn't see where his life was going or where he wanted to be. For a while he stopped eating, 'food became the biggest bugbear of my life', which didn't help his recovery.[11] In his autobiography, written forty years later, he glosses over this period, claiming that he was 'quite happy', but there are indications in other sources from that time that this was untrue. Norman's concerns about food and the frequent 'bilious attacks' he was prone to at times of stress, raise the question of whether he had some form of anxiety-related eating disorder.

There were women at Linford – some girls around Norman's own age. He had a brief crush on a girl called Anne, but it quickly petered out since he was bed-bound and couldn't go out walking with her. They remained friends. The second relationship was more serious. Her name was Sylvia Lubelsky, she was four or five years older than Norman and the daughter of a wealthy Jewish furniture manufacturer. In his autobiography he refers to her as Celia and plays down the relationship, denying that he had ever fallen in love with her. This too was untrue. At first it was a matter of recommending books and music. It was Sylvia who introduced Norman to Bach. She encouraged him to listen to the Promenade Concerts broadcast on the radio and one night she sent him a note via one of the maids saying, 'Tune in now and listen'. When he turned on the radio he heard music he'd never heard before. '…instrument after instrument – violin, oboe, perhaps bassoon – kept running up and down and looping over and over in delicious patterns of dissolving and re-forming sound'. It was his first experience of counterpoint. 'I had become a Bach fan before I learned Bach's name'.[12]

When Norman wasn't well enough to get out of bed and sit on the terrace, in what was called 'the shelter', with the other patients, he and Sylvia sent each other pencilled notes. It's impossible to date, but at some point during the long, dark nights at Linford, Norman had begun to write seriously, scribbling poems and pieces of prose. And it was to Sylvia that Norman confided his private thoughts about becoming a writer and asked her advice. She urged him to use his powers of observation when he was finally allowed to walk out into the woods and gardens. After one expedition, when Sylvia was confined to her chalet with a relapse, he wrote to her:

'I tried to exercise my imagination after the fashion you advocate. Before me was a patch of heather in the luscious, rich, purple of full bloom, sprinkled on the intense, deep, dark, living green of its own leaves, beside the lighter, wearier green of the sparse grass. I thought how it was like red wine poured on a green carpet; I thought of Scotland, of the blood of the martyrs shed on the wild moors… It was something infinitely more beautiful than either of those. It was heather on a windy

CHAPTER FOUR

hillside.'[13]

When both of them were well enough, they walked out together, exploring the woodland, sometimes accompanied by a young Jewish man, Maurice Elvey, who was also a friend of Sylvia's.

Norman began to fall deeply in love with her and it caused a rift in their relationship. One of the notes reads 'Is our friendship at an end?'[14] It's clear from the letters that Sylvia liked him very much, enough to spend a lot of time with him and encourage him. He told Sylvia that she had 're-awakened' in him 'the realisation that life is worth living'.[15] She was a mature woman of twenty three; he was by now a boy of eighteen. In some of his letters he addresses her as 'Big sister' and that seems to be how she wanted to be seen. But given the fact that she kept all his letters and notes, even at this early stage, and maintained a friendship with him for the rest of her life, there has to have been something more. Norman was very attractive – tall, with soft, dark, wavy hair and an animated face. He was intelligent, charming, needy, and very articulate.

Sylvia challenged him about his feelings for her and he responded defensively; 'When you carefully explained the "symptoms" which had led you to ['believe' crossed out] think, that I was in love with you, did it not occur to you that the same arguments which had convinced you, might also convince me, against my inclinations, my will, my feelings?' He argues that he isn't in love with her, adding, 'but do you believe me?'[16] The denial is transparently false and Sylvia was not convinced.

Norman had a relapse in the early summer and coughed up blood. He was immediately put back to bed and spent a week lying completely still. But despite the fact that his tuberculosis remained active, he was told that he was going to be discharged. Norman was horrified at the thought of leaving and aware that he was still not well enough for normal life. But Joe's money had run out. He had expected Norman to stay in the sanatorium for a few months, but he'd now been there for nearly two years. Norman didn't realise, until his father died in the nineteen fifties, just how close to insolvency his finances had been.

The doctors gave Norman detailed instructions on how to live a sanatorium life at home. While received medical opinion stated that it was impossible to achieve the same standard of care in a home environment, there were dissenting voices, including Dr Isaac Burney Yeo, who wrote that:

'We believe an intelligent patient, anxious to be cured, and convinced of the curative power of the conditions prevailing in sanatoria, and with the means needed to secure constant medical supervision, can be provided with "open-air" treatment at home as well as in such institutions, although, no doubt, a temporary residence in a well directed sanatorium would serve as a useful introduction and education for home treatment.'[17]

1932 'glowed into a ripe and complacent September',[18] and Norman vowed to follow the instructions he'd been given as carefully as possible. He was to stay in bed for a few days to recover from the journey home and keep to the same regime as Linford, taking his temperature and watching his weight, going to bed before meals and retiring every night at 6 o'clock. The window of his room at home had been altered to allow it to open to let in the bracing, if somewhat polluted, air. Norman's parents, who came for him in Dick Sobey's car, were told to allow him to set his own pace. Leaving Linford was a huge wrench – his friends gathered on the drive to wave goodbye and Norman felt sadder than he had felt on his departure from Millom almost two years earlier.

He travelled north, from Bournemouth via London, on train after train, 'in a state of numb apprehension'. The first sight of Black Combe beyond the Duddon Estuary, 'looking dark and smudgy in the grey evening', lifted Norman's heart for a moment, but then the landscape of Millom Ironworks came into view 'grim, gaunt and bony'. Thirty years later, he could still recall the anger and resentment he had felt. 'The fells looked flat and listless as a stage backcloth ... The slagbanks were the frozen excreta of the earth – huge, fossilised medieval middens. The tarmac and concrete and pavements seemed to seal off the living pulse of the soil. The smoke spread over the town like a dirty umbrella blacking off the sun and the sky. I was appalled ...'[19] At that moment, Millom was just as he had pictured it in Linford – 'small, dark, drab, damp and mean'. It seemed impossible that he could recover his health in such a place. 'There was not, I feared, a lungful of breathable air in all those streets and back-alleys.' The walk from the station to the house was almost more than the exhausted boy could manage. His thoughts were in turmoil. 'I did not know what was going to happen; I did not know where I really belonged.'[20]

Chapter Five

Norman quickly bounced back from his initial depression and reported to Sylvia that although his return to Millom had been a surreal experience, he was now settling in. At the end of his first week he was already planning Sylvia's promised visit to Millom and sent her two maps he'd drawn of the town and its surroundings, so that she could see the important places he was going to write about in his letters. 'The Mines (very interesting and even beautiful in their way) the Estuary, Haverigg, Lowscales, most certainly Black Combe, and the mysterious place marked on Map 2 as the Mains … I can only say that within an area of about 1½ x ¾ miles one can find dunes, rocky coast, sea-washed sand, heather, shingle, and patches of appalling drabness.'

He talked about the Duddon Valley, 'the most wildly romantic & exquisitely beautiful district I have ever seen.' Its main attraction for Norman was that there was 'not a single tourist'. He told Sylvia that he was staying in bed a lot, reading a book on music and talking in his sleep about major thirds and imperfect fifths. He was playing the piano again, trying to learn the meaning of counterpoint and had asked his mother and father for a gramophone. He ends the letter with a request for photographs: 'I would give a great deal for one hour of your company, just to cuddle up against you & talk about nothing in particular… My regards to Maurice & my love to Anne, and absolutely everything you would like from me for yourself, you darling. …'[1]

Norman took his own temperature several times a day and if it rose by even half a degree he went to bed and stayed there until it came down. His weight continued to increase and by January he weighed nine and a half stones. He filled his time by reading and writing. When he plundered his old school exercise books, for scrap paper to write on, he told Sylvia that he 'was surprised' to find how clever he had been. The tone of his letters to Sylvia is chirpy and upbeat, confident, sometimes demanding; this is a young man who is used to being the centre of attention, very sure of his own abilities – almost to the point of arrogance. He told Sylvia that the sooner she realised that, in looking after herself, once she left the sanatorium, she would have to be completely selfish, the better. She would have to 'disappoint, & annoy, & offend other people', in order to protect her health. 'You simply must not consider other people's feelings,' he told her. It came more easily for him, he admitted, because he had never 'joined in' and nobody expected him to. He was, he told Sylvia, a loner by nature.[2]

Norman's affection for Sylvia showed no sign of being dimmed by distance – at one point he talked, half joking, about eloping with her. On another occasion he sent her a postcard with one of George Bernard Shaw's love letters to Ellen Terry inscribed on the back. Sylvia was not amused; Norman was undeterred. The avalanche of letters continued. He was using the time in bed to study – his old headmaster Walter Wilson, a part time student himself, had given Norman the catalogue of the Cumberland County Education Committee Library for Teachers, and he offered to get him any books he wanted from it. Norman was glad to accept.

This was the most important period of his life – the years that made him a poet. He read, he wrote, he practised, and he had willing critics around him to read his work and provide feedback. His old school friend Bessie Satterthwaite helped him out when she was home from Manchester University. Ted Fisher was at Durham and he also came back for university vacations and shared what he was learning there. But the most influential of all his friends was Sylvia Lubelsky. Norman showered her with letters – some up to twenty pages long – containing poems and stories and ideas for stories with requests for her opinion. He told her about Bessie, describing her as a girl about his own age with whom he talked 'about literature and Shaw', but reassured Sylvia that he was not attracted to her.

The contents of Norman's letters are interesting, because they show his development as a writer. From the beginning he was working on fiction and drama as well as poetry. There are pages of dialect speech; an idea for a historical novel about a siege at an isolated pub at Seathwaite in 1890; a short story; a play set in the time of Moses. But it was poetry that was the biggest challenge. He practised relentlessly; 'If I am ever to try and write any poetry,' he wrote to Sylvia, 'it is obviously necessary to get some practise in versification. I think I will try experimenting in various rhythms and metres in order to get used to the handling of various verse forms. I am not very attracted to free verse which, to me, savours too much of decadent

CHAPTER FIVE

romanticism.'[3]

He began experimenting by imitating other poets and by seeing what could be done 'with modern diction and subjects in the old classic forms of quatrain, Shakespearian sonnet and Papal couplets.'[4] He sent Sylvia a Bach sonnet, complaining that he couldn't get rid of the phrase 'ceaseless longing', and asked her if she knew any magazine that might take the poem, once he'd polished it up.[5] Norman was still only nineteen, but from the very beginning he appears to have been focused on getting into print.

Norman's first publication was in March 1933, *The Radio Times*, in a section called 'What the Other Listener Thinks'. It was a short, humorous piece on George Bernard Shaw called The Silver Nickel. He wrote proudly to Sylvia that it was quite an event, seeing his name and 'Millom' in the Radio Times; 'After all, I don't suppose I have seen the name of Millom printed in a London newspaper more than twenty times'.[6]

The gramophone Norman had asked for never materialised, which wasn't surprising, given the straitened financial circumstances of his parents. There were still doctor's bills to pay – Norman needed regular check-ups and no bout of influenza, or even the common cold, could be neglected. And there was always the possibility of another stay in a sanatorium which would have to be paid for. Joe and Rose were watching the pennies, with no idea how long it would be before Norman could support himself.

Norman's only source of music became the radio. He regularly listened during the day, up in his room, but particularly in the evening since he often retired to bed at 6 o'clock. He loved listening to the Third Programme, as it was then, with classical concerts and academic discussions. This section of the BBC was quite proud to be what was called 'Highbrow', and became Norman's window on an intellectual world he was cut off from. His letters to Sylvia were full of enthusiastic comment and at one point he copied four bars of Beethoven onto the page to illustrate a point. He recorded his delight in the Brandenburg Concertos. His study of counterpoint was giving him more of an insight into Bach's method of composition, and he observed that 'each movement is purely a progression of musical thought'. Bach wasn't the only composer he was discovering. He experienced total ecstasy listening to Mendelssohn's violin concerto. In a letter to Sylvia, he compared it to kissing his first girl friend in the sand dunes aged fourteen, or hearing the New World Symphony for the first time. Norman liked listening to the radio at high volume and one of the neighbours complained, resulting in a visit from the police.

It was a discussion that Norman heard on the radio that first introduced him to the subject of provincialism versus metrocentrism. It was a debate between Eric Linklater and John Bone with the title, 'I want to abolish London'. Linklater argued that London was sapping the life of the whole country. 'London, he said, has cornered the theatre, & the press, & the publishing business, so that any actor, or dramatist, or author has to work with an eye on London if he is to succeed.' Trapped in Millom by circumstance, Norman found himself in agreement. 'Abolishing London … would also mean abolishing Provincialism.'[7] Norman had found himself a philosophy. All the intellectual and social snobberies Norman had encountered at Linford and elsewhere, could now be rebuffed by cogent argument.

In April 1933, seven months after Norman had left Millom, he went back to Linford for a check-up. His friends Sylvia and Anne were still there, as was Maurice Elvey. Norman was ecstatic about the opportunity of seeing Sylvia and Anne again. He indulged in a little flirtation. Anne, he wrote, should 'Please wear the bed-tick if still in existence. Respectability not necessary, nor even desirable.' Sylvia was instructed to book him into 'Campions' bed and breakfast in the village, and he was very exacting in his requirements. 'Lunch for me must be at 1.0pm … dinner at 7.15 or 7.30pm.'[8] There was a catalogue of misunderstanding over the booking. Norman's dates kept changing – Sylvia seems to have been uncertain about the timing of his visit or perhaps uncertain whether she wanted to meet him again – it's impossible to be sure with only one side of the correspondence in existence. In the end he wrote her a very angry letter. 'For God's sake make things definite this time. You have continually changed my plans about this visit and I am miserable with worry.'[9]

There are no words of gratitude for Sylvia's hard work finding him somewhere to stay, and no apologies for his rudeness. In another letter, undated, but apparently in response to Sylvia's protest at the tone of one of his, Norman wrote: 'I don't think it should be necessary for me to conceal any gusts of bad temper I may have. Our friendship is not of so frail a growth that it needs to be sheltered like a hot house plant.'[10]

Norman travelled to Linford alone and seemed to have enjoyed his holiday. The quarrel with Sylvia was made up, and Norman came back to Millom more in love with her than ever. In one letter he confessed that he wrote to her because he was lonely and writing was like chatting to her. He had extracted a promise from her to come and visit him in September. He warned her that he couldn't arrange for her to stay at his house in advance because his step-mother Rose would become too anxious about it and

CHAPTER FIVE

couldn't cope with the upheaval. There would have to be some subterfuge – a hotel booking that fell through at the last moment perhaps. Norman was clearly in awe of Rose.

In the summer weather Norman's strict regime was relaxed. The long hours of daylight made reading more of a pleasure. He had a hatred of artificial light and its influence on him, which seems to have brought on a kind of 'SAD' syndrome – his mind wandered – he couldn't concentrate and felt 'in a state of suppressed anxiety, for something I don't know & can never know.' A 'trouble of the lower levels of consciousness … unpleasant nervous excitement'. In the summer he didn't suffer at all.[11] He went out for walks and discovered the great pleasure of lying naked among the sand dunes, returning 'absolutely drunk on air & sunlight'. He told Sylvia that, 'Unless you have tried it, you can have no idea of the freedom of complete nakedness in the open air. I have never been so conscious of the knowledge that throughout me & the birds, & the whole of nature there is the same [kind] of life. It was a profoundly religious experience.'[12]

Norman's love of the natural world, which he had discovered at Linford, was becoming stronger. His old headmaster, Walter Wilson, was a keen botanist and began to introduce Norman to the wild flowers – some of them quite rare – which grew on the hillside and around the iron-works. The Linford regime included 'light exercise' and so, every day when the weather permitted, Norman had to go out for a short walk, usually across the cricket field.

He continued to send Sylvia his poems and she was now trying to find magazines to send them to. Although Norman asked her for feedback, he wasn't always pleased with the edits she suggested. 'To my mind the best title for the Orange poem is "Recitative". The "Loudly" must remain. Please ask them to publish it under a pseudonym', though it seemed unlikely that it would be published at all. The working title for the poem was the rather Georgian phrase: 'Bring me not Chrysanthemums', and it included the lines; 'If I were God/ I would take the world in my fingers/ and squeeze it like an orange.' The poem was proving difficult to finish. 'I am trying to keep to a strict metrical pattern (while by no means keeping to conventionally poetic ideas) & they are giving me a lot of trouble.'[13]

Norman had been asked to give a talk to the Weslyan Guild, which he regarded as an honour, but struggled to find a subject for it. Sylvia suggested Haydn and Norman's letters are full of discussion of the talk. Sylvia was by now in and out of Linford, as her condition improved, followed by a relapse after she was discharged resulting in re-admission, but in September 1933 Sylvia came to Millom for the much discussed holiday, and it seems to have been a great success. She got on well with Rose, which made things much easier for Norman. Millom is a very small town and news that Norman had 'a girlfriend' from the sanatorium soon spread. Sylvia became the object of discreet curiosity and was subsequently referred to as 'Norman's girl'. Norman was thoroughly miserable after she left to return home to London and his time seemed difficult to fill; 'there still seems a big blank in the day. I can't help feeling that it is an awful waste of time, being alive, & on the same earth as you, & yet not being with you.'[14]

In another, much more jokey, letter he sent '10,000 X 10,000 thanks' for a photo which was, apparently, better than the 'tired woman' photo resembling a 'poor housewife at the end of a hard day's work before she had Persil' which was all he had had previously. He added: 'Ich Liebe dich/je t'adore/I love you', and then in brackets, anticipating Sylvia's reaction, '(shut it yourself!)' The letter ends 'love & kisses dearest', and in a postscript he admits that his 'enthusiasm' for her 'has gone on so long that it may almost be called an obsession'.[15]

In the early summer of 1934, Norman went down to stay with Sylvia at her parents' home at Dalston in north-east London. Apparently his parents couldn't take their own summer holiday unless Norman was safely catered for elsewhere, but it was a good excuse for Norman to see more of Sylvia, who was now temporarily discharged from Linford and living at home. This was only Norman's second visit to London, after the trip to the Great Exhibition when he was a small child. He appears to have been very happy and wrote to Sylvia in July, after his return to Millom;

> '… each time I meet you again I seem to get to know you still better. I venture to say, Mr Chairman, that between the young woman before mentioned and myself there exists an intimacy & an understanding which has rarely been attained between two people of the same or of opposite sex. C'est a dire, Sylvia dearest, I love you, I am completely satisfied in my love. In fact I love you better than little onions…You are a darling; you are an intellectual; you are a perfect friend; you are a bloody fool; I love you in each capacity.'[16]

But things were far from perfect. There were long silences when Sylvia failed to reply to any of his letters, almost as though she had begun to wonder whether to break off the correspondence. Norman continued to

CHAPTER FIVE

write, though he did add irritated remarks to the bottom of his letters, sometimes berating her, sometimes re-iterating his affection; 'I still love you, Sylvia, even though you don't write to me now…'[17] For some time, Sylvia's friends had known that she was emotionally involved with Maurice Elvey, the young man she had met at Linford and who had shared so much of her time there. They all knew that she was planning to marry him as soon as they were both free from the threat of tuberculosis. Norman had always been very jealous of Maurice, and felt excluded by the fact that they were both Jewish and spoke to each other in Yiddish. At one point he had begged Sylvia to teach him the language. Sylvia seems to have been afraid of Norman's reaction to their engagement, because of his own intense affection for her, but in early 1934 her friends urged her to tell him before he found out from another source. During Norman's visit, Sylvia seems to have made some attempt to prepare him for the news of her unofficial engagement, though his loving letter above seems to have been written in complete ignorance of it. Shortly after his return home, Sylvia wrote more explicitly about her intention to marry Maurice, but Norman carried on corresponding as if nothing had changed and seems to have remained hopeful that the marriage would not take place. Occasionally he signed his letters 'Your adoring, and eternally damned, Norman', before adding a thousand kisses.[18]

In October 1934, Sylvia came to visit Millom again, and on November 3rd Norman wrote to her, telling her how he felt and enclosing a poem 'in the manner of Lovelace'.

> The oak tree sheds her yellow leaves
>   And sobbing sighs the pine
> And Phoebus knows, when Sylvia goes,
>   What needs him then to shine?
> Diana puts not forth her ray
>   When Sylvia disappears;
> The wild winds wail, with no avail,
>   And clouds dissolve in tears.

Norman's letter was needy and self-pitying. He told her he was ill with a 'vile bilious attack' which had developed as soon as Sylvia left and that he felt wretched, miserable and 'depressed'.[19]

It was during this period that Norman appears to have published his first poem, under the pseudonym of Anne Blundell Sims. It was called

A Child's Thoughts on the Moon and Stars. It's only possible to establish that the poem is Norman's from the correspondence with Sylvia Lubelsky. At one point he writes to her 'Please do not send [the poem] to any paper under any name or initials whatever.' How the pseudonym was arrived at is unknown. 'Anne' was the name of their friend at Linford, but the surnames are a mystery. Whatever Norman's injunctions to Sylvia, the poem was published in a newspaper and Sylvia kept a cutting. Later, Norman and Ted Fisher wrote a spoof on it in their hand-written, hand-illustrated notebook of satirical poems called 'Limitations'. Under the title 'Upon Mrs A. Blundell Sims – Her Limitations as an Interpreter of Juvenile Astronomical Conjecture', there is a quote from the poem:

> Of course I like the wee stars, too,
> But they are never still
> And twinkle, twinkle all night through,
> And all the sky do fill.[20]

Norman never admitted to authorship. During the years 1934 and 1935, he was hard at work on poetry 'in the best Modern manner ... which even the most enthusiastic modern couldn't make any sense of' interspersed with a few lines 'in the Rabindranath Tagore manner'. Sylvia sent him T.S. Eliot's *The Waste Land* for Christmas 1934 and it had an effect on Norman which he likened to a religious conversion.[21] He described how he and Ted Fisher sat on the edge of the cricket field, declaiming 'Sweet Thames, run softly ... We read on in growing excitement, though neither of us understood a word... I went about for weeks in a dither of enthusiasm, my head whirling with the new words and images'.[22]

He immediately began to read Jessie L. Watson's *From Ritual to Romance* and Fraser's *Golden Bough* in order to understand the references in *The Waste Land*. It was, the twenty year old Norman wrote, 'One of the greatest poems I have ever read'. He thought its layers of meaning were 'contrapuntal' and talked about it in musical terms. 'Form, balance, growth & development, crescendo & diminuendo, such as is very rarely found'. But there was also 'magnificent poetry' and symbolism 'complicated and subtle'.[23]

Norman had a publishing success with one of his own poems, in the *North Western Daily Mail*. Ted Fisher remarked that the first two lines were 'indistinguishable from Eliot' which Norman took as a compliment rather than a criticism. One of the poems that he sent to Sylvia for comment demonstrates the extent of Eliot's influence on his work at this point. It is

CHAPTER FIVE

also a precursor of one of his most important poems, The Pot Geranium. Morning Voluntary [a reference to Wordsworth's Evening Voluntary] describes the dawn seen from the window of his room.

> Indefinite vague grey motes of light
> Co-ordinate and straighten out
> To long grey lines of slate
> And antic shapes of chimney pots.

The next verse describes the roofs coming into view, and telegraph wires that

> Etch their recurring patterns on the sky…
> While muttering below, the street
> Stretches sulkily like a dog
> And scratches its returning consciousness.[24]

Norman was now spending a great deal of his time writing and beginning to think more critically about it. He told Sylvia, who was now in Switzerland, that he was deleting and revising a lot. Norman had no money that didn't come from his parents and wasn't free to buy books, or even paper to write on. Sylvia sent him reams of foolscap, because that was what 'real' writers used, she told him. Norman wanted to buy her a copy of the T.S. Eliot that had been such an epiphany for him, but couldn't; 'my people could not understand why I should want to give you a book when it is neither Christmas nor your birthday'.[25]

Norman had another epiphany when he read Virginia Woolf's *The Waves*, 'the most important (for me) literary discovery of the last few years … the most beautiful prose I have ever read'. Norman was writing a lot of prose and had told Sylvia in March that 'for the last 3 weeks, I have been hard at work on a novel… all the characters are bloody fools' – perhaps his first novel, *Love to the N'th*, completed in the late thirties.[26] Now he sent her an excerpt from a short story he was writing which was a blatant pastiche of Woolf's style. It was, he told Sylvia, written in the first person, present tense, and was the picture of a woman 'seen through indigestion, as it were'. It began:

> 'Waking within sleeping. Pale glimmer of half-awareness. One over two. One stomach over two buttocks. Pale glimmer of half-

awareness that brings dawn-ache to belly-consciousness and the brain-unconsciousness. Grey prelude glow, that gleams now on the mirror's faint remembrances of what the moon may perhaps have looked like and on these two unseeing eyes that stare. Low, blue-bottle buzz of light, ineffectual against the window panes.'[27]

A letter to Sylvia contains further excerpts from the story with the comment, 'You will agree that it is pretty good... I am very satisfied with it myself'. But he wasn't happy with the feedback he was getting from Sylvia, who wasn't writing as often as Norman thought she should, and when she did complained that his letters to her were too long (up to twenty four pages long) and 'boring in parts'.[28]

Sylvia was having her own problems – her health had broken down again and her father had sent her to Switzerland, to a sanatorium in Montana. Her marriage to Maurice Elvey had been indefinitely postponed and it seems that Norman believed the engagement to be at an end. There's no discussion of their relationship in his letters and Norman may well have assumed that she was no longer going to marry Maurice.

In July 1936 Norman wrote her a letter full of anger. 'About a couple of weeks ago I learnt from Sally that you were married and that your married name was Elvey.' Sylvia had married Maurice at the beginning of 1936, but she had failed to tell Norman and he was 'at a loss to understand' and very, very bitter. Just why Sylvia hadn't told him that she and Maurice were married, isn't clear, though it seems to have caused her some anguish. The other half of the correspondence is missing, but in one of Sylvia's letters to Norman she told him that she had 'lived 2 lives ... in heaven & in hell' during the last year. Perhaps she had been afraid of the way in which the news would affect him. Norman wouldn't accept excuses. In a letter he talks of 'bitterness sublimated'. What has upset him most is that even the postman and the man who delivers the milk knows her address and her marital status – but she hasn't told him. This was a major rupture between them and although Norman continues to write to Sylvia, the letters become less frequent and less personal. Maurice generously sent Norman a gramophone, perhaps as a way of mending bridges.[29]

From this date, new influences are apparent in Norman's work. In 1936 a new vicar came to Holy Trinity Church in Millom. Sam Taylor was a relative of Aldous Huxley, and an avid reader, particularly of modern poetry, and very happy to share books with like-minded people. A discussion group formed at the vicarage, 'where a group of us, mostly very young, could meet

Norman Nicholson aged about 4 with his mother Edith, nee Cornthwaite
Photo © the Cornthwaite family, with permission.

Norman in his sailor suit, aged about 6
Photo © the family of Yvonne Nicholson, with permission

Millom in the nineteen forties.
Photo author collection

The grave of Edith Nicholson and
her infant son Harold.
Photo © Kathleen Jones and Neil Ferber

Norman's grandmother,
Maria Nicholson
*Reproduced by courtesy of the University
Librarian and Director, The John Rylands
Library, The University of Manchester*

14, St George's Terrace in 2013.
The dormer window was Norman's attic room.
Photo © Kathleen Jones and Neil Ferber

Rosetta Sobey, 'Rose', at the piano.
Photo © the family of Yvonne Nicholson, with permission

The wedding of Joe Nicholson and Rosetta Sobey.
Photo © the family of Yvonne Nicholson, with permission

Joe and Rose Nicholson with Norman aged about 18
*Reproduced by courtesy of the University Librarian and Director,
The John Rylands Library, The University of Manchester*

Linford Sanatorium where Norman spent almost 2 years
Photo author collection

Norman with a young woman who may be Sylvia Lubelski
Photo © the family of Yvonne Nicholson, with permission

Enrica Garnier at the time of her engagement to Norman
Reproduced by courtesy of the University Librarian and Director, The John Rylands Library, The University of Manchester

Cockley Moor, the home of Helen Sutherland, where Norman met Kathleen Raine
Photo © Kathleen Jones and Neil Ferber

Brother George Every SSM, who brought Norman's poetry to the notice of T.S. Eliot
Reproduced by courtesy of the University Librarian and Director, The John Rylands Library, The University of Manchester

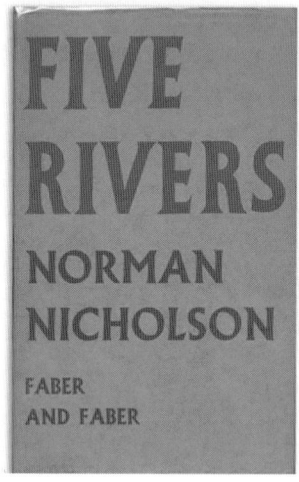

Norman's first collection of poetry 1944.
Photo author collection

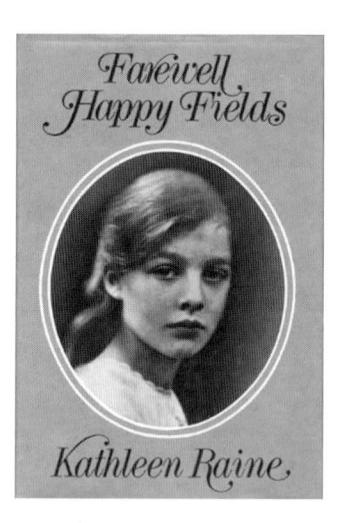

Kathleen Raine as a young woman on the cover of her autobiography
Photo author collection

. The Old Vicarage, Martindale, where Kathleen Raine lived in 1941 and where Norman wrote 'Above Ullswater'.
Photo © Kathleen Jones and Neil Ferber

CHAPTER FIVE

and borrow books and argue.'[30] Sam Taylor lent Norman W.H. Auden and Louis MacNeice and also read and commented on Norman's early verse. Also, at some time in 1936, Norman met a friend of Ted Fisher's, called Enrica Garnier, who gave him feedback on his verses, typed them out for him and helped him to find suitable outlets for publication. Perhaps most important of all, through the Student Christian Movement, Norman met Brother George Every – a literary monk who would later provide him with an introduction to T.S. Eliot.

PART TWO

FLOWER AND STONE

1936 – 1948

>
> Earth's heart is shown –
> A cold round stone.
> Earth's heart is bare,
> And no fire glows
> Nor flower grows there …
>
> The anatomy of desire
> Is only a stone.

Norman Nicholson, 'The Anatomy of Desire'

Chapter Six

In 1936 Norman was twenty two and most of his friends were coming to the end of their university terms and beginning to consider embarking on careers and romantic relationships. Norman was still at home, his clothes provided for him by his father, his meals put in front of him by Rose, living to a strict schedule in his attic room. He read and wrote for several hours a day, went for a short walk after lunch if his temperature was normal, avoided human contact as much as possible in order to prevent infection, and went to bed early – sometimes at 6pm. There seemed little prospect of any other kind of life.

Not surprisingly Norman was lonely and, at times, deeply depressed. Most of his contemporaries had left Millom – there were few people with whom he had anything in common other than a shared childhood. He had little opportunity to meet new friends, especially women, given his reclusive life-style. One part of his personality remained immature, while his intellectual precocity continued to develop. Norman's invalid life-style had cut him off from the normal practising we do in human relationships, between men and women, by dating – the adolescent processes Norman had begun with 'Maureen', adoration, kisses in the sand dunes, then a more mature affection with Sylvia, friendship that deepened into love, unfortunately unrequited. Norman had never had the opportunity to develop a relationship where love and friendship evolved into a physical expression of emotional attachment.

But, at some point in 1936, Norman was introduced to one of Ted Fisher's friends, Enrica Garnier. The following year he spent a holiday in Sheffield with Ted and his girlfriend and Enrica. They stayed in bed and breakfast with the wife of one of Ted's professors – Mrs Hamer and her daughter Janet. Enrica, like Ted, had just qualified as a teacher and was about to take up a post at Walthamstow Hall school in Kent. Enrica was the same age as Norman, born in England, to French Cathar parents, and described by those who knew her as 'exquisite'. She loved poetry and, by 1937, had already taken over Sylvia Lubelsky's role as Norman's amanuensis and chief supporter. The neatly typed sheets of poems which Norman was sending out to magazines and friends for criticism were now being produced by Enrica.

A whole clutch of these was sent to Mrs Hamer – who had been a published author – for advice and comment. The resulting critique provoked a long, defensive response from Norman. He accepted that a poet should 'take it and be damned' but insisted that he must 'put in a good word for my generation as a whole', following his protest up with a short lecture on modern poetry. The insinuation is that Mrs Hamer is old-fashioned in her judgement. Norman, with all the brashness of twenty three, is quite patronising in his remarks. Mrs Hamer has accused him of 'jotting down images merely because they are unusual and startling'. There are sometimes too many images, creating confusion. One of the poems she singled out as an example contained this stanza;

> Square-shouldered fells like firemen (taut
> Snow gleaming chromium on their helmets)
> Pass a concatination of cloudy pails
> To douse the larch-leaf embers of autumn.[1]

Norman was vigorous in his rebuttal of her criticism, defending himself on the grounds that 'I don't consciously choose my images at all'. The relationship of the image to the poem is for him 'the very life of the poem to me'. The tone is injured, the voice of someone who has been misunderstood.

But although many of the poems Norman sent to Mrs Hamer were flawed, the tautly controlled No Man's Land (remembering a walk to Swinside stone circle before he went to Linford) belongs to this period, and a poem he wrote for Enrica, Poem in Pencil, which begins:

> Your photograph
> Is a map in relief
> Its frame the periphery
> Of a beloved territory...

Both poems were eventually published in American magazines.

CHAPTER SIX

Another very personal poem, written around the same time, Sonnet for an Introvert, eventually published in *Poetry* (Chicago), is a revealing account of the poet's internalisation of emotional conflict and a plea for a shield that will protect

> ... the crumbling nerves
> Against the explosion of the grenade Love
> That cracks the brittle facade of reserve.
> Bolt fast my body, seal from roof to toe;
> What others do not see I need not know.[2]

Enrica's parents had been missionaries in China. She was deeply religious and it may have been through her that Norman became more involved with the Student Christian Movement. Enrica was certainly a big influence in the direction Norman now took, but other friends were also persuasive. Bessie Satterthwaite was an active member of the SCM and attended the conference in 1937 where she met George Every, who was giving a lecture on modern poetry. 'Brother' Every was a poet and high churchman, only five years older than Norman, who was part of an Anglican monastic order – the Society of the Sacred Mission – at Kelham in Nottinghamshire where T.S. Eliot went on regular retreats. Bessie showed some of Norman's poems to George, and he was so impressed by them, and by the story of Norman's isolated situation and struggle with ill-health, that he sent them on to T.S. Eliot who was cautiously approving. 'I do think there is very likely something here, if he is young enough, and I am pleased by an interest in a variety of things outside himself, and a livelier experimentation with varieties of metre than is usual. It is still very unformed, of course.'[3]

George Every also sent Norman's poems to Michael Roberts, a teacher at Newcastle Grammar School who was a poet and who had just edited the 1936 edition of the *Faber Book of Modern Verse*. Michael generously responded by sending Norman three pages of technical commentary, including the manifesto of the Imagist poets, and recommended that Norman should send a selection of poems to *Poetry* (Chicago) – which was one of the leading poetry magazines of the time. Norman, in his isolation, welcomed the suggestion.

Norman wrote to Mrs Hamer again in February 1938, arranging an Easter weekend in Sheffield for himself and Enrica, but also telling her that he had now 'taken to heart' her remarks about 'overloading and confusion' in his verse and that *Poetry* (Chicago) had accepted Song for 7pm which was going to be published in March.[4] Norman also wrote to Sylvia, congratulating her on the birth of her daughter Jacqueline, and to tell her about acceptance of the poem which was to be his first publication 'in any magazine of note'.[5] Norman had begun to believe that things were going to happen for him.

But the appearance of his poems in *Poetry* (Chicago), and the encouragement of Michael Roberts and T.S. Eliot, failed to have the effect that Norman hoped for. Despite the fact that Michael's wife Janet was the literary editor of *The Listener*, and even though Eliot was editor of *The Criterion*, his submissions were rejected by both periodicals. Eliot's recommendation also failed to get him accepted by *New Verse* or *Twentieth Century Verse*. The editor of *Life and Letters* apparently didn't even bother to read what Norman had sent him. Norman felt the rejections keenly. He was fully aware that he was an aspiring poet, living in an area remote from the centres of literary influence and without any formal education, at a time when University was seen as an essential gateway to literary life. The gate-keepers seemed determined to keep him out for reasons that Norman believed had to do with snobbery. This was becoming a visible chip on the virtual shoulder.

Norman's programme of self-education continued. In 1937, the chairman of the Millom Workers Education Association had invited Norman to attend a course they were running on modern poetry. The lecturer was almost as young as Norman and equally enthusiastic. It soon became evident 'that the two of us were the only people present who cared tuppence about modern poetry' and each session became a lively debate between them – the kind of intellectual tug and pull that Norman so badly needed. The following autumn Norman was surprised to be asked to prepare a series of lectures for the WEA. 'The impudence of it now staggers me!' he wrote later. 'In twelve weeks I proposed to slap down a dozen or so authors in front of the class with the confident belief that I was covering the main trends of Twentieth Century literature.' But he did, even though the 'physical and nervous effort taxed me to the utmost'.[6] He was also paid £12.00, which was the first money he had ever earned.

It was so successful that, in 1939, he was asked to teach the same course in Whitehaven, and St Bees, to the north of Millom, and extend it into two twenty-four week courses on modern literature. Norman also proposed another course on the seventeenth century – a favourite period for him. Throughout the early years of the war, until the end of 1943, Norman

CHAPTER SIX

travelled up and down the Cumbrian coast, teaching evening courses for the WEA at £1.00 per night.

A WEA lecturer never knew what to expect, and Norman quickly discovered that it was 'no good trying to assess the value of the classes by numbers'. Sometimes an obscure subject would find a hall packed full of enthusiastic people; at other times a supposedly popular theme would attract 'only the vicar and the man who was going to operate the magic lantern'.[7] The WEA was all about offering the opportunity of self-advancement and it also provided entertainment at a time of deprivation as well as the possibility of an escape from the harsh realities of rationing and sombre news reels. The war, Norman observed, gave the audience a 'special character' because it changed the demographic of the area. The village of St Bees, where Norman was running courses, was home to one of the oldest public schools in the country – dating back to the sixteenth century – and during the war it also became home to teachers and pupils from Mill Hill School near London. Norman found himself lecturing to the teachers and their wives. It was stressful, but Norman recorded later that 'the stimulus of their interest was of immense value to me, coming, as it did, after years of intellectual isolation'.[8]

Norman later identified this period as a significant point in his development as a writer – he was forced to read more widely, and engage in debate. But it also enlarged his knowledge of his native country – the train and bus journeys to Whitehaven and St Bees showed him more of the industrial landscape of West Cumberland. It gave him 'a new landscape and new imagery'. The title poem of his first collection, Five Rivers, began as a description of the train journey southwards along the coast from Whitehaven towards Millom 'where cliffs of coal/Slant like shale to the low black mole' and 'the railway canters along the curving shore/Over five rivers'. It's a long poem describing the origins and characteristics of each of the five, and it ends:

> Brown clouds are blown against the bright fells
> Like Celtic psalms from drowned western isles.
> The slow rain falls like memory
> And floods the becks and flows to the sea.
> And there on the coast of Cumberland mingle
> The fresh and the salt, the cinders and the shingle.[9]

He wrote later that the poem 'managed to define, in more ways than just the topographical, the main boundaries of what was to be my life's work'.[10]

The years on either side of 1940 were not only the years that Norman began a career as lecturer and literary critic, it was also during this period that doctors believed him to be free from Tuberculosis. There was still no reliable cure for TB – that wouldn't come until the introduction of streptomycin in 1944 – but by 1940 doctors had become better at diagnosing and treating it by isolating patients in sanatoriums and performing pneumothorax operations to collapse affected lungs in order to allow them to recover. Norman's regime of healthy eating, rest and fresh air, had allowed his immune system to get ahead of the disease. He told a friend that, 'I discovered, almost to my surprise, that the disease had been killed'.[11] Later, the new antibiotics would quash any fears of a recurrence.

Norman was twenty six in 1940 and the world was opening out in front of him. He was like an animal that has been kept in captivity for six years and suddenly finds that the door to the cage has been left open. Why he did not run joyfully out into the new freedom is a question that has to be asked, but can probably only be answered by psychologists. He could have gone to university – during the years that he had been at home he could easily have studied for and passed his Higher Certificate. And, though Joe and Rose could not afford the fees, there were bursaries which – given his earlier academic record and his recent studies – he would almost certainly have won – and which would have paid for his fees and his subsistence. But Norman was now much older than the average intake and he had settled into a routine of invalidism and was genuinely afraid that if he relaxed that routine he might become seriously ill again and die. He may also have been afraid to step out into the competitive hurly-burly of the world outside the comfortable cocoon of his own home. The timid motherless boy who couldn't 'say boo to a goose' had not completely gone away. Norman's parents had, by his own admission, 'molly-coddled' him from birth and continued to encourage him in his dependence on them. Someone who had known him well described him as 'spoilt, very spoilt'.[12] The emotional and financial pressure exerted on him was to stay put.

For an intellectually hungry, emotionally needy young man in his early twenties it was a lonely and repressed existence. Not for Norman nights out on the tiles with friends and adventures with women. He continued to go to bed after tea on the evenings that he wasn't teaching a class, and in his single attic room he read, dreamt, listened to the radio, and wrote. But it had its advantages. As many women writers had found in the 19th century, ill-health facilitated creativity because it released them from the day-to-day

CHAPTER SIX

responsibilities of their sex. Norman had become institutionalised, first by his stay at Linford, and then in the years of confinement at home. Changes in routine caused enormous stress and provoked 'bilious attacks'. Norman was generally seen as a lively, sociable young man – a witty conversationalist and charming companion. But the effort of talking to people and the stimulation of social events drained his nervous energy and risked bringing on the dreaded 'busts'. He told Sylvia Lubelsky that an hour's animated conversation was more tiring than a long walk. After one meeting with a friend he commented, 'I nearly wrecked myself with talking'.[13] He was sometimes very depressed, particularly in winter, without any clear idea of the cause.

Norman was still in touch with George Every and T.S. Eliot, who continued to comment on his poems. Eliot kindly arranged for Norman to have a subscription to the *New English Weekly* – an influential periodical containing prose, poetry and reviews – which Eliot thought might help Norman to develop as a poet. There were frequent letters to and fro – often from T.S. Eliot's secretary Anne Ridler. Anne had just published a collection of her own poetry, which had been generously reviewed, and she was one of the rising stars among the younger generation of poets. She was an intellectual, who had studied journalism at Kings College London, deeply religious, and so had a great deal in common with both Norman and Enrica. She was also upper middle-class, brought up in a very academic and literary environment. Her father had been a house-master at Rugby School, and various of her relatives were authors and publishers. Anne had recently married Vivian Ridler, who would later be Printer to the University of Oxford.

In 1939, through the influence of George Every, Norman was eventually granted an interview with T.S. Eliot – an event that filled him with fear and excitement, not just because of the reverence he had for Eliot's poetry, but also because he knew that it could be a turning point for him as an author. Eliot's influence, as both publisher and poet, was immense. Enrica arranged to go to London with Norman and be with him when he went to Faber's office. She immediately got on well with Anne Ridler and the two women sat downstairs and chatted to each other while Norman had his talk with Eliot. The poet must have treated Norman with great kindness, because he wrote afterwards to Sylvia Lubelsky: 'I have met Eliot … and may, I think, claim him as a friend'. He was, Norman said, 'A delightful companion, and a most lovable person'.[14]

But despite the euphoria of Norman's meeting with Eliot, there were further disappointments to come. During the past three or four years, Norman had been at work on two novels – one provisionally titled *Love to the Nth*, the second – more humorously – *The Cat's Got the Toothache*. In 1939 *Love to the Nth* was rejected by two publishers, Chatto & Windus and Longmans, in such a way that Norman put it to one side. Eliot had apparently given him some encouraging words about the second novel, but though Norman redrafted it several times, Eliot criticised it so drastically the following year that Norman gave it up, though not without considerable pain – 'I haven't the heart to start again,' he wrote to a friend.[15] He told George Every that he felt 'like a cart without a horse – or perhaps a car with a driver but without any petrol'.[16]

In July 1939, as Europe lurched towards war, Norman went – with George Every's encouragement – to the Student Christian Movement's summer conference at Swanwick near Derby. The conference was held at a sprawling country house called The Hayes, where several hundred young people from all over Britain and abroad would gather once a year to listen to inspirational talks, play tennis, go for long walks, join in debates and enjoy an intense social and spiritual experience. Many young people felt 'called' to the ministry or other forms of religious service as a result of going to Swanwick. For Norman it was overwhelming.

After he left Swanwick, at the persuasion of George Every, he accompanied him back to the Anglican monastery at Kelham in Nottinghamshire for a week's retreat. Kelham was a gothic extravagance, built by the same architect who designed St Pancras station. It was, in practice, a theological college, founded in the 19th century as an Anglican monastic order – an off-shoot of the Oxford Movement – and still run by the Company of Brothers, training priests for the Church of England, some of whom remained at Kelham as celibate monks. It housed about 100 students at any one time and the regime was very strict – almost militaristic. Not everyone was happy. One priest who trained there described it as,

> 'a very rigid and compartmentalised hierarchy … in the late 1930s [Kelham] had certain built-in authoritarian terrors comprising histrionic monologues, directives on notice boards, and a general atmosphere under one roof and round one holy table of a great gulf fixed between them and us … the Society was too concerned with its own satisfactoriness and permanence to think that communication with people not actually enclosed behind its hedges needed much attention.

CHAPTER SIX

Nor was there any awareness that (apart from subscriptions) we needed anything of love, sympathy or care from them...'[17]

But the asceticism appealed to some; George Every had been there since he was twenty and was a fully professed, celibate, brother; T.S. Eliot went to Kelham on regular retreats. And it spoke to Norman Nicholson. There, he finally became a spiritually committed Christian, rather than just a ritual observing Anglican. The boy who had resisted every Methodist mission that asked for his surrender to Christ, now gave his soul's allegiance in a different form. Norman explained it in this way: the Methodist religion was one of emotion but the Anglican religion was one of reason and logic – it was something that could be learned like a mathematical principle. Norman wanted to be swayed by reason – something he could justify by argument, rather than by emotion. It was a very considered decision.

In December he wrote to Sylvia Lubelsky, telling her about the conference and his conversion. 'Slowly, gradually, I have found myself veering towards the Christian point of view and towards the complete acceptance of the Christian dogma. It has been neither easy, nor impulsive...'[18] Norman wrote about the profound experience of his first communion as a professed Christian in a poem that wasn't published until years later. It addresses the new responsibility that he feels as a writer and poet – no longer fulfilling the demands of his own ego, but as an instrument of God.

> Now that I have made my decision and felt God on my tongue
> It is time that I trained my tongue to speak of God,
> Not with pretended wisdom, not with presumption,
> But as a tree might speak of him, that no resumption
> Of yesterday's words may sour the sweet grapes of the blood.

There is a note of surrender to a higher will – giving up his own goals and ambitions and acknowledging, with relief, that his life is now being directed by someone else.

> Now that I have burned my boats on an ebbing sea
> That once was quicksand but returned to would-be sand of hell,
> It is time that I cease to stare towards the horizon for a goal,
> But gear my step to the near path cogged out for my soul,
> Or step if need be through the black bracken of the untracked fell.[19]

Chapter Seven

Norman's newly found faith was tested straight away. May 1940 found Norman working 'steadily and persistently' but 'without any success and very little encouragement'. The rejections that he was still experiencing were very painful. 'Poems, short-stories and 2 novels have been praised and admired, but they haven't been published', he told Sylvia Lubelsky, and admitted that over the winter he had had another 'breakdown' being very unwell. 'I'm afraid I've lost most of the hope I ever had for the future, and have been inclined to fear that I was on the edge of a final breakdown'.[1]

Apart from his WEA work, Norman was now reviewing for the *Times Literary Supplement*, at Eliot's suggestion, as well as the *New English Weekly* on George Every's recommendation. Reviewing helped Norman to think through his own views on modern fiction and poetry, and to evolve a personal manifesto of what he wanted to achieve in his own writing. He wrote to George Every that he was seeking to eradicate 'the introspective element in my earlier work'.[2] There must be no more baring of the soul, as in Sonnet to an Introvert; Norman was trying to de-personalise his poetry. There were other stringencies. Although he admired the technical skill of Dylan Thomas, the pyrotechnics of his language irritated Norman 'to the extent of disgusting me'. It was 'what I do not want from poetry', and was a direction 'I feel the poetry of the immediate future must at all costs avoid'.[3] Keen observation – urged on him by Sylvia Lubelsky – and absolute truth were the two things he aimed for. 'The first article of faith for me as a poet is a complete and unreserved belief in the objective reality of the world around me, and in the general trustworthiness of my senses to inform me about that world.'[4]

A few years later, Norman would put his ideas into a poem, published in *Outposts*, but not included in any of his collections until after his death.

CHAPTER SEVEN

It's called, quite simply, Poem.

> I would make a poem
> Precise as a pair of scissors, keen,
> Cold and asymmetrical, the blades
> Meeting like steel lovers to define
> The clean shape of the image .....
>
> I would make a poem
> Solid as a stone, a thing
> You can take up, turn, examine and put down;
> Bred of the accident of rain and river,
> Yet in its build as certain as a circle,
> An axiom of itself.[5]

A poet needs not only technique, but a recognisable personality – a 'voice'. Not only did Norman feel that he now had a clear idea of what he was doing, he also felt that he was finally discovering his own voice. The first time he was aware of this, was in autumn 1939 when he wrote a poem called The Blackberry. 'I can clearly remember the poem which seems to me ... the first Nicholson poem ... and it wasn't till some months after ... that I found ... I had begun to write in the way I was going to write.'[6] The poem employs metaphysical conceits and is composed in the octosyllabic couplets that Norman had begun to explore. He felt that the 'discipline of octosyllabics' helped him both to see his way through a poem and, 'also, when necessary, to distance oneself, slightly, from the subject when it's too close for comfort'.[7]

If 1940 was the year in which Norman found his 'voice' on the page, it was also the moment when he became part of a wider social group, as personal circumstance and war brought new people into the remoter areas of Britain. The poet Michael Roberts, editor of the *Faber Book of Modern Verse*, who had been so helpful in critiquing Norman's poetry, had been evacuated to Penrith in East Cumberland with his school in the autumn of 1939. Michael's wife, Janet Adam Smith, had been assistant editor of *The Listener* and was still reviewing for its literary pages, as well as for other periodicals, such as *The Criterion*. They rented a house in Wordsworth Street and in the spring Norman was invited to visit. Here he met warmth – a crowded house full of the paraphernalia of family life and literary activity, 'Michael's books and his typewriter and gramophone and the late Beethoven quartets he loved'. It was also a place where visitors found 'friendship of the mind, the best of talk'.[8] Having people of this intellectual stature to talk to made a great deal of difference to Norman, though the Roberts seem to have remained little more than acquaintances and useful contacts. Both Janet and Michael came from a wealthier, more traditionally academic tribe than Norman, and there were other, subtler differences. Norman and Janet did not 'take', perhaps based on Norman's feelings of injury that she had not published his poems in *The Listener*, and the two men had little in common except poetry – Michael was a Communist and a passionate mountaineer, and Norman a Christian whose physical boundaries were circumscribed. Michael was working on a new book *The Recovery of the West*, an analysis of everything that he felt was wrong with western civilisation, and liked to argue his political viewpoint robustly. He was also an ardent ecologist and may have helped to influence Norman's increasingly ecological stance.

One of the other new arrivals was a woman called Helen Sutherland, who had known the Roberts family when they lived in Northumberland. Helen was in her fifties – single and wealthy – an early marriage had been annulled, her two brothers had died in the First World War and her parents had died while she was still young. In the north east she had become the patron of the Pitman Painters, and she admitted that her associations with artists and writers were 'a kind of family life given from above'.[9] Her generous patronage was made possible by the fact that she had inherited a considerable fortune from her mother – so large that her father had left his money elsewhere. Helen Sutherland was a rather austere looking person – she wasn't beautiful, having a sharp nose and a small mouth, usually pursed up in a prim expression that deterred people. She was diminutive – less than five feet tall with size 3 feet, and very shy. Her speech and physical gestures were sometimes hesitant, giving the impression of nervousness, but she was actually quite formidable. Her voice was a surprise – 'as small as her person, but clear and musical, and she had a delicious laugh.'[10] Her life was ascetic. According to the painter Winifred Nicholson, Helen had a cold bath every morning, walked up to twenty miles a day and lived on grapes, apples and a little lettuce.

Helen had moved to Cumberland in 1939 from the north east and decided to buy a house called Cockley Moor, occupying an isolated position on the fells above Ullswater – a strange, elongated line of traditional stone and modern glass buildings – a hunting lodge that had become a farmhouse with haphazard extensions built for need rather than aesthetics. Its position was glorious, south facing, twelve hundred feet above sea level, with views

CHAPTER SEVEN

out across the lake and a beck flowing through the garden. It had been altered so that, sitting in Helen's drawing room, 'those bare hills and wet clouds, the moon and the stars, became a part of the world of art she had created',[11] inside and outside in counterpoint, just as Norman described in his poem Cockley Moor;

> Outside, the cubist fells are drawn again
> Beneath the light that speaks extempore;
> The fur of bracken thickens in the rain
> And wrinkles shift upon the scurfy scree…
>
> Inside, are cows on canvas, painted bloom
> Fresh as a girl's thin fingers burst to flower,
> Bright leaves that do not fall, but fence the room
> With the arrested growth of a June hour.[12]

Helen's aim at Cockley Moor was to establish the same kind of cultured circle that she had enjoyed in Northumberland – and she quickly began to gather round her a group of artists and poets whose patron she became. These included the painters Winifred and Ben Nicholson (not related to Norman), the poet-painter David Jones, Kathleen Raine and, later, Elizabeth Jennings. It was a strange mixture of the lower and upper classes. Winifred Nicholson was the grand-daughter of the Earl of Carlisle. Her divorced husband, Ben Nicholson, now married to the sculptor Barbara Hepworth, also had a titled father. But David Jones was the son of a printer's overseer from north Wales and Kathleen Raine the daughter of a Methodist school-master.

It's not clear how Norman met Helen, since they didn't mix in the same social circles, but it was probably through Janet and Michael Roberts. Whoever made the introduction, Norman soon became one of the select group Helen Sutherland invited to stay at her house-parties. Helen's aim was to create a nurturing environment for creativity. She liked to think of her house as 'a place of contemplation … a stimulus … from Nature and from human meetings – and with something of a Divine influence too – I love to feel this house full of the people I love'.[13] But for the guests, visits were daunting affairs. It was very far from anything that Norman had ever encountered. The rooms were filled with elegant antique furniture, and the walls were hung with valuable paintings. Helen was a devotee of the modernists – a friend of Jim Ede at Kettle's Yard – and she collected abstract art – including Mondrian and Matisse, with a preference for the art of the High Modernist movement. Apparently she kept two Picassos in a drawer because she no longer liked them. Norman, who had loved the poetry of high modernists such as Eliot, now had the opportunity to examine the art produced under its influence – strong on structure and sparing with colour. His poem Cockley Moor refers to the cream paintings of Ben Nicholson, 'Square laid on circle, circle laid on square', which hung on Helen Sutherland's walls.[14] It was here that Norman's taste in art was developed, as well as his conviction that it was necessary to have structure in art and poetry.

There was a rarefied atmosphere – some people described it as almost monastic – and the house rules were strict and inflexible. No muddy shoes, no loud noises, no special requests, no staying up late. Guests had to be absolutely punctual at meal times, and were expected to join in with everything that was organised; regular activities included going for walks, reading Wordsworth, and sometimes P.G. Wodehouse, aloud after dinner, going to church, and listening to music. They also had to provide intelligent conversation and Helen was apparently 'ruthless' to those who she felt didn't come up to scratch. She could be intolerant, jealous of her house and possessions, angry and defensive. David Jones, whose health had been precarious since World War I, almost had a nervous breakdown over a bottle of spilt ink. But Helen could also be generous and she was much loved. Kathleen Raine said that Helen had been like a mother to her; Helen felt that Kathleen's friendship had been sent to her by God. There was a very deep emotional connection between the two women.

Kathleen Raine had also come to Cumberland during the winter of 1938/1939 to stay with the Roberts family in Penrith. Her life had reached a point of crisis. Kathleen's first marriage had broken down when she had fallen in love with the poet Charles Madge and left her husband to live with him. Now that relationship too had broken down, because she had fallen in love with another man. Janet had already published Kathleen's poetry in *The Listener* and a small anthology *Poems of Tomorrow*, which she had edited, and Michael was a close friend and admirer of Charles Madge. They had offered a sanctuary and Kathleen had come north, with her two children by Madge, to make a new life. She spent the winter months with Janet and Michael in the small terraced house in Penrith, but in the spring, when their lease ended, she rented the old vicarage near a village called Martindale, on the opposite side of Ullswater to Cockley Moor.

Martindale is one of the Lake District's hidden treasures – a small

CHAPTER SEVEN

hamlet in a concealed valley among some of the area's most beautiful scenery. It is remote and peaceful. Despite the implications of its name, the old vicarage was, and still is, an eighteenth century cottage. Kathleen Raine fell in love with the house on first viewing; 'the most beautiful little white house imaginable, stood in its own field, with a great lime tree at the gate and a beck fringed with birch and alder bounding its little domain'.[15] It is incredibly remote – the nearest neighbours are a brisk walk away and there is not even a track to connect the house to the road. Behind it, the fellside rises steeply up to crags overlooking Ullswater.

At the Vicarage, Kathleen was surrounded by ancient history. On the other side of the valley was the old church whose foundations probably date back to the Vikings – it was certainly in existence in 1220. A yew tree in the church yard is believed to be over a thousand years old and the altar came from a Roman shrine on the fellside. Roman legions had marched on nearby High Street, past the stone circles and burial mounds of the more ancient dead. Surrounded by beauty and these connections to the distant past, Kathleen found it perfect.

Helen and Kathleen met over a wartime supper at the Roberts' house in Penrith, where Kathleen impressed Helen with an improvised chestnut soup. Although Virginia Woolf had described Kathleen as having 'the mind of a lovely snowball'[16] it wasn't long before Kathleen too, was invited to one of the gatherings at Cockley Moor and it was there that she and Norman met each other. It was a collision of opposites; Norman, impressionable, needy, insecure, full of repressed sexual energy, and Kathleen, passionate, spiritual, uninhibited and sexually experienced. They both shared a Methodist childhood, a common love of landscape and poetry and all things spiritual. Both were writing, though neither had produced a collection of poetry yet. Kathleen Raine was very beautiful – six years older than Norman – and it was probably inevitable that he would fall in love with her, as friends say that he did, despite the fact that he was unofficially engaged to Enrica Garnier. Kathleen was also still very much in (unrequited) love with another man and not, perhaps, able to respond. Neither have left many traces to shed light on what was, for Norman, a very private and painful relationship. Kathleen mentions him briefly in her autobiography. There are a few cards and letters. In Norman's case, there is a group of poems about love and the failure of it that interconnect with some of Kathleen's poems – both groups written over the same period of time. They indicate a close creative collaboration. A line in one of Norman's poems from this period, 'Stone and flower', is also the title of Kathleen Raine's first collection of poetry, published in 1943. In return she supplied the title to Norman's second collection, *Rock Face* and 'provoked' Norman into writing the title poem.

Kathleen's title, *Stone and Flower*, comes from a poem Norman wrote, called Above Ullswater, written when Kathleen was living at Martindale on an occasion when he was staying there with her and her children. Norman told Philip Gardner that the 'you' of the poem was Kathleen Raine. That the poem is definitely situated in the old vicarage and not Helen Sutherland's house at Cockley Moor is demonstrated by the references in the poem, which include one to 'the spore box of the moss' which Kathleen always kept on her table. The poem talks of the impossibility of holding things still – the collision of two worlds that must inevitably separate. It's a poem of parting. 'What remains' Norman asks, 'When the hour-old past flies off like a cloudy comet?/What remains, now, in the world/Of stone and flower, the world/That hand and eyesight know?' The flower, the moss, the lichen, and the stone, will all remain, but 'It is the eternal that never stays'. And then the poet addresses the person with whom he has just spent 'two days of sun';

> Oh but you
> To whom the angels speak in colours,
> Was the silence singing, and the shining air
> Snowy with angels' feathers?
>
> The stones are hard beneath my feet; the water
> Clinks its little teaspoons in the beck;
> The world that I belong to nudges back again.
> But still your hair is trembling in the draught of angels' wings,
> And paradisal colours are rising in your eyes.[17]

There is an echo here of another poem dedicated to Kathleen Raine around this time, called The First Day of Autumn, which ends 'Angel and man and beast and flower and stone'. These are the motifs that recur like a heartbeat through Norman's Kathleen Raine poems, and through those of Kathleen herself.[18]

Among the poems that Kathleen wrote during her stay at Martindale are The Waterfall, written after a walk along the fell behind the house, and her poem Good Friday, which may have been written in parallel with Norman's Sonnet for Good Friday. She also wrote The Hollow Hill, dedicated to Helen Sutherland, and Stone on High Crag. Then there is the

CHAPTER SEVEN

lovely Night in Martindale which seems to respond directly to Norman's poem Above Ullswater.

> Not in the rustle of water, the air's noise,
> the roar of storm, the ominous birds, the cries –
> the angel here speaks with a human voice.
>
> Stone into man must grow, the human word
> carved by our whispers in the passing air
>
> is the authentic utterance of cloud,
> the speech of flowing water, blowing wind,
> of silver moon and stunted juniper.
>
> Words say, waters flow,
> rocks weather, ferns wither, winds blow, times go,
> I write the sun's Love and the stars' No'.[19]

The evidence of Norman's emotional involvement is circumstantial; the location, the timing, the content of a group of poems, two of which mention Kathleen by name, anecdotal evidence from friends (he told Sylvia Lubelsky jokingly that he had fallen in love with Kathleen's little daughter). Nevertheless, it has to be addressed, and there can be no doubt at all about their close creative collaboration. Another poem, The Candle, was written when Kathleen suggested a theme and imagery to Norman and gave him the first line, 'Poetry is not an end'. Her contribution is openly acknowledged by Norman in a footnote to the poem in his second collection *Rock Face*, published in 1948, which connects the poem deliberately to Kathleen. But, although the first stanza was apparently written from her suggestion, the poem takes off on its own trajectory and becomes a love poem.

> The beloved is not love,
> Nor poetry the grammar and the theme.
> But when the beloved – oh with hair
> Like seaweed on the rocks
> When desire flows back at the turn of the night –
> Then she seems
> All that love is
> And being herself is loving. So the song

Seems cause and crown of singing, and the dream
The body and bride of longing,
To one who seeks thought's lips with his tongue.[20]

During the period when Norman knew Kathleen Raine, there is a new element in his poetry that has been missing so far – very personal – confessional – even erotic. It is exactly what he had told George Every he was trying to get away from and marks out his second collection, *Rock Face*, as different from the rest of his work. Critics have treated it as an aberration. Most rated the poetry in it as being of a lower standard than the rest of his work. But this has much to do with the fact that poetry at that time was expected to be impersonal in order to be universal. A more personal poetics was being evolved in America, but had not yet reached Britain.

Kathleen Raine's time in the Lake District didn't last long. A year later, the need to earn a living took her back to London, leaving her children behind with Helen Sutherland. From then on she came back only for visits. But in London she met someone very important for both herself and Norman Nicholson. This was James Meary Tambimuttu, always called Tambi by his friends, a Tamil poet and critic who came from an aristocratic family in Ceylon. He came to live in London in 1938 and quickly surrounded himself with artists, musicians and writers, frequenting the bars and restaurants of what came to be known as 'Fitzrovia'. Tambimuttu had published poetry in Ceylon, and shortly after his arrival in England he established Lyrebird Press and began a monthly magazine called *Poetry* (London). It was beautifully designed and illustrated and featured many of the very best contemporary poets – such as Stephen Spender, Dylan Thomas, Louis MacNeice, George Barker and Lawrence Durrell.

Tambimuttu was an inspired editor, but utterly chaotic both in his public and his private life. Manuscripts were lost and contributors went without pay, but poets were queuing up to appear in the magazine. Norman was among those who submitted frequently and was very depressed to be rejected. He managed to get a few poems into the *New English Weekly*, as well as two American literary journals, the *Southern Review* and *Poetry* (Chicago), but his poems failed to find an English market. Kathleen Raine was one of the lucky ones to find publication with *Poetry* (London) and 'Tambi' became a personal friend.

Norman felt an increasing sense of hopelessness. But, at the beginning

CHAPTER SEVEN

of March, 1941, something extraordinary happened. Norman, who had not as yet published much of either prose or poetry, was asked to compile an anthology of religious poetry for Penguin. It was described as 'Tongues of Men – an Anthology for the Times' and Norman was given an advance of £100 for it.[21] It is not known whose influence was behind the request, but it could have been George Every, T.S. Eliot, or even Anne Ridler. It was quite a coup for Norman, as a relatively unknown author, to get this commission, which would be published in 1942 under the title *An Anthology of Religious Verse, Designed for the Times*.

Norman had firm views about what he wanted to include. He was determined to avoid 'moral uplift in rhyme or pious verse about the Good Shepherd', containing the kind of conventional images and clichés which might suggest that Christianity had ceased to be 'a living thing'. His own poems were examples of the new, forward-looking contemporary approach and offended many readers with their colloquial expressions and everyday images. Carol for Holy Innocents Day begins:

> The cat was let out of the bag by the angel,
> Who warned them and planned their get-away,
> And told how Herod would make holy with death,
> The day that a birth made a holy day.

In the poem, Norman makes an analogy with the current war.

> We have hurried our children from a German Herod,
> Whose bombs stretch further than a city's roofs:
>
> ... on the frozen cradle of Europe
> The infant Jesus is left to die.[22]

The selection that Norman made also proved to be controversial. He ignored the obvious historical choices – George Herbert, John Donne, Christina Rossetti – to concentrate on contemporary poets. All his particular friends were included – T.S. Eliot, George Every, David Gascoyne, Anne Ridler and two new acquaintances, a clergyman called Andrew Young whose poems had caught Norman's eye in the magazine *New Verse*, and Tambimuttu. The most controversial choices were W.H. Auden and D.H. Lawrence. Norman justified their inclusion by saying that 'the structure of the book is Christian, in that it deals with the modern man's conception of

God, and his life in relation to God. I have not, however, asked any poet to say his catechism before he was admitted to the volume, and the reader will find some who are not professing Christians, but ... seem to express a Christian point of view.'[23]

The use of the male pronoun in the introduction highlights the fact that, like most anthologies of this period, it is predominantly masculine – Anne Ridler and Ruth Pitter were the only women represented – 5 poems out of 80 contributions. The non-inclusion of Kathleen Raine is a surprise, given the spirituality of her poems, but it's possible that she would not have wanted her work included in such an overtly religious collection.

Norman suddenly found that there was more of a market for his work. He was asked, for the first time, to contribute to John Lehmann's *New Writing and Daylight*, published by the Hogarth Press. This was a crusading periodical, committed to publishing the younger poets who had grown up after the First World War, many of whom felt alienated, and it was determined to represent the poetry of the future. John Lehmann was to become one of Norman's advocates. Tambimuttu also began to take note and Norman was finally accepted into *Poetry* (London).

Requests also came in for contributions to two anthologies of war poetry to be published the following year, *Poetry in War Time*, edited by Tambimuttu and *Poems of This War*, edited by Patricia Ledward and Colin Strang. Tambimuttu's collection was by far the best and Norman found himself in the company of Kathleen Raine, Anne Ridler, Alun Lewis, Laurie Lee and George Barker. Although Norman was prevented by his tubercular lungs from taking any part in the war, and Cumberland was one of the few areas remote from German bombing raids, Norman's poetry reflects the social problems and the changes that war brought to rural communities. In the poem Cleator Moor, men are working flat out for the war effort, now that coal and iron are such important raw materials. Declining industries are suddenly booming.

> But now, the pits are wick with men,
> Digging like dogs dig for a bone;
> For food and life we dig the earth –
> In Cleator moor they dig for death.
>
> Every wagon of cold coal
> Is fire to drive a turbine wheel;
> Every knuckle of soft ore

CHAPTER SEVEN

A bullet in a soldier's ear.[24]

The RAF used the quiet bays of west Cumberland for bombing practice, and Norman described seeing the bombs dropping from the planes like seeds into the water where they sprouted trees of water 'silver as willows/ or white as a blossoming pear'. Even the Home Guard got a mention – several of Norman's relatives were members – training beside the railway line, hiding their torches when they heard the drone of a plane and praying for bad weather and moonless nights to keep the German bombers at home. Wartime metaphors began to scatter his poetry – snow becomes a 'parachute invasion' from the sky, streets are dug as 'deep as trenches'. Evacuees was written in 1943, four years after Millom had seen its first trainloads of women and frightened children. The Lake District was full of evacuees – even Helen Sutherland took five small boys from the slums of Newcastle. As the poem records, many of them quickly got bored and, when the invasion failed to materialise, went home again, preferring to risk the bombing of their homes, than live like 'cuckoo's eggs' in the homes of strangers. Others stayed:

The little girl who wept on the platform then
Now feels her body blossom like the trees,
Discovers tennis, poetry and flowers ...[25]

Reviews for Norman's *Penguin Anthology of Religious Verse* were excellent. It was described in one periodical as 'a bomb shell. It is concise, skilful and passionately conceived'.[26] The *New Statesman* liked 'the unusual flavour' of Norman's choices, and the influential writer Charles Williams thought the collection 'convenient and interesting'. It was just the kind of boost Norman needed and may well have been a factor in the award of another commission that came through the letter box in 1942, this time with George Every's influence definitely behind it. Norman was not an academic, but he was now asked to write a work of literary criticism. He had been talking, since early 1940, about shaping his WEA lectures into a small book and, in September 1942, he signed a contract for a book on 'Modern Literature from the Christian Point of View', with the Student Christian Movement Press. The advance was only £25, but there was a 10% royalty on the first 3000 copies.

Debates about the Nature of Man, and the Doctrine of Original Sin, may seem irrelevant in our multi-cultural and increasingly secular society, but it was still a live issue in the early 1940s, made more so by the brutal realities of the Second World War. Was a baby really conceived in sin and born in sin? Was Man by nature evil? Or was he born innocent and corrupted by his environment? Was he capable of redemption? It depended on whether you believed in the Garden of Eden and whether Eve really did give Adam the forbidden apple. Norman wasn't attempting to address these questions, simply to categorise 20th century literature according to the viewpoint the author seemed to be putting forward. The chapters of the book and their contents were, according to Norman, basically a re-working of his WEA lectures.

In his introduction Norman states that 'This book is not an attempt to measure modern literature by a Christian yardstick', but – as some reviewers pointed out – this is exactly what the author sets out to do; the parameters of Christian doctrine are always evident and its moral principles are latent in the text. Norman goes on to say that 'It is not, fundamentally, literary criticism at all … It is an enquiry into the assumptions as to the nature and purpose of Man which underlie much of modern writing'. There are three categories – Liberal Man, Natural Man and Imperfect Man.

In the end it fails as a method of literary criticism because there are huge numbers of authors who can't be categorised because their work doesn't fit. And it ignores style and form and other literary methods of analysis that might be more illuminating to readers of the text. But it is a remarkable book to be written by a young, self-educated man, scrabbling for intellectual stimulus in Millom. What is interesting now about the text is what it tells us about Norman himself and where he locates himself with regard to God, Literature and Humanity. But a definite answer is hard to find. The reader senses where his sympathies might lie when he quotes Aphra Behn's *Oroonoko or The History of the Royal Slave* – 'simple Nature is the most harmless, inoffensive, and virtuous mistress' and Nature herself 'better instructs the world, than all the inventions of Man'.

He is scathing about D.H. Lawrence and *Lady Chatterley's Lover* – a daring choice for discussion in 1943. There 'is to be found the most complete attempt yet made to portray Natural Man entirely in sexual terms and to put forward sexual love as the key to all experience'. Norman criticises the ending, where Lady Chatterley and her lover decide to go away together and the novelist wants us to believe that this apparently happy ending 'is the ultimate right choice'. But Norman can't accept that this is true. 'We cannot believe this, not even within the framework of the novel, after such violence beforehand' and he doesn't believe that Lawrence – 'a very sick

CHAPTER SEVEN

man both in body and mind' – believed it either. Sin, he implies, can never produce a happy ending.

Norman is interesting on Elizabeth Bowen, whose skill he equates with Jane Austen, and on Kafka, whose 'parabolic' narrative structures he admires. But where his categories really fall down is when he approaches the section on modern poetry which, he admits, 'does not fall so easily into three "periods" as does the prose'. He discusses Yeats and Eliot, Auden, C. Day Lewis and Stephen Spender and manages to find space for a mention of various friends – David Gascoyne, Anne Ridler, Andrew Young, and Alex Comfort. They are the 'Younger Poets' who have emerged since 1939 (though Andrew Young had been born in 1885). In their work Norman detects 'a new humility, and the new realisation that man is an imperfect, sinful, dependent being'. He ends with a quote from Anne Ridler:

> Life is your lot, you lie in God's hand,
> In His terrible mercy, world without end.[27]

With the publication of *Man and Literature*, as it was eventually called, Norman could now say that he was a recognised editor and literary critic.

Chapter Eight

Even though Norman's literary reputation was gathering momentum, his personal life remained solitary and he was often lonely. Norman wrote to Sylvia Lubelsky again, lamenting that all his contemporaries had gone to war. There was no-one he knew left in Millom. In addition, most of his friends were now married, and he complained that it was 'cramping their style', even Ted Fisher was becoming domesticated. Kathleen Raine was in London, working for the Ministry of Information, and Michael Roberts had accepted a wartime position with the BBC and moved south with Janet and the children. Norman was still an occasional visitor to Helen Sutherland, but not at home among her elite guests, except on one occasion when the Roberts brought T.S. Eliot to stay in 1942.

But 1943 would mark a big change in Norman's fortunes. During the previous year he had begun to be accepted in more and more magazines, perhaps because of his reviewing, or perhaps because of the Penguin anthology. He was earning an average of three guineas for his contributions, and bigger publications like *Horizon* paid five. Some of his poems were included in the *Best Poems of 1942*, published in 1943 by Jonathon Cape. He also appeared in *New Road*, edited by Alex Comfort, and Norman's contributions were specifically mentioned in the *Observer* review of the anthology. The *New English Weekly* grouped Norman together with Anne Ridler and Kathleen Raine, calling them 'neo-christians' though Norman thought that their work was not particularly similar. David Gascoyne's name was also sometimes linked to theirs.

There was a big breakthrough for Norman in fiction. Having ditched his first attempts at the novel, he had been working on another throughout 1942, initially called 'The Holy Winter' and he was finally offered a contract in March 1943, with a publishing company called Nicholson and Watson, on very good terms. He would have a royalty of 20% on the

CHAPTER EIGHT

first two thousand five hundred copies. It was wonderful encouragement. Very few novels were published during the war because of the shortage of paper. But for Norman, the best news of all came when he was asked to be the third poet included in an anthology of *Selected Poems* alongside Keith Douglas and J.C. Hall, in the Modern Readers' Library series. Hall, one of the Oxford poets, was the driving force behind *Selected Poems* which was supposed to show-case his work and that of his friends, so Norman was very lucky to be included. It didn't matter than he was a second choice – the slot was originally to be occupied by a poet called Alan Rook who was offered separate publication elsewhere at the last moment. The anthology contained twelve of Norman's poems, including some of the war poems, The Blackberry, and two long poems Garden of the Innocents and The Holy Mountain. Eight of the twelve would be included in Norman's first collection the following year.

Selected Poems was well received and Norman was often singled out for special mention. *Time and Tide* even carried a verse letter by Charles Williams on 'Men and Books' which praised Norman's 'fabulous couplets' and his knowledge of myth - he is 'better with it than many another' because he can treat Faith 'as a myth and love it so/Piety alone is not poetry, nor can be.'

Norman was continuing to collaborate with Kathleen Raine. He helped her to put together her first collection and supplied the title, *Stone and Flower*. It was duly sent to T.S. Eliot at Faber and turned down. Eliot later told Kathleen that this had been a mistake on his part, but at the time she was very hurt by his rejection. She then sent the collection to Tambimuttu who was happy to accept it. *Stone and Flower* was published in 1943, in the kind of beautiful edition Tambi was famous for, illustrated by Barbara Hepworth, the second wife of Ben Nicholson, whom Kathleen had met at Cockley Moor. It all emphasised the importance of knowing people, in this small, enclosed world of literature and art.

Kathleen was also advising Norman on the compilation of his first collection. Encouraged by her experience and now wary of Eliot's judgement, Norman sent *Five Rivers* first to Tambimuttu, who unexpectedly turned it down. Norman, fresh from the success of the *Anthology of Religious Poetry* (which had included poems by Tambimuttu) and *Man and Literature*, had believed that acceptance would be a formality. Encouraged by Anne Ridler, Norman sent the collection to T.S. Eliot in October and was delighted when Faber and Faber offered to publish it. He wrote to

Sylvia Lubelsky that he was more excited about that than any of the other books. Norman joined the most prestigious poetry list in the country, and *Five Rivers* was scheduled for publication in May 1944. It was dedicated to Enrica Garnier.

Man and Literature was published in the autumn of 1943 and attracted thirty reviews, including a two page spread in the *Times Literary Supplement*. Norman had an article in *John O'London's Weekly* in January 1944 flagged as being written by 'the author of the remarkable book *Man and Literature*' and it was accompanied by a photograph of Norman, subtitled 'Critic and Poet', showing a handsome man with long wavy hair blowing in the wind. Predictably *The Church Times* thought it 'brilliant', and it proved very popular with a conservative establishment. The second-hand copy I own was originally given as a school prize and it was widely used for this purpose, as George Every had hoped it would be – a Christian literary text suitable for schools and colleges, able to influence young minds. A review in *The Presbyter* put it very succinctly; 'Ministers should find it particularly useful for putting into the hands of young people who are beginning to read these authors for the first time and who find them very unsettling'.[1] Norman had no idea, at this time, that he was being recruited as a lay brother for the Society of the Sacred Mission - a missionary for literature rooted in Christian values.

But *Man and Literature* wasn't universally liked. *The Listener* disliked the rigid classifications and the straitjacket of having to measure literature against the 'Christian yardstick'. They felt the lack of 'illuminating revelations of the essential quality and significance of any author's work'. Authors should be judged on 'their actual merit as artists' rather than their 'conformity to some outward political or religious orthodoxy'. Nor could Norman rely on his friends. He had reviewed Kathleen Raine's collection enthusiastically, but she didn't allow friendship to get in the way of intellectual honesty. Kathleen reviewed *Man and Literature* for the *Dublin Review* in July 1944 and was kind but critical, pointing out that there was 'nothing original'. She criticised Norman's treatment of Lawrence's 'blood and soil mysticism as a huge joke', and asked why there was so little on Virginia Woolf. *The Manchester Guardian* thought the book was 'symptomatic of intellectual trends within the Church of England', and that Norman's criticism was extremely weak, particularly in the chapter on D.H. Lawrence and Natural Man. The 'imposed superstructure' of the book was 'inevitably shaky'.

Most of these comments Norman could deal with, though he

CHAPTER EIGHT

complained wryly that he was being criticised for not doing what he had not set out to do in the first place. Hadn't he stated quite clearly at the beginning of *Man and Literature* that it was not a work of literary criticism? And he had already anticipated that he would be pigeon-holed as a religious author and the religious content of his work would not find favour with the growing number of agnostics and militant atheists among the Marxist literary critics. T.S. Eliot himself had remarked, in a book that Norman had drawn on extensively for *Man and Literature*, that 'amongst writers the rejection of Christianity – Protestant Christianity - is the rule rather than the exception'.[2] Norman was never going to see eye to eye with poets and critics such as Michael Roberts.

Alex Comfort was one of those who wrote personally to Norman. Alex was an anarchist, doctor, scientist and poet who was, like Norman, just at the beginning of his career. He had published his first novel while still a student at Cambridge in 1941 and his third novel *The Power House* was published in 1944, just as he graduated from medical school. He was also a prolific poet – but ultimately to be most famous for the *Joy of Sex*, published in 1970. Alex Comfort had a dazzling intellect and was often controversial. In 1944 he was heavily involved with the Peace Pledge Union – a Pacifist organisation – and produced political pamphlets for them throughout the war. Alex felt that the writer as a human being, was 'charged with the terrific task of speaking for the voiceless', and compared writers to the 'canaries taken down mines' – they were sensitive to changes in the atmosphere which they had a duty to draw attention to.[3]

So it was no surprise to Norman that Alex disliked *Man and Literature* – the big surprise was that he had read it and felt it worth criticising in detail. Very little of Norman's correspondence has survived, because he had a habit of writing prose drafts and poems on the backs of the letters he received – 'no letters; no poems!' – but this was one of the letters that Norman kept. Alex went through his objections point by point. He didn't think the classification of writers according to their attitude to Man was valid. The whole concept was fundamentally flawed. '… you don't seem to grant that a poet is his work. You give the impression that you think that a writer's attitude to man is voluntarily chosen – it isn't… A man writes what he is' and this, following Freudian principles, is the outcome of his childhood. Alex asked if Norman had intended it as a textbook for the WEA and felt that to be useful it should have included analysis of the 'aesthetics of style'. His beliefs were so fundamentally opposed to Norman's that there could be no meeting of minds at all. 'Original sin is self-evident, but there is no doctrine of Grace, because the conception of immortality is simply not factually true.'[4]

Norman could handle Alex Comfort's carefully argued objections – just – but he took issue with an anonymous review in the *Adelphi*, almost identical to the review that had appeared in *The Listener,* which Norman believed to have been written by one of Alex's friends, Derek S. Savage, a left-wing poet with very strong views on modern literature and an active member of the Anglican pacifist movement. Norman ignored the unwritten rule that an author should never respond to a bad review and objected forcefully in a letter, particularly to the use of the phrase 'lacking insight, integrity and intellectual capacity'.[5] Norman never forgave him.

Nor could he forgive the mauling he got at the pen of George Barker. George was the same age as Norman, but their paths had been very different. George had been published by Faber in his early twenties and gone on to become Professor of English Literature at a Japanese university. At the beginning of the war he had gone to America where he had a long affair with Elizabeth Smart, the author of *By Grand Central Station I sat Down and Wept.* Together they had four children, produced at a time when he was also having children by his wife. George had returned to England in 1943 and was making a name as an author and literary critic. His review appeared in *The Spectator* in February 1944 and it was deeply personal. Called 'Parochial Criticism' – George Barker went on to refer to *Man and Literature* as the 'little thesis with the big title'. He picked out inconsistencies in the arguments, particularly the contrasting of Eliot and Joyce, and pointed out that Eliot was migrating towards Christian doctrine, as Joyce was recoiling from it 'Eliot was merely half a journey of disillusionment behind Joyce'. He also found some of Norman's literary judgements either 'naive' or 'intolerant theologically'. There is 'a kind of parochiality of judgement that probably goes back to theological origins'.[6] It was, perhaps, the word 'parochial' that cut deepest, but Norman was deeply hurt and it was the beginning of a literary feud that would last a lifetime.

Norman had another 'bust' in March. He told Sylvia Lubelsky that he wasn't well enough to see anyone and that he had to take things very quietly. It seems to have been a combination of his winter depression, anxiety about the reception of his forthcoming poetry collection and the new novel, as well as the chest infections to which Norman was so vulnerable. Millom was very industrial and the air was thick with smoke from the coal fires that still heated every house. Winter was a dangerous time for viruses,

CHAPTER EIGHT

flu and bronchitis. Even a common cold could be perilous for Norman. Apart from the depression, Norman had a small haemorrhage and feared that the tuberculosis had recurred. Fortunately there were now good antibiotics to treat any remaining bacteria, but he was quite ill and very low psychologically. He gave up the WEA lectures after the publication of *Man and Literature* telling friends that he felt he had been over-doing it and 'would have to give it up if I did not want a second break-down'.[7] The failure of his health occurred at a time when the last and most loyal of his friends told him that she was getting married. In the summer of 1944, Bessie Satterthwaite, who had read his work, given him feedback, showed it to others, championed his cause and bolstered his courage, married the Rev Leonard Schiff in County Durham and settled down to the life of a vicar's wife. Both Leonard and Bessie remained friends with Norman until the end of their lives, but Bessie was no longer able to give Norman the attention that he had enjoyed before her marriage.

After the controversy over *Man and Literature* Norman was braced for negative criticism and was unprepared for the storm of approval that broke over his head when *Five Rivers* eventually appeared in May. It was reviewed everywhere from the *Irish Times* to the *Quarry Manager's Journal* – even Vita Sackville-West liked it. In the *Times Literary Supplement* he was a 'brilliant and original talent', and John Betjeman thought he was 'a real poet' even though there was 'too much imitation of T.S. Eliot'.[8] *New Poetry* commented on 'minute exactitude', but the best review came from *New English Writing* which was wholehearted in its recommendation of Norman's collection. 'You will not find a single woolly word, a single worn poetic phrase, throughout this book.' They commended the landscape of 'scree, beck, fell, tarn, moor and dale' – the exactness of local words – 'of flora and fauna'. The reviewer found parallels to John Clare, and added that, 'It is difficult to believe that Norman Nicholson is not going to be a major poet'.[9]

There were other, private, letters of support. David Gascoyne, whose work was often grouped with the 'neo-christians', wrote to say that he thought the success of *Five Rivers* was due to the poetry being 'rooted in physical spiritual reality'. David Gascoyne differentiates in the letter, between Christian 'ethical, moral, social code and standards' and genuine Christian spirituality, which is a bedrock rather than a veneer.[10] The clergyman poet Andrew Young had been writing to Norman since 1939 on the subject of nature poetry, which he thought was very badly done in England. He had recommended Robert Frost to Norman, as the best writer about the natural world. Norman's acquaintance with Andrew was developing into a firm friendship, based on shared religious beliefs and a love of botany. Andrew wrote to Norman on the publication of *Five Rivers*, saying that he liked the poems best that were 'about that "bloody" country of yours' which Norman has made him see 'with a new vision'.[11]

It was this 'bloody country' that was the key to the success of the collection. The industrial edgelands of places like Millom were rarely the subject of poetry. The combination of stark scenery and industrial activity was highly original and the 'great vitality and colourfulness' of the language was also remarked on. Norman was not afraid to use the dialect words of Cumberland's Viking heritage – a 'dialect crisp with the click of the wind'. From the miner with his 'segged' hands, to the 'thieving heifer and yow and teg' living 'Here where the Norsemen foraged down the dales… /Leaving their names scotched on the flanks of the hills', the poems were vibrant with new images.[12]

The first edition of *Five Rivers* was sold out by July, to the surprise of everyone – even Faber, who rapidly printed a new edition. The poetry included in the collection was a mixture of new material and work that had appeared in *Selected Poems* and the anthologies of war poetry. Norman's more accomplished religious poems sat alongside his topographical poems relating to the West Cumberland landscape, the war poems, and one or two that were more personal. The poems with explicitly religious themes formed the largest group. They included three long poems that Norman felt were among his most important work – Garden of the Innocents, The Bow in the Cloud and The Holy Mountain – written in lyrical sections influenced by Norman's passion for music. As one critic observed, 'long unrhymed descriptive lines' give way to 'ballad quatrains to octosyllabic couplets' which lead in turn 'to exultant Psalm-like passages' like the 'recitative, aria and chorus in an oratorio'.[13]

All three poems deal with biblical myths from the Book of Genesis – the Garden of Eden, Noah and the Flood, and the Fall, transposed to the Cumberland landscape. Norman had never forgotten how his Uncle Jim, one afternoon at Sunday School, had re-told the parable of the Good Samaritan, and how the man 'went down from Jerusalem to Jericho, just as it might have been from Broughton to Foxfield'.[14] It was a lesson in making distant events relevant by re-locating them to a familiar landscape. But, despite Norman's innovations and the musicality of the different sections of each poem, T.S. Eliot wrote to Anne Ridler, saying that he still thought

CHAPTER EIGHT

that the long poems were a failure.

Two of the personal poems in *Five Rivers* refer to Norman's continuing involvement with Enrica Garnier, though the poems that reference her are curiously cool, unlike the poems written during the Kathleen Raine period. Anne Ridler was one of those who commented on the lack of passion in Norman's relationship with Enrica. Walthamstow Hall, where Enrica taught, had been evacuated from Kent to Shropshire and Norman went to stay with her on more than one occasion. Both the poems that can be directly connected to Enrica were written on a visit to her during the war. One is called Wales and describes looking, with regret, across the border at the Welsh hills. The other poem, September in Shropshire, has an even more elegiac feel. The poet has left Shropshire behind and is travelling north 'To a winter of slag and frozen mountains', remembering the time he has just spent with 'you who already have so much'. He describes the large Victorian house the school was inhabiting, 'Where Mrs Radcliffe haunts the hearth like a downdraught'. There are views across to Wales and the September sun is 'hot as a kiss of parting'. All is withering into winter, but the 'you' the poem is addressed to, knows 'the nudge of the catkin beneath the drying leaf,/The spring intentions of the swallow', as well as 'the fantastic/Sting of love in the blood, the brutal wooing of God.' Norman ends the poem in a minor key:

And so I leave you
To hoard the bright pods of a dying summer
In the brown and poignant winter of this war.[15]

The other personal poems that Norman selected for *Five Rivers* also included one dedicated to Kathleen Raine, The First Day of Autumn, a poem written for Janet Roberts' children, Hokey and Henrietta, and another to Anne Ridler and her newest baby, Alison. Both Kathleen Raine and Enrica Garnier were invited to be Alison's godparents, but Kathleen – who was about to be received into the Catholic church – had travel problems and arrived too late for the service. Enrica had made friends with Norman's friends. There is a mention of her lunching with Kathleen Raine. She had also kept up her connection with Anne Ridler after their meeting in T.S. Eliot's office and the two women had become close. Anne was very fond of her. 'Rica', as they called her, stayed with the Ridlers to help out after the birth of their second daughter in 1943 and was a big hit with the entire family. Enrica liked to be needed. One of the subjects she taught was needlework and she was always happy to help out with Anne's overflowing mending basket. She also adored babies. Anne wrote to Norman that – 'all children would trust Enrica at once, of course (like their elders for that matter)'.[16]

Norman and Enrica were engaged and the relationship seemed permanent, if at a distance, though that was a common experience during the war years. They communicated by letter and saw each other for brief visits during the school holidays. Enrica's influence was important for Norman because it broadened his horizons. She had family connections in Italy and spoke good Italian. With Enrica's encouragement, Norman also began to learn the language, intending to read Dante in the original. He became good enough to translate from the Italian, publishing his first contribution – a short story called 'Il Piccolo Patriota Padovano' [The Little Patriot of Padova] by 19th century Italian author Edmondo de Amicis, in a magazine called *The Wind and the Rain* in 1945. It helped to bring Norman's work to the notice of Italian critics.

In 1943, Norman and Enrica spent a summer holiday together in Coniston. It became a favourite place, but the poetry that sprang from it has a curiously elegiac feel. In The Boathouse, Bank Ground, Coniston, the poet watches Enrica, 'a girl in a heckberry frock', dip her arm in the lake,

> Till the clouds swim round her fingers. Ragwort and rose,
> Wetherlam, weather and the yellowy wind
> Pour through her eyes like water in a beck,
> Leaving the memory smooth as stone.[17]

In 1944, when Norman was thirty, he cut a cartoon out of the newspaper and posted it to Enrica. It depicted an elderly man standing in a sea of paper calling out to a woman in another room 'Mary! Where's that novel I was writing? I can't have published it can I?' Over the top, Norman has written 'NN in 40 years?' and he has crossed out 'Mary' and substituted 'Rica'. The event referred to was the publication of Norman's first novel, *The Fire of the Lord* (originally called The Holy Winter) only a few months after his first collection of poetry. It was a book that Enrica knew well – having laboriously typed out all the various drafts from Norman's illegible handwritten manuscripts. So notorious was Norman's handwriting that T.S. Eliot was reported to have suggested that Norman's friends should club together to buy him a typewriter.

CHAPTER EIGHT

The Fire of the Lord is set in 'Odborough' which, the author admits 'is not entirely imaginary' and is only a loosely disguised Millom complete with 'parlour shops' like those in St George's Terrace, and an ironworks at the end of the street. The characters are slanted towards caricature – the slightly comic policeman who can't see in the dark, the plump female baker with her dusting of flour, the elderly vagrant preacher and the boy who is not quite 'right in the head'. The central character, Jim, is married to Maggie Birker, who is a lot older than her husband. Although Jim is unaware of it, Maggie had married him while still married to someone else – a man she believed to be dead. Meanwhile, their marriage has soured and Jim has fallen in love with Maggie's assistant in the shop, a young girl called Elsie.

Most of the book is taken up with the moral question of their relationship – their love and desire for each other which is prohibited by their religious faith because Jim believes himself to be married. But unknown to them, Maggie's husband has returned to the town as an itinerant preacher and Maggie has recognised him. She, too, is in moral jeopardy. Towards the end of the novel, Elsie, overcome by her feelings, offers herself to Jim, who righteously refuses. Humiliated, Elsie makes up her mind to leave Odborough. In the last pages, Maggie's inconvenient husband is killed at the ironworks, revealing the invalidity of Maggie's second marriage, and Jim and Elsie are free to find each other.

It is tempting to see in the plot of the novel and Jim's situation, a parallel with Norman's unsatisfied desires for the women in his life, particularly for Kathleen Raine – a woman who is married but not married because she is not living with her husband, or even the lover she had left him for. Is sex when someone is technically, but not actually, married always sinful? Kathleen Raine believed that love was the only criteria – sex without it was wrong – and marriage without love was, in itself, a sin. Jim tries to discuss this with Elsie in the novel in a very unsatisfactory way, but the conclusion is firmly stated. Sex without marriage is wrong. Adultery is always sinful. Lies will always find you out. The sexual frustration in the novel is palpable and the religious debates on the moral questions it deals with are often tedious. Stephen Spender's revealing comment that Norman's work was 'a mixture of sex, sin and sanctitude' is certainly relevant to the novel.[18]

Reviews were not encouraging. There was, *The Times* thought, 'Too little imagination and experience at work here, to hold the reader's interest'.[19] *The Observer* was one of the most favourable, but noted that 'Mr Nicholson's vision has not been clear enough to focus all his elements with a balanced whole'.[20] *The Guardian* found the story wholly unbelievable, the characters unconvincing and the ending 'most unsatisfactory'. Pamela Hansford Johnson implied that Norman should stick to poetry, stating that 'The theme of this story and its narrow construction are destructive of Mr Nicholson's talents'.[21] The religious papers, such as *The Church Times*, were more enthusiastic, since it was a novel with a clear moral message, quite suitable to put into the hands of the young. The novel was also popular with the local northern papers with headlines of the 'local boy makes good' variety, and it quickly sold nine thousand copies (an amazing amount for a first novel by a relatively unknown author) and Norman's agent was able to sell the American rights for publication in 1946.

With the combined successes of *Five Rivers* and *The Fire of the Lord*, Norman should have been ecstatic. He had another novel under way, a commission to write a play in verse – *The Old Man of the Mountains* – and a big commission from Robert Hale to write a book on the topography of Cumberland and Westmorland. He was now earning regular money as an author and marriage to Enrica had become a real possibility. By 1946 they had known each other for ten years, the war was over and there was a new atmosphere of optimism. But Norman was in personal turmoil. 'Bilious' attacks occurred frequently, particularly when Norman was under stress, and may well have been nervous in origin. Depression, particularly in winter, was a feature of his life. His life during the 1940s was full of stress. For any writer the publication of a book causes great anxiety – the fear and dread of how it's going to be received and the relentless need to produce another. Norman was no exception. And on top of his creative anxieties, there was also the unresolved conflict of his personal life.

In order to marry Enrica he would have to leave home and be prepared to support a wife and family. Norman felt unable to cope with the disorder that children would have brought into his life; Enrica loved them. He was also deeply afraid of the prospect of making his own way in the world and being responsible for another person. Norman had never had to fend for himself in any way – his parents provided for him completely – the roof over his head, his food, his clothes. He was still in every way the dependent child. And we don't know how much discouragement Norman faced at home from the dominant Rose and the cautious Joe who were afraid to lose him, sceptical of his ability to stand on his own two feet. Joe was still running the shop, though past retirement age, partly because he had spent all his savings on medical treatment for his son and partly because Joe was a man whose work was his life. Joe would willingly have worked himself into

CHAPTER EIGHT

the grave to keep his son out of it.

Norman's personal conflict is recorded in a poem, published in *Five Rivers*, called Askam Unvisited, which begins 'All through the summer I planned to visit Askam'. But in spite of summer's opportunities, when autumn arrives, 'Askam remains an intention and a goal,/Or perhaps a sin of omission, an opportunity missed… A letter lost/ In the post'. Askam is real enough, but somehow unattainable.

> The greater commandments I readily know,
> Not to kill, nor steal, nor love incontinently –
> These have not always to be thought of. But the lightning scores no
>
> Signposts in stone beside the choices that lie
> Like a spreading maze before me – whether to go or stay,
> Whether to speak or be silent, whether to raise an eye
>
> To an eye, a hand to a hand, turn this or that way.
> Among these I walk haphazard, like a bird pecking crumbs,
> Aware of the wild importance of each moment, though
>
> Unaware of the meaning of the moment when it comes.[22]

Enrica went on waiting for Norman to feel secure enough to marry her. Norman carried on living at home.

Chapter Nine

In May 1944, Norman had begun writing a play in verse for a group called the Pilgrim Players. It was to be a religious drama, based on a biblical event. Since the success of Eliot's *Murder in the Cathedral*, and the *Family Reunion*, there was a new demand for plays in verse. Anne Ridler had had some success with *Cain* in 1943 and was now working on a nativity play called *Shadow Factory*, for production in 1945. Through George Every, Norman's work had come to the notice of a theatre producer called E. Martin Browne, who had created the Pilgrim Players in 1939, with the object of touring his productions. On a tour of the East Midlands, Martin and the company had stayed at Kelham and met George Every, who had mentioned Norman and one or two others and urged Martin to think about 'the younger poets', meet them and build up a repertory of verse drama. Martin was directing Eliot's plays and he and Norman met for the first time in Ulverston, a small town close to Millom, at a production of *Murder in the Cathedral*. 'We found ourselves at one in having a special love for the Elijah story. "Nic" had already the germ of an idea for a play, transferring it to the fells. We talked as long as time allowed about the practical problems of constructing and setting the play; and then had to carry on by letters to and from that remote spot.'[1] After seeing *Murder in the Cathedral* in Ulverston, Norman wrote to Eliot with an enthusiastic description of the production. Eliot wrote back saying that 'I have myself lost all desire to see the play or to hear the words again'. In the letter he describes Millom as a village then crosses it out and substitutes 'town' – and one can't help but think that he wasn't much interested in Millom. Though Norman liked to regard Eliot as a friend, his letters to Norman are always signed formally, sometimes 'Eliot', more often 'T.S. Eliot' – never Tom.[2] There is no hint in the correspondence that Norman was getting any encouragement for his project from Eliot.

CHAPTER NINE

Norman's play was at first destined for the touring company, but in 1945, Martin Browne leased the tiny Mercury Theatre in London and began a series of productions of 'new plays', which included work by T.S. Eliot, Christopher Fry and Anne Ridler – Norman's play was going to be one of the first to be produced. Norman had always been interested in the theatre, since he had read Shaw's plays as a student, and he had attended almost every play put on by the local amateur dramatic society. There was always something of the actor about Norman, that part of him that had revelled in performing poetry as a child. While convalescing after Linford sanatorium, Norman had begun to write a drama with a biblical theme, much discussed with Sylvia Lubelsky. It had been set in the court of the Egyptian Pharoahs and based on Jewish/Gentile conflicts represented by Moses and Aaron, but it was a juvenile effort that came to nothing. Now the idea of verse drama based on biblical stories attracted him once again.

But, as Martin Browne was quick to point out, most poets have no working knowledge of the theatre, and they are at a disadvantage. Unlike words on the printed page, oral performance has to be capable of immediate comprehension. 'During a performance the audience cannot ask the actor to go back over obscure lines. Their meaning is irretrievably lost. That is the major and perhaps the most difficult lesson a poet has to learn when he adopts the drama as a means of expression.' In Norman's case there were additional difficulties with dialogue in the Cumbrian idiom; 'dialect is inhibiting to many actors who cannot characterise freely if they are trying to master unfamiliar sounds'. The cast had coaching from a woman from Westmorland, but were still 'not at ease' with the language.[3] Not all of them found it a problem. Robert Speight, who had played the lead in Martin Browne's production of Eliot's *Murder in the Cathedral*, played Elijah and he wrote to Norman to say that the characterisation was so good that 'Every word that Elijah says rings true'.[4]

Norman was still sharing work with Kathleen Raine and he sent her the play for comment. She wrote back full of enthusiasm. 'It bears the impression of authenticity that the old, anonymous Morality plays have, and I see you, less as a poet of the 1940s, than as one of the artist-craftsmen whose trace is to be found all over England'. She thought that 'the dialect, the details of rock, water, cloud, tree and plant' were timeless. Kathleen thought that he had found his 'true medium' in the play, and that it contained 'the best moments of the novel and of the poems'. There's a reference in the letter to a forthcoming visit to Cumberland and she is looking forward to being able to discuss it with Norman and Helen Sutherland. But she ends the letter on a more critical note. The play is not without its faults. 'Too many lines from TSE ... my pen drying up falls in with my own impulse to say no more ...' And the ink obligingly fades out.[5]

The play was eventually called *The Old Man of the Mountains* and, like Norman's long poems, it provides a modern Cumbrian setting for a biblical story. The Old Man is Elijah, a 'statesman farmer' living up in the fells and keeping himself to himself. The Raven is the narrator, the voice of 'something older', opening and closing the play. Martin Browne used a split stage for the performance. One half was the inside of Ruth's cottage, with a door in the wall, and the other side was her garden with a beck running along the edge of it. The beck is a character in the play, and the running, chattering, repetitive dialogue is read by three women, functioning like a Greek chorus.

The play can be seen as a parable about man's custodianship of the natural world and from the beginning, it has a very distinct environmental message. The Raven accuses the audience of having abandoned the idea of Earth as a mother, worthy of care and respect, telling them that now 'your guts are tight with greed'.

> You tear the crops like hair from the living skin;
> You drive the earth like a slave; you wring
> The last drop of blood from the land till the soil is dried into dust.
> The hills which were your altars have become your middens;
> The becks which were your temples have become your sewers.

And the beck answers 'You have shackled and fouled us... you have tipped your slag in us, dipped your filth in us ...' The human race stands accused of having forgotten 'that water is a gift'.[6]

The other characters, Ruth, Ben, David, Rebecca, Martha and Obadiah, are tenants and workers on land owned by Ahab who 'knows how to look after the brass' and is 'living on the fat of the land' with his wife Jezebel. As the play opens, the foreman Obadiah arrives at Ruth's cottage to instruct David, the labourer, to chop down the big ash tree at the bottom of her garden on Ahab's orders. This causes a great deal of distress to Ruth, who protests. 'You've chopped down half the woods... can't you leave us that one tree?' She tells her friend Martha, 'they don't plant even a shrub in place of the trees they fell. The rabbits are getting in and the whole place is going to ruin'.[7] Worse is to come; Ahab has decided that Ruth's orchard must also be grubbed up to plant crops. His philosophy is that the land

CHAPTER NINE

must be treated as any other commercial enterprise.

> We must see that the land is made to pay ...
> Dig chemicals in your soil, comb the fields
> Till the last ear of corn is hooked from the grain;
> Make your beasts earn their keep, squeeze the last pint
> Of milk from the cows, and work your horses
> Till they are only fit for the knacker's yard.[8]

This is an extraordinary play to be written in 1944, well ahead of the ecological concerns raised in the fifties and sixties about the dangers of modern farming methods. Rachel Carson's *Silent Spring*, the book credited with launching the environmental movement, wasn't published until 1962. Norman, whose knowledge of botany and birds had been growing since he left the sanatorium, admitted that he had been influenced by the *New English Weekly*, a subscription paid for by T.S. Eliot, which contained articles by writers who 'were already thinking about those ecological and environmental dangers which were not to become popular preoccupations until years later'.[9] Norman was also writing from a concern with the way that the land had been treated during the war effort. The need to grow the maximum amount of food to feed the British population during the war, led to the felling of old orchards, the ploughing of important habitats for wildlife, the indiscriminate draining of wetlands and widespread use of artificial fertilisers, herbicides and pesticides. Some farmers in marginal areas like the Lake District, farming in a traditional, sustainable way, were deeply concerned about the consequences. Norman picked up on this and worked it into the story of Elijah. In the biblical story, Ahab is told that there will be a catastrophic drought because he has forsaken the Lord God and allowed Jezebel's priests of Baal to erect altars in Israel. In *The Old Man of the Mountains*, the ways of 'the Lord' are equated with the nurture of the earth and respect for all living things. Ahab's commercial exploitation of the land is the equivalent of the worship of Baal. Despite Elijah's warnings, Ahab continues his destruction in the name of progress; there is a drought and the beck dries up.

At the beginning of the play Elijah has almost forgotten he is a prophet and it takes the prompting of the Raven to remind him that he has a voice and can perform miracles. He restores Ruth's son, Ben, to life and makes sure the flour bin and the milk jug are always full. But he still doubts that he is responsible. Ruth and Ben never lose their faith in him and, as a result, they are evicted by Ahab. At the end of the play, Ahab is asked to change his ways and agrees to do so if Elijah will bring rain. When the rain eventually comes, at Elijah's bidding, Ahab is – almost – convinced; the tenants all get their jobs and houses back and Ahab has a new scheme to build a dam to conserve water in times of drought. It is a commercial enterprise, of course. The entire plot could be summed up as a conflict between environmentalism and consumer capitalism.

The Old Man of the Mountains was scheduled for production at the end of September 1945, and in June Norman signed a contract with Faber and Faber for a printed edition. It was to be one of his most popular works in the amateur dramatic repertoire, until the vogue for religious drama dissipated. Then, just as the play was going into rehearsal, Norman had some very important news. A letter arrived from the Royal Society of Literature informing him that he had been given the prestigious Heinemann Award for *Five Rivers*. Not only did this mean a cheque for £100, but it also put Norman among the leading poets of the day. The letter also went on to invite Norman to put his name forward in order to become a Fellow of the Royal Society, and indicated that his application would be sympathetically received. Norman wrote to Sylvia Lubelsky that he thought himself 'an odd choice', but he was very conscious of the honour, making preparations to go to London for both the presentation and the opening of his play at the Mercury. The new honour was hastily added to the programme notes. There was considerable coverage in the national and local presses and Millom town council sent Norman a letter conveying their 'esteem and admiration'. Millom now had a Royal Literary Fellow living in the town.

Norman was delighted by this recognition of his work, which came from much further afield than Britain. Kenneth Rexroth in America voted Norman 'one of the ten most vital poets under forty in Great Britain'[10] and a Scandanavian publisher wrote to enquire about translation rights for *The Old Man of the Mountains* as well as *Man and Literature*. Norman's trip to London for the first night of the play was a celebration. T.S. Eliot came with Norman to watch the production, but his comments afterwards were rather disappointing. 'Promising, Nicholson, promising' is apparently all he said. Norman felt deflated. And the critics were also lukewarm in their response. Robert Speight wrote to Norman saying 'I am sorry that the critics were so idiotic in their incomprehension'.[11]

Most had focussed on the play's flaws. Norman's handling of the dramatic structure was uncertain. Although he had read plays for pleasure and attended a lot of local amateur dramatic events, he had no depth of

CHAPTER NINE

experience of live theatre. As Martin Browne had pointed out, a play on the page is very different to the living thing on the stage. Norman had trouble with the ending – what was true biblically, and what made a good story, did not translate into a satisfying dramatic conclusion. The final act of Elijah's story takes place on the mountain where the prophet invokes 'the fire of the lord' to light his altar and the priests of Baal are killed by the lightning bolts as the rain begins to fall. It's a moment of high drama. Norman did not quite know how to render this theatrically and 'more important, had not adjusted the characters' view of the happening to accord with their reality as twentieth century people'.[12] The merging of biblical and contemporary was incomplete.

After the production Norman worked on the last act to remedy this, but the result wasn't completely successful. The scene on the mountain was omitted, replaced by an 'interlude' where Elijah and Ahab are glimpsed in stylised conflict on the mountain top. Norman then opened the third act with Elijah's arrival back at Ruth's cottage after descending 'Carmel' Fell. Rain is promised, but hasn't yet come and Elijah's powers are doubted. He himself has a crisis of faith but it is eventually resolved as the rain begins to fall and Ahab does his abrupt, not particularly convincing, *volte face*. Friends told Norman that although it now worked dramatically, they preferred the first ending. Andrew Young was one who liked the original inspiration – telling Norman that it would have been a '*tour de force*' if he could have brought it off. But the new ending worked well enough for Martin Browne to encourage Norman to write another play, even though he had lost money on it, 'half of my very small capital'.[13]

Buoyed up by his new success and the recognition of his gifts by the literary establishment, Norman continued to write with new conviction. Between 1945 and 1948 Norman signed contracts for four non-fiction books and was busy working on his second novel, *The Green Shore*, as well as poems for his second collection *Rock Face*. He was also reviewing regularly for the *Times Literary Supplement*, contributing articles to a variety of magazines and doing occasional radio broadcasts.

The Green Shore had been commissioned on the strength of Norman's earlier successes and *The Fire of the Lord* had sold moderately well for a first novel. Norman and his publisher had hopes that this second novel would establish him as a writer of fiction. The cover was designed by Graham Sutherland who wrote to Norman saying that he aimed to get 'in a more abstract manner, something of the "brightness" of the spirit of your writing'. He produced a striking, abstract design in green, on a stone-coloured ground, that became a collector's piece.[14] It's now almost impossible to get hold of a copy.

The novel is set in the nineteen thirties and there are two main characters in the book; Alice, a young girl whose legs have been damaged by rickets and who has to wear a leg-iron, and Anthony Pengwilly, an eccentric, isolated character, who lives in an abandoned building on the sea shore and is regarded as something of a bogeyman by the local children. In the opening pages, Alice is out walking with a friend and they are being bullied by local boys who tease Alice about her leg-iron. The girls go out onto the rocks to evade the boys, but are followed and then the entire group is cut off by the rip tide. Most of the children manage to leap across the rocks to safety, but Alice is unable to do so. Someone fetches 'Old Pen' and he rescues Alice by carrying her across on his shoulders.

Alice goes to see him to say thank you and a strange relationship is struck up between them. As Alice grows older and becomes independent she continues to think about him and goes to visit him again. Gradually 'Old Pen's' story is revealed. He had once loved her mother but had been too shy to do anything about it and she had married someone else. There are rumours that Alice is his child, which he strongly denies. Alice believes him. Old Pen tells her that he lives in his isolated house to avoid temptation. His greatest temptation is that of sex – with others, such as drink, he tests himself regularly to make sure he is able to resist, but he has always avoided sex.

There's a strange scene where he asks Alice to take her clothes off in order to test him. He promises that he will turn his back and not look. After a lot of deliberation she agrees and he keeps his promise. Alice too is having problems with sex. She has a boyfriend of her own age, but she is uncomfortable with physical contact. Alice makes up her mind to go and live with Old Pen, but when she arrives at his house it's locked up and he has gone away.

One of the best things about the novel is the character of Anthony Pengwilly's mother, which is a portrait of Norman's grandmother Maria Nicholson. He includes the scene where, on first seeing Millom, she tells the carter to turn around and take her back home again. Mrs Pengwilly is uncompromising and severe. Like Maria, she has a crippled leg and must sit in the kitchen, where she gives orders to the young girl who 'skivvies' for her, waving her crutch to back up her commands. There are also some good descriptions of the scenery, but the dialogue is tedious and the plot

CHAPTER NINE

lacks drama. As in *The Old Man of the Mountains*, Norman's work is not particularly strong on psychological and emotional motivation – it's not always clear why his characters behave as they do.

Montague Slater wrote to Norman to say that he'd been reading his poems and 'the Millom novel' and they had made him want to re-visit Millom. He warned Norman from his own experience that people in the town as well as his family would 'identify local characters in his work even if they are not'.[15] Although there were some who liked the novel, *The Green Shore* was almost universally panned by the critics. Norman's old enemy D.S. Savage sharpened his knife before applying it in the *Spectator*. He referred to it as 'This inept and callow novel … so bathetically commonplace as to defy criticism'.[16] In *The Listener* P.H. Newby referred to 'amateur monasticism' and said that Norman's central character withdraws from the world as a way of 'escaping from sex' and that the whole novel has 'a sort of pervading sexy itch'. He found the central situation unconvincing and added that Anthony Pengwilly's difficulties 'are never too great for an energetic and intelligent parish priest to have cleared up in a fortnight'.[17] Sylvia Lubelsky wrote to Norman advising him to stick to verse. He wrote back; 'I agree with you … Fiction isn't my line'.[18] But this admission of failure, after four novels, was painful.

In 1946 Norman had acquired an agent for the first time. He was signed up by Pearn, Pollinger and Higham whose offices were in The Strand and he would later move with David Higham when he set up his own agency. Having an agent had immediate benefits – Norman now had someone in London who could sell his work and generate publicity for him. One of Norman's poems, The Raven, was read on the BBC radio Home Service in a programme of verse and prose called 'By Lake and Fell'. A few months later an entire programme was devoted to extracts from *Five Rivers* and there were two more programmes – the first of Norman's talks on the Lake District, 'Man and the Country', in July and one of his short stories 'The Island in the Lake' was featured in November.

In 1946 Pearn, Pollinger and Higham negotiated two contracts for biographies of William Cowper and H.G. Wells on Norman's behalf, and another the following year for a Wordsworth anthology in the 'Poets on Poets' series as well as a collection of Cowper's verse. These biographical studies were a new departure. By 1948 Norman, perhaps advised by his new agents, was re-thinking his whole approach to writing. Fiction was dropped in favour of non-fiction, and his poetry, from being consciously religious, exploring religious themes and subject matter, became less obviously so – Christianity remained its bedrock, but on the surface it had a much wider appeal. The Canadian academic Philip Gardner thought that this was a deliberate decision, prompted by a reviewer's comment that 'part of Nicholson's fascination is that he exacts not even a temporary belief from the unbeliever'.[19]

Whatever the reasons, after *Five Rivers* there is a definite shift in Norman's work. Philip Gardner in his critical study maintains that 'he continued to treat religious themes, but he did so in verse plays where their individual human relevance could emerge more fully. In his poems, he concentrated on landscape and man's relationship to it'.[20] My own view is that Norman was growing more and more concerned about the 'pigeon-holing' of his work as that of a 'religious poet', grouped with poets such as Anne Ridler and David Gascoyne. He knew that this would stand in the way of his recognition as a major poet. Eliot's remarks about the rejection of poetry that was recognisably Protestant and Christian in his controversial book *After Strange Gods* – a work Norman very much admired – bit deep. He could see that this was a cul-de-sac where the poetry mainstream was concerned, and Norman wanted very badly to be part of the mainstream, like Eliot, whose faith is inherent in his work, but who could never be fettered as a 'religious poet'. Kathleen Raine too, was evading classification by adopting a more 'transcendental' poetry – spiritual but not specifically Christian. She had been adopted into the Catholic Church, persuaded by friends, but later lapsed.

Norman's second collection, *Rock Face*, was published by Faber in 1948. Philip Gardner, who discussed the poems with Norman, observed that 'the influence of Kathleen Raine's thought can be positively felt in the volume as a whole'. But he felt that the influence of 'her rather abstract style' took Norman away from his usual path of expressing the objective world through detailed observations. Gardner thought that the 'transcendental method of Kathleen Raine' wasn't natural to Norman.[21] But the collection was praised by Howard Sergeant, who liked this move from overt theological and biblical themes towards a poetry growing organically from the strong bedrock of Christian values he sensed underpinning the poems. 'As a result, his work not only shows a greater depth of thought and imaginative quality, but is more authentic in expressing the Christian interpretation of life through his own poetic experience.'[22]

Rock Face is a strange collection, less coherent than *Five Rivers*, containing a very diverse group of poems. There is no one thread to hold them all together. Kathleen Raine described it as a kind of 'winter Georgic'

CHAPTER NINE

and she approved what she saw as 'a kind of mysticism of the bones'.[23] Some of the poems are topographical, others – Cowper, The Tame Hare, Thomas Gray in Patterdale, Emily Brontë – flag up Norman's current interests. He was already at work on his biography of Cowper and he was also reading Thomas Gray as part of his research for *Cumberland and Westmorland*, which had been commissioned by Robert Hale in 1944. Emily Brontë's poetry and fiction had been read for a new introduction to the 1946 edition of *Wuthering Heights*.

The collection also contains the poems that Norman wrote for Kathleen Raine, Above Ullswater, The Candle, and Rock Face, as well as others that show her influence, Song at Night, and The Anatomy of Desire. But the majority of the poems reflect the turmoil that Norman was going through and his depression – what he refers to in Frost Flowers as 'the Arctic circles of the soul' – a bleakness that led some reviewers to draw a parallel between Norman and the Finnish composer Sibelius. But these bleak periods can be very productive. In St Luke's Summer:

The soul, too, has it brown October days –
The fancy run to seed and dry as stone,
Rags and wisps of words blown through the mind;
And yet, while dead leaves clog the eyes,
Never-predicted poetry is sown.[24]

What comes out of many of the poems, is pain. In Song at Night, one of the poems that may be connected to Kathleen Raine, but could equally refer to Enrica Garnier, the poet longs for something to 'Resolve the brawls of rhyme/That chord within my head', but it ends '… then let me pluck one name/And echo clear proclaim/Not I, my dear, not I.' In Song for a Play the face of the woman who loves him haunts the poet both night and day. 'When night is bandaged round my pain/The full-faced moon is raised,/Brazen in the breath of the sun,/And lights my sleep with the light of a love unseen.' The anatomy of human desire is, in the end, 'only a stone'. Several of the poems examine doubt. In Songs Unheard, the poet is caught in conflict between the blood and the brain, only 'the heart that shares/(Knowledgeless still in knowing)' will endure 'Longer than memory and hard as bone'. And in the Grass of Parnassus, the heart, as well as the lover, is restless and unsatisfied 'beneath the catastrophic sky'.

Probably the most important poem in the collection is, like Askam Unvisited in *Five Rivers*, about moral choices. Across the Estuary describes a walk across Morecambe Bay – a treacherous estuary of mud and quicksand. The changing paths are marked daily by the official guides with cuttings – 'brogs' – of broom and local history tells many tragic tales of walkers lost when they deviated from the paths and were caught by the rip tides. In the poem, the traveller is in a place where the familiar landscape is 'blurred away … under the canvas of fog'. There is only the sand, and a 'dead, purple turf' and 'gulleys in the mud where now the water/Thrusts flabby fingers'. There are wild geese feeding and cormorants 'curl black question-marks/Above the threshold of the sea'. The traveller follows the ruts of cartwheels, now filling with water, along the track marked by the 'brogs' of broom and is suddenly lost.

> But now – where is the track? Where are the ruts? The broom
> Skulks back into the dark, and every footstep,
> Dug deep in mud, draws water through the heels.
> Each step goes wrong.

As the mist and the sea wrap their 'cold, wet nets' about him, he realises that it is pointless to wonder where he left the path, or why he came here. It isn't the past that stares at him through the gloom, for the past is forgiven;

> It is not then but now
> That tightens like mist about me:
> Not how I came
> But where I am,
> Not what I was,
> Nor how I grew
> From that to this,
> But merely
> My being I.

And the sea pushes relentlessly in as the tide spreads across the estuary.

> Gulleys and gutters are confiscated now
> Into the grey acreage of the sea; for a while
> The inevasible choice of wrong and less wrong
> Is forgotten or deferred …
> There is no sign of traveller on the flat waters.[25]

CHAPTER NINE

Although the whole of *Rock Face* declares the influence of Kathleen Raine in Norman's life, it was typed out by Enrica Garnier and Norman had originally intended a dedication, but the collection was printed without it. The outcome of Norman's long personal conflict was not happy. Sometime before *Rock Face* was published in 1948, Norman broke off the engagement and Enrica was devastated. According to Anne Ridler, to whom she had confided details of the relationship, Enrica had always hoped that 'the time would come when he proved able to break away from his father and stepmother to marry her'.[26] But, in the end, he was unable to do it. Anne and her husband never completely forgave Norman. Enrica was by now in her thirties and had invested all her youth and her love in a man who was unwilling to leave his sheltered environment to make a relationship with her. She had no further contact with Norman, never married anyone else and remained a dedicated, much loved teacher at Walthamstow Hall School, where a prize for Religious Studies has been created in her name. According to the Ridler family there was always a 'wistful' tone to Enrica's voice when she spoke of Norman, and she remained convinced that when he was on his deathbed, she would be the person he asked for.

PART THREE

PROVINCIAL PLEASURES

1948 - 1960

My ways are circumscribed, confined as a limpet
To one small radius of rock; yet
I eat the equator, breathe the sky, and carry
The great white sun in the dirt of my fingernails.

The Pot Geranium, 1954

Chapter Ten

The break-up of Norman's long-term relationship with Enrica Garnier came at a time when his work was in considerable demand. He had contracts for four non-fiction books and another play. Urged on by Faber, he was also trying to put a new collection of poetry together. The deadlines for his non-fiction books, commissioned three or four years earlier, were the most pressing. Almost the last manuscript Enrica typed out for him was the topographical study *Cumberland and Westmorland*, one of Robert Hale's County Book series. Norman acknowledged Enrica's struggle with 'the longest and most illegible script I have ever written' and dedicated the book to his old schoolmaster Walter Wilson whose advice he had regularly sought during the writing of it. *Cumberland and Westmorland*, published in 1949, is an account of Norman's passion for his home country. It's a poet's book, lyrically written and full of striking images and metaphors. Unlike the clumsy verbiage of the novels, the prose sings.

The title was somewhat misleading because Norman idiosyncratically included a portion of Lancashire he felt belonged more naturally to Cumberland and Westmorland and he excluded both the border country beyond Hadrian's Wall and the eastern Pennine area because they were 'really foreign to the Lake system'. What he is actually describing is the Lake District: 'a huge cart-wheel pattern of lakes and valleys which focuses somewhere … in the Helvellyn Range'. It is also a very personal account, often written from memory and imagination. Norman didn't have a car, and neither did his parents, so any exploring he did had to be by public transport. He was also not in good enough physical condition to walk very far. He went to Carlisle and borrowed books on ecology, history and archaeology, and he re-visited the places he could reach easily by train or bus. Where he has intimate knowledge of a location the detail is rich – Coniston where he holidayed with Enrica, the Penrith area where Janet and Michael Roberts had lived, Ullswater where he stayed with Helen Sutherland, Castlerigg Stone Circle which he had visited with Kathleen Raine, and of course the west coast which was his homeland. Other areas are less well described, but it would be difficult for a reader to guess which was which. For someone with impaired lungs who had not stood on a mountain top since he was a boy, the descriptions are marvellous. Norman had been warned by a friend, the librarian at nearby Barrow-in-Furness who was helping him with the research, that some earlier writers on the Lakes – including Defoe and Leland – hadn't always visited the places themselves, and it had led to glaring errors. It was essential to get the details right.[1]

Norman revealed a passion for the geology of the Lake District. 'In no other part of England,' he wrote, 'has the life and character of a district and its people been so controlled by the nature of the rock and by the forces which have acted upon it'. He went even further; 'to look at the scenery of Cumberland and Westmorland without trying to understand the rock is like listening to poetry in an unknown language – you hear the beauty of the sounds, but you miss the meaning. For the meaning is the rock.'[2] His imagery is original and often colloquial. Black Combe is a 'round, gumboil of a mountain'; the great screes on the mountain sides have been created by a kind of 'geological rheumatism', while limestone 'goes on the razzle at Grange'. It was the beginning of a deep interest in geology that would find expression in his poetry – particularly the collection *Sea to the West* thirty years later. The seeds of one of his most famous late poems – 'The wall walks the fell' – are already here on the page, when he describes how the 'walls and barns ... seem to have grown like trees' from the landscape – 'for they are of the very stuff of the rock on which they stand ... and they keep their footing and balance on the steepest slopes, climbing high over crags'.[3]

Another passion illuminated the book – there is real joy evident in the naming of the wild flowers of the region – a subject Norman knew well. He had first become interested in botany through his school-master Walter Wilson and then through his reading at Linford. In 1938, his contact with the clergyman-poet Andrew Young revealed a joint interest and their correspondence was more often about the identification of flowers than about poetry. Andrew was much older than Norman and his complete opposite – 'hale and hearty and outdoorsy'[4] – but they shared a love of plants that drew the two men together. In *Cumberland and Westmorland* the pages are filled with litanies of flowers particular to the Lake District – the details of which Norman had discussed with Andrew. Norman writes lyrically of the flora of the edgelands in which he lives. 'I remember the half-tame flowers around old cottages which have crumbled and fallen ... and I remember with special joy the flowers of railway sidings and cuttings; colts-foot along the banks in March and primroses in April.'[5] He also draws attention to the role that plants play in healing the landscape. 'Some of the pits are caving in, the water is breaking through the dykes, the old buildings and pithead gear are falling, but the cresses and the buttercups reclaim the soil. Man struck the rock and the rock gushed blood, but the bloody crane's-bill grows on the red scabs of rubble.'[6]

When the book was published reviewers focussed on Norman's account of the industrial side of the Lake District – one not often discussed. The geology is rich in minerals – even rare metals such as silver – and it has a long history of exploitation dating back to the Romans and beyond. Norman catalogues the industrial decline of the twentieth century and its consequences for the affected areas. In 'an underworld landscape of Miltonic horror', all is 'dark and damned'. It is a ravaged landscape, scored by industrial history, now decaying. But the abandoned pits and iron-works 'stand like ruined abbeys' in the twilight. Even slag-banks, he argues, 'can be gravely beautiful under snow'.[7] He defends quarries, which many people felt defaced the landscape. They were 'true to the very nature of the rock' and they were no different from screes in appearance and would be reclaimed by nature in the course of time. Equally controversial was his view of forestry. They were trees after all, even if planted in straight lines. It wasn't industry that would ruin the Lake District – 'it is the sentimental and the sham which are the great dangers'. Norman was against the 'preservation' of the Lake District as an outdoor museum. The Lakes were becoming a 'beauty spot', a 'shrine', a 'national heritage', a curiosity, even 'a prodigy to be exhibited like a fat woman in a circus'. It was the way to turn the area into a 'beautiful invalid'.[8] He believed that its only way forward was as a 'living economic unit', and he raised a lot of hackles, both locally and nationally, when he wrote that he 'would rather see the whole of the dales covered with mining shafts and chimneys than with select verandas for tourists and aesthetes'.[9] In particular he railed against the construction of houses in materials not native to the Lake District and declared that he 'would cheerfully put dynamite under most brick buildings in a slate country'.[10]

For authors of non-fiction, inevitably there is always a reader out there who has more up-to-date information and can pick up the tiniest mistake. The Barrow librarian had been right to warn Norman. After publication, the Cumbrian archaeologist Mary Fair wrote to him to point out some of his errors. Herdwick sheep, she told Norman, have white faces, not black ones – an embarrassing mistake for a supposedly observant poet, but one which underlines the fact that he was essentially a town dweller without the knowledge a country bred person would have had. And there were other mistakes – his paragraphs on early Britain, carefully researched in the Tullie House library, were completely out of date – 'that Goidel Brythonic stuff is no longer used'. She added that, since the 'industrial portion is so out-standingly good', it was important that the ancient history should be equally 'good and modern'. Mary hoped that Norman would revise the text in a second edition and wrote to his publisher to reinforce the point, telling them that 'the pre-history of the book is very poor indeed'. But her biggest complaint was that Norman had criticised the owners of Calder Abbey for neglecting the historic structure and allowing it to fall into decay. Apparently they were 'very distressed' by his comments. Mary explained that they had little money and during the war it had simply not been possible to find workmen, or funding, for this kind of project.[11] Whatever his personal feelings towards the negative criticism, Norman was glad of the contact and dealt patiently with the corrections. Mary Fair became a very useful advisor for future books.

Every poet born and bred in the Lake District has to come to terms with Wordsworth. Norman, in an interview, described him as 'a big obstacle ... a huge mountain of a poet',[12] but Norman wasn't intimidated by him. His opinion of Wordsworth's poetry hadn't altered since he wrote to Sylvia Lubelsky at the age of nineteen, but his method of expressing it had grown much more sophisticated, if boldly unconventional. Norman was commissioned to produce a selection of Wordsworth's poetry accompanied by a five thousand word essay, in 1947, for the flat fee of £75.00. He begins his introduction to Wordsworth with scathing remarks about tourists who visit the Lake District from the south and get no further than Windermere. (Bowness on Windermere was one of Norman's bugbears, and he hated the commercial 'touristification' of the Lake District.) Applying this to Wordsworth he goes on; 'In the same way I believe that the modern reader approaches Wordsworth from the wrong direction' – they get lost in a 'Windermere country' of lesser poems and never reach 'the heart of the poetry'.

Norman recognised Wordsworth as a fellow Cumbrian, descended from Scandinavian stock, bred from the rocks which 'helped to make

CHAPTER TEN

Wordsworth what he was'. Yet, Norman comments, 'their direct influence on his poetry seems to be small. He turned away from them to the rocks of the dales, and surely this very choice, this rejection, is significant'. There are other omissions in Wordsworth's poetry that Norman finds surprising. The Wordsworth children often went to Whitehaven to visit their uncle who was a customs agent at the port, but 'the sea seems to have meant little'. The poet's father was agent to the Lowther estates and 'must have heard much about the iron mines'; Wordsworth's son married into the Curwen family – 'Workington coal owners' – and yet 'all this is ignored in his survey of the background to his life'.[13]

Norman is also critical of Wordsworth's lack of direction. As a young man, he complains, Wordsworth 'made not much attempt to provide for himself'. And he misunderstands the nature of Wordsworth's relationship with Mary Hutchinson, whom he eventually married, believing Annette Vallon to have been Wordsworth's only experience of 'passionate love'. He also believes that Wordsworth was driven by guilt about his abandonment of Annette and attempted to heal himself 'by his early feeling for nature and the religion of the heart'.[14] His love for Dorothy is described as 'certainly romantic and perhaps sub-consciously incestuous'. Several readers protested about this assumption.

Wordsworth had little interest in geology and described a geologist, with 'heavy-heeled irony' in *The Excursion*, but Norman uses the different rock strata of the Lake District to draw a 'topographical parallel with Wordsworth's poetry'. Old Skiddaw Slate stands for 'the basic Wordsworth, plain, bold, solid verse', and the Volcanic rock of the middle period represents 'the soaring poetry of Tintern Abbey'. The 'long anti-climax' of the poet's later years is characterised by the more recent Silurian rock.[15]

Norman uses a very sharp knife to dissect Wordsworth's reputation. *The Excursion* is referred to as 'those dreary Sunday School rambles'; the Ecclesiastical sonnets as 'sanctimonious, didactic pieces' which are the products of Wordsworth's old age. Norman agreed with Coleridge that Wordsworth descended too often from 'sentences of peculiar felicity ... to a style, not only unimpassioned, but undistinguished'. He accused Wordsworth of sometimes being self-important and pretentious and complained of 'flat-footed lines, redundant or obvious words, forced rhymes and platitudes'. 'Even Milton could not be living at this hour without dragging "bower" and "Dower" after him like the chains of Marley's ghost'. But Norman praises Matthew, the Lucy poems and Michael – 'here is the bedrock of Wordsworth' – and included sections of the early draft of *The*

Prelude in his selection of the poetry.[16]

Norman is not inclined to believe Wordsworth's manifesto – the much quoted Preface to Lyrical Ballads, in which he proposed to use the language 'really used by men'. 'What men?' Norman asks. 'Certainly not the common people of the dales whose language it was supposed to be'. Not only was Wordsworth not a member of the 'common people', he didn't use Cumbrian dialect or the Norse vocabulary available to him. What Norman doesn't acknowledge is that the use of such language at that period would have cut Wordsworth off from the educated, southern audience he courted. Wordsworth may have spoken in dialect to his neighbours – he certainly spoke with a strong northern accent – but the language he used in the poems was a hybrid – colloquial, plain, though not too colloquial. Norman has to admit that, 'when he speaks in his own voice using language quite as simple but less colloquial, he achieves some of his greatest successes'. And in his best poems it is possible to see 'everyday words shining even as pebbles shine like jewels with the sun on them'.[17]

Norman was currently reading Charles Williams on the Affirmative Way and the Negative Way for a radio broadcast he was planning to write and he had clearly absorbed some of Williams' ideas. He assumed that his readers would also be familiar with them when he began to compare Wordsworth's Way of Nature with Dante's Way of Romantic Love. As Grevel Lindop, Charles Williams' biographer puts it, all 'aspects of created reality could lead to the spiritual', traces of the divine were to be found in everything. The Affirmative Way stated that aspects of God, images of God, could be found everywhere in the created world. Such things could be regarded as either a pathway to the divine, or a distraction from it. The opposite path was The Negative Way, a path of asceticism and self-denial, which led ultimately to withdrawal from the world because it was a sinful trap for the unwary. Both paths were valid ways to God, but Williams felt that the Church had stressed the validity of the Negative path far too strongly, particularly with regard to sex. God had created pleasure, as well as pain, Jesus had fasted, but he had also given food and wine, and it was necessary to have a balance. Williams' interpretation of Dante was particularly controversial. The image of Beatrice, the revelation of the divine in her, was essential to Dante's knowledge of God. Romantic love was, he insisted, a 'method of process towards the inGodding of man'. Williams went further, into what some thought to be heretical territory, believing that the sexual act, if celebrated in the right spirit, was a sacrament like Mass or Holy Communion – not just between man and wife, but between any man and woman who truly loved.[18] Norman had conversations with Anne Ridler (who had been taught by Williams and later edited his work) on this subject and Anne was intrigued to find that Norman thought that Charles Williams understood man as a lover, better than man as a social being.[19]

Norman makes comparisons, based on his reading of Williams, between Dante's and Wordsworth's visions of the correct Way for mankind, and he manages to bring in an environmental aspect. Both Dante's Way of Love and Wordsworth's Way of Nature had their own particular pitfalls. Dante had provided a clear picture of the perversions of his own path and their bitter consequences in the torments of Hell; Norman goes on to ask what the perversions of the Way of Nature might be. He suggests that they should include, 'Dust-bowl-farming, artificial insemination, slag-banks, village slums, atom bombs …' and he describes a scenario as graphic and depressing as Dante's Inferno, arguing that how we walk the Way of Nature is a vitally important question because, 'on making up our minds depends, perhaps, the future of man'. Wordsworth's vision is therefore 'of the utmost importance to us'.[20]

Norman was almost overwhelmed with work. Hardly had *Cumberland and Westmorland* and *William Wordsworth* had time to settle on the bookshelves than Norman's critical study of H.G. Wells was published. A modest thirty thousand words, it was one of a series of introductory monographs called 'The English Novelists' brought out in the nineteen forties and fifties. Norman begins unconventionally, by asking the question, 'What makes a man?' and then uses it as a mechanism to explore, very briefly, how much Wells' impoverished childhood influenced the pathway he took as an adult. Unusually, for this kind of book, Norman puts himself into the text. The Home Counties, he remarks, seem to him as a Northerner 'strange and indeed romantic. I never cease to be surprised by a red roof on a hill', and he goes on to discuss the flora and fauna in a personal digression. There's a slightly jocular tone to the book, that also sits uneasily with the genre, as in this description of Wells' father – 'the man who could go one better than a hat-trick in County cricket, could never entirely lose faith in himself'.[21] Norman should have been on home territory with Wells, who came from a small town, albeit in the south, and was the child of a small shop-keeper, later apprenticed to a tailor. But somehow the prose fails to catch fire. The book is simply a critique of Wells' novels and there is little information about Wells the man in it at all, but perhaps as a critical work intended as an introduction to the author, suitable for schools, that was appropriate. It gives no impression that Norman enjoyed writing it.

H.G. Wells is not a biography. Almost the only biographical information is a section in the first chapter about Wells' early life and some of the most important parts of this are glossed over. Wells' period of wearisome apprenticeship, his struggle to educate himself and his subsequent scientific training get little attention, given how important they are to his development as a writer – particularly a writer who made science so central to his work. The commentary is distant, impersonal and the reader gets a sense that the author isn't exactly enamoured of his subject. And there are some odd insights and opinions. Norman didn't rate Wells' craft as a novelist very highly – 'Wells never really learned how to construct a novel' – though Norman thought that the *Invisible Man* was a masterpiece. Neither did he like Wells' literary style, observing that Wells had 'little feeling for the shaping of a sentence' and was a slipshod editor of his own work. 'He tied himself frequently into grammatical knots and he was careless and could not be bothered to revise.'[22] But Norman's colloquial approach to literary criticism occasionally breaks through like a ray of sunshine. Shaw, Norman observes, 'hacks off his opponents' arguments like a diker trimming thorns with a bill-hook'.[23] He describes the forces he believed to be destroying Wells' ability as a novelist as 'dry rot within and a smothering ivy outside'.[24] But it is only when he talks about the creative force of Wells' imagination at the end of the book, that we get the first hint of why Wells' novels might be worth reading; 'words run together like savage beasts, mate and bring forth wild, heraldic creatures that leap off the page and go flying or galloping through our memory'.[25]

Norman's critical appraisal of Wells received muted approval. Reviews were generally favourable, but there were dissenting voices. His opinion of Wells' prose style was described as 'ungenerous' or even 'unjust' by reviewers and some questioned the lack of biographical information. Norman's *H.G. Wells* suffered a little because it came out at the same time as Vincent Brome's full biography, which was a Book Society choice.

In 1949 Norman was thirty five – exactly in the middle of the biblical lifespan of three score years and ten – and there had been years when Norman had never expected to get even this far. The possibility of death had been a very real companion, only recently banished, and he was still going for regular medical check-ups. It was time to take stock of his life. In the poem On My Thirty-fifth Birthday, it is Time that is the poet's

CHAPTER TEN

preoccupation.

> There is no time now for words,
> Unless the words have meaning; no time for poetry,
> Unless the poem has a purpose; ...
> There is no time for love,
> But love of the world in the one; no time for joy,
> But joy that is secreted between shells of pain; no time for hope ...
> No time for you, no time for me; ...
> No time for time,
> But only for eternity.[26]

Time was one of Norman's problems. He was reviewing regularly for various literary periodicals and broadsheets, contributing poems to anthologies and magazines, writing articles, radio broadcasts, plays and works of literary criticism. The sheer amount of reading that he was being forced to do was daunting. There was little space in his life for anything else and his output of poetry began to suffer. During this period Norman was in the process of writing his biography of the 18th century poet William Cowper and had been working on several other books simultaneously, including his critical study of H.G. Wells and *A Choice of Cowper's Verse*. Norman had also signed a contract in March 1948, for a play that he had already been working on for some time, to be completed by August 1948 for a flat fee of £150, payable on delivery.

Despite the biblical character of the title, Norman's second verse play, *Prophesy to the Wind*, is a secular drama, written for the Little Theatre Guild, who wanted 'a play about a post atomic age'. The play shows the very strong influence of H.G. Wells' futuristic 'scientific romances' – as Norman called them – and Well's warnings about the possible consequences of scientific progress form the germ of the plot. Norman wrote that 'Wells was aware from the first that the development of scientific knowledge was not in itself any guarantee of progress ... and ... divorced from the wisdom that sees beyond the first line of consequence, may bring disaster to mankind'.[27] In the programme notes for the first performance, Norman explained that he was interested in 'the problem of reconciling the need for scientific investigation with the need to control science's discoveries', with particular reference to the bombings of Hiroshima and Nagasaki.[28]

Norman had learned from reading Wells that certain futuristic plot devices failed to work. He had observed, while reading *The Time Machine*, that 'because it was not possible to transmit more than one person of our own age into the future' the result was 'rather cold' and the book suffered from the 'lack of humanity'.[29] Since Norman chose to have only one human being transported into the future, he knew that he would have to solve this problem. John, the main character, is whirled away from an atomic cataclysm, into the future 'up the chimney of time', but finds that in the future, human beings have regressed more than a thousand years to a time before technology. The future is almost identical with the past. The setting Norman chose resembles Viking Cumberland closely. His characters have Viking names – the girl is called Freya, her father is Hallbjorn and the man he wants his daughter to marry is called Vikar. They talk like Vikings – Cumbrian dialect is very close to Old Norse – and their lives could be taken from one of the old Scandinavian Sagas. Some critics felt that this decision 'to flesh the future on the bones of the past' was wrong because it gave an archaic rather than a futuristic feel to the drama.[30]

The story is simple – John arrives in the future and falls in love with Freya. He tries to improve life for the people, constructing devices with all the skill and knowledge he has brought from an age of advanced technology. But Hallbjorn does not want his help and distrusts the machines John makes, telling him that 'Destruction, boy,/Lies like disease in man's blood'. Fearing contagion, Hallbjorn declares that 'Here in this dale/Man shall retain something of his true health' and orders John to 'Go,/Break up your machine'.[31] Earlier in the play, Hallbjorn had given the reasons for his distrust of the works of his ancestors;

> ... and when you venture inland,
> As I did, moving south, in search of tin,
> You come across a country where the land
> Is dead as slag or cinders. Not even a rat
> Lives there; a worm, a snake: not even a bird flies over,
> The dust stings the eyes. Drink of the gulleys
> And soon you'll vomit rotten flesh and maggots
> And die within the hour ...
> This is the land of the people who once were great.[32]

In the play, John stands for the power that has destroyed civilisation and which would, if allowed to go on, re-enact both its creation and destruction. Ordered to destroy his machine, John is unable to do so or to give up his passion for scientific knowledge. He believes in progress;

CHAPTER TEN

Hallbjorn believes in living with nature. When Hallbjorn discovers that his daughter is in love with John, he arranges to have him killed by Vikar. Then Freya reveals that she is pregnant with John's child, and Hallbjorn, stricken with guilt about John's death, decides not to break up the machine. He admits that perhaps, after all, technology might not be totally evil. The play ends as Freya makes a plea to the audience to think carefully about their gift to the future; 'you,/to whom he has returned,/What do you send for his son?'

Prophesy to the Wind was previewed at the Newcastle People's Theatre in 1949. The People's Theatre was a very forward looking, left-wing, company who performed a lot of experimental drama – a good place to begin, and the play had a positive reception in front of a provincial audience – a significant number of whom were descendants of the Viking settlers in northern England. From Newcastle it went to Questors Theatre in Ealing and from there to the Watergate in London where it was played in front of a more sophisticated audience unfamiliar with much of the source material. T.S. Eliot, who attended the Ealing performance, thought the play technically more advanced than Norman's first and commented as he left that Norman 'ought to be a very happy man'. Unfortunately the play was panned by the critics who pointed out careless borrowings from Shakespeare, infelicities of language, the stylistic imbalance between the different tonalities of prose and verse within the play, as well as the clunky plot. Philip Gardner disliked the excursions into humour which were characteristic of Norman's work and which Gardner felt detracted from the seriousness of the play's message and created an uneven texture. *The Observer* commented that it read on the page better than it played on the stage and was likely 'to do the cause of today's poetic drama little service'. It wasn't particularly successful from Norman's point of view either. He was less passionate about this play than he had been about *The Old Man of the Mountains*, and confessed to George Every that he felt a degree of detachment, 'as if … I didn't quite own the play'. He was bitterly disappointed in the critics' reaction, however, since he felt he had given his best and it hadn't been good enough. 'I can't but be more and more aware of the gap between what I have to give and what even the most sympathetic expect'.[33] It was his last attempt at secular drama.

Norman was often referred to as 'a recluse', but he had rather more of a social life than people were aware of. There were visits to Andrew Young in Sussex, and to Anne Ridler in Oxford, as well as journeys to Manchester to record programmes for the BBC. He also went to London to see his agent, his publishers, or attend performances of his plays. After his break-up with Enrica, he sometimes stayed with Sylvia Lubelsky, though his habits made him a difficult guest. He warned Sylvia in 1952 that he often went to bed at 6 o'clock. Norman had lived as an invalid for so long that he had become one. During the nineteen forties he occasionally stayed with Kathleen Raine. A letter to Norman from Phyllis Bentley was addressed to Norman at Kathleen's house in 1949 and, since she was aware of his correct home address, she must have known that he was going to be there. Kathleen's daughter Anna mentions Norman's visits, which she and her brother looked forward to. Anna was clearly Norman's favourite. 'He was a very polite, kind man,' she remembered – a man who noticed children and would talk to them. She also recalled that he was in poor health and needed to rest a lot. But her mother 'didn't care for him coming to stay' and was beginning to be impatient with Norman – 'She could be very sarcastic' – and Kathleen was also beginning to disapprove of the poetry he was currently writing – 'She disliked the "mystic" element in it which she felt he was looking for'. On one visit, possibly the last, Norman gave the children a book and wrote in it 'When will we three meet again, or rather, when will I meet you again!'[34] They continued to exchange Christmas cards and notes for another decade, but the relationship had cooled.

Norman was in love again, this time with a local girl, Sylvia Gendle. Sylvia was a Millom girl, considerably younger than Norman, who was by now in his late thirties. She had gone away to read physics at university and returned to take up a post teaching science in Barrow-in-Furness. It's possible that their relationship dates from 1948, just after Norman broke off his engagement to Enrica Garnier. Sylvia sent Norman a photograph of her graduation ceremony for his thirty fifth birthday in January 1949 with a message that suggests friendship rather than romance. 'A very happy birthday and may each one in the future be the milestone marking the course of a happy and successful life – successful in the things that make for fullness of life, peace and contentment of mind'. It's signed very simply 'Sylvia'.[35]

The friendship quickly became a love affair. Her cousin, Dr Ian Davidson, recalls coming back from a fishing trip at Haverigg one evening, when he was a young boy, and meeting Sylvia walking through the dunes hand in hand with Norman, clutching a bunch of wild flowers, obviously in love. But Sylvia's parents were horrified by the fact that she had begun a relationship with an older man. They regarded Norman as quite unsuitable. A great deal of pressure was put on Sylvia to end it. Like his other love

CHAPTER TEN

affairs, Norman has left few clues to his feelings, or to the events that took place. There is a fragment of poetry in a letter he wrote to Sylvia.

> Sweet liar, who say you love me
> And lie because you love,
> Not me, but the salty-blooded sea,
> The blue above, the green below, –
> Not me, but the unfilled mould of me –
> That is what you love.[36]

It is signed, 'To my dearest and only one'. Whatever happened, Norman again broke off the relationship and Sylvia married someone else in 1952.

Chapter Eleven

The biography of William Cowper took Norman five years to write, between the first outline and the completed manuscript, but it was finally published in 1951 and is, many people believe, still the best and the most sympathetic biography of the poet available to the reader.[1] Norman portrays Cowper as a lovable, gifted recluse, and plays down the darker side of the poet's nature. Reviewers perceptively described Norman as 'the right man for the right subject'. The reasons behind Norman's choice of Cowper as a biographical subject become obvious a few pages into the text. There are multiple parallels between the two poets, though they were living centuries apart, and Norman's own experience gave him a tremendous empathy towards his subject, which illuminates the text. The first great tragedy in Cowper's life was the death of his mother when he was only six, and Cowper wrote a poem, On the Receipt of my Mother's Picture, about his memories of her. Norman comments that 'no modern poet would dare write such a poem for fear of what the psychologists would say',[1] which is a sad reflection on the state of contemporary poetry in 1950 and the constraints that Norman felt himself to be under. He talks about the fact that, after an early disappointment, Cowper remained unmarried and speculated that the poet had lost confidence in himself after the loss of his mother and that he may have been seeking 'for what would now be called a mother-substitute' in all his relations with women, 'it was this surely . . . which led him to shy away from the sort of intimacy which led to marriage'.[2] Another revealing comment is Norman's statement that the death of Cowper's mother 'destroyed his trust in the world. He felt cheated, and the kindly meant efforts of the servants to keep him from the full realisation of [his loss] only increased this sense of having been deceived'.[3] It is difficult not to connect this statement with Norman's own childhood distress at the euphemisms he

---

1. A new one is being written by Neil Curry

CHAPTER ELEVEN

himself had received, when his grandmother told him that his mother had 'gone to live with the angels' and his subsequent outburst when he saw the angels depicted in the church windows.

There were other parallels. There's a glancing reference to Norman's own Methodist memories when he discusses Cowper's legacy from the Evangelical faith; 'its moralising and its prejudices remained with him for the rest of his life'.[4] Cowper, like Norman, liked to live in one secure place; 'he lived in an out-of-the-way village, meeting scarcely anyone but a few selected friends',[5] and, like Norman, he wanted to write about the ordinary, homely details of his life, 'the usual, the everyday, the humdrum'. Not romantic landscapes of torrents and mountains, but 'hedges, walls, roads, ditches, puddles, plough-land and pigsties'. Cowper, Norman wrote, was 'the poet of the commonplace, the common-sensible and the sane'.[6]

But Cowper's sanity was much debated – his mental health was fragile and he suffered from depression, spending time in an asylum. Yet, as Norman described, 'in spite of all his fears and illusions, his heart turned to life and longed for it and loved it when he saw it'.[7] Cowper found, as Norman had discovered for himself, that his health benefited from a strict domestic routine. He lived with friends, in the village of Olney in Buckinghamshire, and their lives revolved round a regular pattern of meals, religious devotions, country walks and quiet time for reading and discussion. 'I need not tell you,' Cowper wrote in a letter, 'that such a life as this is consistent with the utmost cheerfulness'.[8] He kept tame hares, dug his garden, and wrote poetry, including the comic ballad of John Gilpin, and some of the hymns that he is now most famous for – God Moves in a mysterious way, and O for a closer walk with God. He also wrote The Castaway, which includes the lines 'We perish'd each alone', famously chanted by Mr Ramsay in Virginia Woolf's novel *To The Lighthouse*. Cowper thrived creatively in this sheltered environment. Norman comments that he 'took root like a cabbage' and that he 'felt he belonged to Olney and would have been incapable of writing anywhere else. To be in a familiar place and among familiar objects gave him a sense of stability in what was otherwise a tottering world'. He harboured there because he was afraid 'to turn anywhere else'.[9] But, Norman speculated, there may have been another, more controversial, reason for his seclusion. Cowper apparently had doubts about his sexuality and 'suspected himself to be a partial hermaphrodite', though there is no evidence for it and this seems to have been only one of his illusions.[10] But whatever the reasons for it, Cowper's sense of alienation was strong. Norman quotes from his long poem, *The Task*;

> I was a stricken deer, that left the herd
> Long since; with many an arrow deep infixt
> My panting side was charg'd, when I withdrew
> To seek a tranquil death in distant shades.
> There was I found by one who had himself
> Been hurt by th' archers. In his side he bore,
> And in his hands and feet, the cruel scars.
> With gentle force soliciting the darts,
> He drew them forth, and heal'd, and bade me live.
> Since then, with few associates, in remote
> And silent woods I wander, far from those
> My former partners of the peopled scene.[11]

Norman's first biography – referred to as 'a study' and published in 1951 – was well reviewed. It was generally felt that he had presented 'a balanced view of the poet' and he was praised for having 'steered clear of the morbid study of [Cowper's] neurosis so fashionable in these days'.[12] It was welcome praise, but it would be the last work of biography or literary criticism that he would ever write.

Norman's reputation as a poet now seemed very secure. Alan Ross included a study of Norman's poetry in the chapter 'Language and Landscapes' in a book called *Poetry 1945-1950*, and Derek Stanford's *The Freedom of Poetry* contained a twenty page, detailed analysis of Norman's work. Howard Sergeant wrote a long article on his status as a 'Northern Poet' for the *Northern Review* and took four poems from *Five Rivers* for his anthology *Contemporary Northern Poetry*. Geoffrey Grigson included Norman in *Poetry of the Thirties and After*. Norman was also being asked to write articles on his own poetry for a number of publications. John Lehmann, who had become a reliable supporter of Norman's work, asked him to contribute to an edition of the magazine *Orpheus*, discussing his work alongside Edith Sitwell, Louis MacNeice and Norman's old enemy George Barker.

Norman chose to write about 'The Image in My Poetry' and what he says expands remarks made in a letter to Mrs Hamer about imagery as far back as 1936. He denies subjectivity. His imagery is taken from the external world around him, and not from 'dreams, myths and the subconscious'. It is the rock that Norman is concerned with, not the world of angels and

CHAPTER ELEVEN

visions he had briefly encountered with Kathleen Raine, or the internal world of mind and emotions. Norman's personal theory is probably informed by the writings of Charles Williams, who believed that images were an essential part of mankind's relationship with God and with other human beings. Each image, Norman explains, has three meanings, firstly the object itself as an object, as it exists in the natural world. Secondly it has a meaning in relation to man and therefore the object selected must have a 'human, communicable meaning'. Finally the object has an over-riding religious meaning derived from its relationship to God. The 'true meaning' of an image 'is in itself and is known only to God', and does not depend on the poet or the poem. What is really interesting in Norman's essay is his admission of the extent to which scientific fact – particularly geology – fed into his poetry. 'Science … instead of destroying my conception of the world, enriches and clarifies it, and it is when I have turned to science to help me understand the world around me that I have found much of the material for my poetry.'[13] The research that Norman had done for *Cumberland and Westmorland*, as well as the strands of thought he had pursued while reading H.G. Wells, had begun to influence his poems. The academic Philip Gardner, working on his own study of Norman's work, twenty years later, had the opportunity to talk to Norman about the direction he had taken. Norman felt that his most significant poem during this period was The Seven Rocks, written during while he was working on *Cumberland and Westmorland*, and published first in *Horizon* in 1948. It is an allegory. In the poem, the seven rocks are not just the geological layers of the Lake District, but also the seven virtues of Christian morality – Faith, Hope, Charity, Fortitude, Prudence, Justice and Temperance. The actual rocks appear in the poem described in their familiar places, from Skiddaw Slate and Coniston Flag to St Bees Sandstone, producing a sense of spatial location, and they appear in strictly chronological sequence which gives another dimension – time – to the movement of thought through the sequence of seven poems, each with different metres and forms. But, though the rocks stand for human virtues, there is no humanity in the poem, except for a single 'I' in one of the stanzas. Norman's poetry has sometimes been accused of giving the impression of landscape with the people left out, and Seven Rocks is one of the poems which could be used as an example.

As the world opened up to him, Norman receded further and further into the familiar cocoon of St George's Terrace, Millom. Rose, who countersigned most of Norman's contracts, was still firmly in charge at number 14, particularly as Norman's father was beginning to decline. But despite his ill health, Joe Nicholson was to be found every morning behind the counter of his shop. His son was now a famous local figure, a Fellow of the Royal Society for Literature, with a row of published books on the library shelves, often featured in the local papers and whose voice was heard regularly on the radio. In October 1950, the local council organised a book exhibition in Millom to celebrate the Public Libraries Centenary year and they asked Norman, as a local celebrity, to open it. Joe and Rose were very proud of him.

As Millom celebrated Norman, he began to celebrate his home town. In 1952 the BBC third programme broadcast his talk 'Millom Delivered', published afterwards in *The Listener*. In the programme Norman takes a look at Millom from beyond the Duddon river, as if seeing it for the first time. He describes the iron works with their alien beauty and the brooding shape of Black Combe behind the town – 'a great hump of a mountain, a large animal shape that sprawls itself over the south west corner of Cumberland ... bald as a badger, yet smooth and almost sleek, scarcely showing a chip of the rock it is made of' – a rock more than three hundred million years old, one of the oldest in the world. It is the rock and its mineral content that have created Millom. He talks about what the town means to him. It is 'a place that seems to belong to me like an outer layer of clothing, so that anywhere else I feel not properly dressed'.

Norman's talk is aimed at the mainly southern, intellectual audience of the third programme and so Norman can go beyond the descriptive to talk about other issues. He makes a parallel between the landscape around Millom and Jerusalem and then links that into a discussion of Charles Williams' Affirmative Way, comprising acceptance of society and romantic love, and Wordsworth's Way of Nature, 'which by-passed hell and purgatory and led straight to heaven'. It is possible, Norman asserts, that Man can find salvation by living according to the laws of nature.

Norman makes his environmental message explicit; 'we are everywhere resisting nature; we are everywhere perverting her ways, felling the woods, burning the coal, blasting the rock, splitting the atom. We are everywhere destroying the fruitfulness of the earth in a despairing desire for physical power.' And he gives a warning. 'If man is to survive he must become once more a farmer rather than a miner, cultivator rather than exploiter. He must turn to the organic world rather than the inorganic, the biological rather than the chemical, to the living world of corn and cows, rather than

CHAPTER ELEVEN

the lifeless world of iron and electricity and nuclear fission.' But the power of the warning is diluted towards the end when Norman, like Hallbjorn in *Prophesy to the Wind*, draws back and asserts that to live fully we might have to compromise and find a balance between the two.[14]

'Millom Delivered' was very well received by both southern and northern audiences. The BBC producer, P.H. Newby, who was also a successful novelist and by no means entirely sympathetic to Norman, wrote a letter to say that the programme was one of the most moving things he had heard in a long time.[15] He was reinforcing the message given to Norman by Andrew Young, who had observed that when Norman wrote about 'that bloody country' of his, he wrote in a much more direct and powerful way – writing out of knowledge and passion. It was a message that Norman was beginning to listen to and he was beginning to recognise his subject.

But Norman was still drawn to verse drama both as a poetic form and as an expression of his ideas. Through George Every and E. Martin Browne he was commissioned to write another play for the Religious Drama Society – not this time for the Pilgrim Players, but for a new group under the direction of Pamela Keily. This was going to consist of 'touring professionals' performing to church audiences, but their remit was supposed to be wide and would not be confined to traditionally 'churchy' subjects. Norman's new play, *A Match for the Devil*, came from an idea he had begun playing with after reading the Book of Hosea as part of his regular bible study. He discussed the outline with Martin Browne, who was the chair of the RDS, and was encouraged to think it was viable.

The story of Hosea and Gomer is a strange choice for Norman, since ritual prostitution is at the heart of it. But his interest in it may go back to his reading of Charles Williams, and Williams' belief that sex between man and woman was a valid sacrament, and that the Negative Way of denial and celibacy was not necessary for the Christian faith. Norman gave a radio talk on Williams' essays which he called 'Yes to the Body' and he was certainly sympathetic to the author's point of view – a considerable change from the more fundamental views put forward in Norman's novels a decade earlier. In the story of Hosea, Gomer is a temple prostitute at a time in history when the sexual act was sometimes regarded as a metaphor for the marriage of God and mankind. Ritual sex is a part of many 'pagan' religions and in the Book of Hosea it seems to be shown as an example of how far the children of Israel have fallen away from the laws of Moses into decadence and corruption, but the moral issues are quite complicated and not always clear. The biblical account of Hosea and Gomer has been the subject of theological and literary debate ever since it was written. Lutheran and Calvinist theologians solved the moral problems of Prophet and Prostitute by insisting that Hosea married Gomer to redeem her, but out of disgust for what she was, never slept with her. Others have seen it as an example of love and redemption. In Norman's version of the story it becomes much more than just a tale of a fallen woman redeemed.

In the play, Hosea is a baker, a single man – a 'scraggy old cockerel'[16] and 'a muddle-headed old badger'.[17] The widow Sarah, who has the shop next door, has a daughter, Gomer, who is in the service of the Temple and whose beauty and personality 'swill the very flagstones with a bucketful of light'.[18] Gomer's fatherless son, David, helps Sarah in the shop and makes friends with Hosea. When David's mother complains that she is tired of her life in the Temple, David persuades Hosea that she is just the wife he needs. However, Gomer isn't happy with Hosea, who provides her with every material comfort, but doesn't make her feel needed or valued. She is bored, describes Hosea as a 'lanky, shanky, comical, cranky, blind-eyed blockhead of a husband',[19] and eventually goes back to the Temple and her old way of life. Hosea, when he finds out, decides against denouncement and divorce and agrees to forgive her and take her back. Gomer objects to being forgiven, because it presupposes her guilt – they must forgive each other in order to be equals – but she agrees to go back to Hosea. In the biblical story, things happen because God wills them, but in drama, the action has to be driven by human emotions and the conflicts they arouse. Philip Gardner states that 'the greatest difficulty' of the play is that surrounding Gomer's motivation in returning to her husband. This was also Norman's biggest problem and he admitted in a letter that 'I nearly gave up the play on account of it'.[20] Gomer's return is the climactic scene of the play and, according to Philip Gardner, 'the least satisfactory'.[21]

Unlike his previous dramas, Norman set the action in Palestine – there was no attempt to transpose the biblical story to Cumberland. He aimed for formal sketches – a kind of tableau treatment that he described as a series of 'charades'. It was going to be written entirely in verse without the colloquial elements of his two previous plays. Although critics detected the influence of Ezra Pound's *Cantos*, which Norman had been reading in 1951, and Christopher Fry's verse dramas, it probably owes more to the Psalms of David. Music was always a big influence on Norman's work and he was very familiar with the rhythms of psalmody. He said that he had tried to create a kind of verse that would carry the sense of 'backward and forward flowing, a balancing, not of stress against stress, but of the whole cadence of a sentence or phrase against another sentence'.[22]

Norman wrote the play specifically for a provincial, religious audience who would be familiar with both the biblical story and its context. He included a lot of comedy, and it was pitched low, rather than directed at the more sophisticated metropolitan audiences and critics who had given Norman so much trouble with his previous plays. He had recently been thinking long and hard about the audience he wanted to write for. Norman decided to target his plays towards the people he knew best – those who attended productions in village halls, schools and regional theatres. 'The standard reached is often surprisingly high,' Norman commented in a letter. He was particularly enthusiastic about local amateur drama groups drawn from the social mix typical of rural post-war England in the forties and early fifties. 'It brings together people differing in age, sex and class. There is always a danger, of course, that it will fall into the hands of one particular clique – the vicarage clique, the educated maiden ladies, or the retired business people – but … when it is really well run it combines class and club, and mixes education with the pleasures of showing-off, dressing, making-up, and even of music and dancing.' This was the kind of audience that was in Norman's mind when he wrote *A Match for the Devil*, but it was an audience that was rapidly dwindling as the demographic of rural England began to change in the second half of the twentieth century.[23]

In retrospect, these decisions were a big mistake. Philip Gardner commented perceptively that 'the circumstances surrounding [*A Match for the Devil's*] composition and production were so unfortunate that any criticism of the play itself is mitigated by sympathy for its author'.[24] The outline was submitted to the 'New Pilgrims' in May 1952 and approved by both Martin Browne and Pamela Kiely and by the end of the year it was in rehearsal. It was at this late stage that the Religious Drama Society 'gave orders to stop production'. Norman's play was effectively banned.

The reasons given were that 'the audience would object to the association of religion with prostitution' and might confuse the Temple with the present-day Church and feel that the Church was being criticised by the play. They also disliked the fact that the prophet Hosea appears in the play as a fool, ridiculed for being a cuckold, and that much of the action is comedy rather than tragedy. There was no apology in the letter, and not a word of thanks to Norman for the work that he had done which they were rendering virtually useless. Philip Gardner, who saw the letter, stated that the attitude was one of 'moral narrowness' and the tone one of 'unpleasant … condescension'.[25] The problem for Norman was that he had a play left on his hands which had been written for a small-town, religious audience, but it was banned from being presented to them and had limited suitability for any other kind of production. It was a very hard blow.

Norman gave a talk about Hosea for the BBC called 'The Comic Prophet', and, perhaps prompted by the radio broadcast, the London Club Theatre Group decided that they would like to perform the play at the Edinburgh Festival. This was a salve to Norman's pride, but he knew that it would expose him to the very audience that had been so critical in the past – and this time it was not the audience the play had been written for. The actors also had reservations about the play, loving the 'vigorously dramatic plot' but less happy 'with the sensitivity of the characterisation on which the play depends', particularly the fact that there seemed to be little rapport between the 'warm-heartedly elusive Gomer' and her son David, 'for which the play cried out'.[26] *A Match for the Devil* was performed at St Mary's Hall, Edinburgh on August 28th, 1953 and was enjoyed by the local audience, which included Hugh MacDiarmid. The London critics thought very differently.

Norman defended the play vigorously. It was not about prostitution, but about the necessity of 'love and reconciliation' rather than 'law and denunciation'. Temple prostitutes re-enacted the love of god for mankind – the marriage of heaven and earth. Norman's thinking, while he was writing the play, had quite clearly been influenced by Charles Williams and by Dante. He makes a reference elsewhere to 'Dante's supreme insight into the divine potentialities of human love'[27] and discussed the 'theology of romantic love' in letters to George Every. Norman's programme notes explained that Hosea was one of the first prophets to see the relationship between God and Man as one of love rather than law – a holy marriage. As Norman saw it, the story of Hosea and Gomer was a metaphor for God's love for imperfect, sinful, mankind.[28] The play was also about forgiveness and the necessity of the forgiver being forgiven – because forgiveness presupposes wrong doing by the person to be forgiven. Gomer insists that for true equality, Hosea must allow her to forgive him for his attitude towards her. Hosea acknowledges that she is right and he asks Gomer's pardon, in front of the priest Amaziah –

> For wanting you not what you are;
> For offering you the consciousness of guilt in part-exchange for love,
> When I speak of sin, Amaziah, I distort her innocence;
> When I speak of forgiveness, I put her in the wrong.[29]

CHAPTER ELEVEN

Feminist literary critics and theologians have found Norman's account of Gomer sympathetic to a feminist revisioning of the story[30] partly because Norman gives Gomer and not her husband, the moral high ground. And in the marriage ceremony between Hosea and Gomer, he suggests that no one can give a woman in marriage 'she is formed of earth, air, sky and water' and gives herself.[31]

A Match for the Devil gave ample ammunition to those who agreed with Stephen Spender that Norman was obsessed with 'sex and religion'. Norman's justification for his controversial choice of subject matter was unconvincing. For the critics there were other problems unconnected with the subject matter; there were difficulties for the audience over the motivations of the characters. Why does Hosea suddenly decide to marry Gomer? And there is little build-up of Gomer's state of mind when she – apparently on impulse – goes back to Temple prostitution. Similarly in the last act, the critics homed in on Norman's main area of difficulty – Hosea's decision to take his wife back and Gomer's to return to her husband – decisions which aren't sufficiently underpinned by any emotional structures. Like a Charade, or a Tableau, the action is simply staged and the deeper, psychological motivations never explored. Then, there was the fact that the play had been written specifically for a religious audience with a knowledge of biblical themes that could be taken for granted. There was little for a secular audience to get hold of.

The Sunday Times greeted *A Match for the Devil* with 'tepid enthusiasm', not because it disagreed with the play's morality, but because of 'its dullness … its wilderness of semi-Biblical metaphors, and its apparent belief that alliterations like "Quicken me with quinces" are witty'.[32] This time, Anne Ridler was also one of Norman's critics. 'In this play,' she wrote, 'Mr Nicholson has … deliberately subdued his talent'.[33] Norman wrote to George Every that their criticism had not only holed the play below the waterline, but he feared that it had ended his career as a dramatist.

What Norman's characters lack, both in his novels and in his plays, is emotional depth; superficial, mechanical motivation isn't enough to convince the reader or the theatre-goer. But perhaps this is symptomatic of someone who didn't want to explore his own emotions too deeply, hiding them even from himself – 'what others do not see, I need not know'.[34] There have been a great many discussions about how the negative effects of remaining in Millom might have affected Norman's work, but, much more damaging than the inability to leave home, was his reluctance to engage in profound and risky emotional connections with other human beings, particularly the opposite sex. The death of his mother and his painful, unrequited, love affair with Sylvia Lubelsky appear to have left him wary of the 'giving of the self' that is necessary in order to make relationships. This had consequences for his poetry. He seemed unable to confront, what Seamus Heaney, in an interview with Dennis O'Driscoll, called 'the necessity to open that inner path'. When Norman wrote about other human beings and their relationships with one another he was an observer rather than a participant. He had never committed himself fully to anyone, but that was about to change.

Chapter Twelve

In July 1953, while he was wrestling with the fall-out from the banning of his play, Norman signed two contracts negotiated by his agents. One was for a new book on the history of the Lake District to be brought out by Robert Hale and the other was for his third collection of poetry, *The Pot Geranium*, to be published by Faber. The title poem of this collection, in the form of an ode, was described by Norman as a kind of personal testimony, the key poem to understanding his work. The Pot Geranium became one of his 'signature' poems. He had spent his whole life in the small attic room he had occupied since he came back from Linford Sanatorium – an indoor plant, like the geranium. Norman had described the view from the window to Sylvia Lubelsky in an early poem – Morning Voluntary – but this poem was much more than a description, it was a philosophical statement, like Blake's view of heaven in a grain of sand, or Donne's 'little room' that becomes 'an everywhere'.

At the beginning of the poem the poet is standing at the window looking out across the 'green slated gables' that 'clasp the stem of the hill' reflecting a 'lemony autumn sun', and he is gazing over chimneys that seem to breathe the yellow smoke of poplar logs even though the fires are unlit. The stone of the buildings is 'brown as bark' and the bakery 'That once was a Primitive Methodist Chapel/Lifts its cornice against the sky'. Suddenly 'like a flight of racing pigeons/Slipped from their basket in the station yard,/ A box kite rides the air, a square of calico,/Crimson as the cornets of the Royal Temperance Band/When they brass up the wind in marching.' The man watches the kite struggling on its leash and can imagine the 'unseen boys/In chicken run or allotment or by the side /Of the old quarry full to the gullet with water,/Pay out on their string a rag of dream,/High as the Jubilee flagpole'.

The first part of the poem is a naming of places – the station yard, the chapel, the model bakery, chicken runs, allotments, the quarry, the Jubilee flagpole – and each place is freighted with the boyhood memories that are the sub-text of this part of the poem. He knows these places; he has listened to the brass band, watched the flag being hauled up the pole for the Jubilee, and he too has run a kite through the allotments on a windy autumn day. But in the second part of the poem, the adult man returns to the reality of his present day interior existence.

> I turn from the window
> (Letting the bobbins of autumn wind up the swallows)
> And lie on my bed. The ceiling
> Slopes over like a tent, and white walls
> Wrap themselves round me, leaving only
> A flap for the light to blow through. Thighs and spine
> Are clamped to the mattress and looping springs
> Twine round my chest and hold me. I feel the air
> Move on my face like spiders, see the light
> Slide across the plaster; but wind and sun
> Are mine no longer, nor have I kite to claim them …

The feeling is one of entrapment. But then the man sees on his window sill 'A pot geranium' which 'flies its bright balloon' of crimson flower and he realises that 'this crock of soil', though small, 'Contains the pattern, the prod and pulse of life,/Complete as the Nile or the Niger'. The mood turns and in the third part of the poem the poet realises that if he cannot go to the world, the world will come to him. He is as much part of it in Millom as he would be anywhere else.

> And what need therefore
> To stretch for the straining kite? – for kite and flower
> Bloom in my room for ever; the light that lifts them
> Shines in my own eyes, and my body's warmth
> Hatches their red in my veins. It is the Gulf Stream
> That rains down the chimney, making the soot spit; it is the Trade Wind
> That blows in the draught under the bedroom door.

The poem looks back to William Cowper. Norman had written in his biography of Cowper that the poet knew his 'personal landscape' as

CHAPTER TWELVE

intimately as 'a limpet its few square inches of rock ... Every door and chair was as familiar to him as the back of his own hand. They were known and real; they did not change ... he felt that his physical life was bound up with them and even dependent upon them ... When he describes them he is almost writing his autobiography'. But Cowper's room was also part of the natural world; 'The house, the chairs, the fire, these were all as much a part of rural life as the birds, the trees, the wind and the snow'.[1] That is the effect that Norman was struggling to achieve in his own autobiographical statement. And he uses the same words that he had used of Cowper, in the last four lines of the poem.

> My ways are circumscribed, confined as a limpet
> To one small radius of rock; yet
> I eat the equator, breathe the sky, and carry
> The great white sun in the dirt of my fingernails.[2]

Few of the other poems in the collection are so deeply personal, but *The Pot Geranium* contains poetry grown very firmly out of Millom. There are poems about Millom Old Quarry, and the main street in Holborn Hill, another, On a proposed Site for Council Houses, which Norman, environmentalist though he was, did not oppose. Other poems describe Winter by the Ironworks, Walney Island, Scarf Gap, Buttermere, Ravenglass Railway Station and On Duddon Marsh. The Coniston poems that Norman had written, remembering his holiday there with Enrica Garnier, are included and provide an elegiac note. In From a Boat at Coniston, the poet looks at his reflection in the lake, where bubbles rise 'from the eyes like aerated/Tears shed there in the element of mirrors'. A light wind 'Lets on the water, paddling like a duck'.

> I wait for the wind to drop, against hope
> Hoping and against the weather, yet to see
> The water empty, the water full of itself,
> Free of the sky and the cloud and free of me.[3]

Two of the poems – Weather Ear and The Buzzer – describe lying in bed and listening to 'the bray/Of the furnace hooter rasping the slates', calling the men to the early shifts. In the second poem it is a 'paleolithic roar' which wakes early memories of other restless nights.

That buzzer, heard in boyhood, meant that nerves
Had stick-o'rogered through a sleepless night,
Promising a party, a girl, or an exam.

Now the poet is older and aware of a dulling of the senses. And there is also a sense of failure, that he is living in the 'now' of that young boy's future.

Age blocks our senses, builds a wall
To shut us on ourselves, until
The streets are rarely heard,

And watching is deaf as sleep. But, with an east wind,
The night slides backward, down a scree
Of memory, the black walls fall in ruin,
And the buzzer wakes the boy whose bed I lie in,
Whose dubious dream is me.[4]

There is loneliness in this collection and a sense of resignation. There's a feeling that Norman knows that he will never leave Millom now. It was recognised by one reviewer who described Norman as being 'wedded to Millom'.

While Norman was reading the final proofs of *The Pot Geranium* and attending rehearsals for a production of *A Match for the Devil*, his father's health deteriorated. On the 13th of February, Joe Nicholson died suddenly, 'sitting in his armchair after lunch – without distress and without pain', beside the fire.[5] He was seventy six.

Norman was devastated. Joe had been the bedrock of his life. Letters of condolence came pouring in from family and friends and members of the wider community. Joe was a member of the local Chamber of Trade and had been much respected in Millom. The Rev Sam Taylor (now Canon), who had been such an important influence when Norman came back from the sanatorium, was now retired and no longer living in the town, but he wrote a comforting letter, acknowledging Joe's essential qualities; 'he never varied in his pleasant, unassuming kindness and interest. Such quiet men are uncommon and a refreshment'.[6]

Norman was now the head of the household and wholly responsible for his stepmother, Rose. In the early days of the Welfare State, older people did not automatically get a pension if they had never contributed to the 'stamp' system. One of Norman's tasks was to go through his father's accounts and

CHAPTER TWELVE

put his estate into Probate. He was shocked to see how little money was left. The shop had been earning very little for years and Joe's savings were down to the bone. But he still had some war bonds left and there was stock in the shop which could be sold with the business if they decided not to carry on with it. There was a lot of discussion about the future of the shop. Norman was earning enough from literature to keep himself, but there was Rose to think about. For two or three months Norman became a shop-keeper. 'I did so reluctantly, knowing very little about it, and feeling the strain on my limited physical powers'. But his time behind the counter also brought a new respect for his father and an appreciation of the things that had given Joe pleasure; 'the satisfaction of giving value, of buying judiciously, of meeting a customer's needs'.[7] Norman's temporary presence in the shop was soon over. A decision was made to rent out the shop space to someone else to bring in a regular income. The stock and the goodwill were sold. After the final accounting, Norman and Rose were entitled to £437.17s.6d each out of the estate – a reasonable sum of money in 1954, but not enough to provide Rose with a pension.

Although Norman was now the 'man of the house' as it would have been expressed in the nineteen fifties, Rose was still in charge of all the domestic arrangements and the household generally. It was Rose who now chose Norman's clothes, not his father, and she shopped, cooked and cleaned as she had always done. Nothing changed, except that Norman's father was no longer there to restrain her forceful personality.

The death of a father is a big moment for a man, but Norman rarely mentioned it. His attitude to bereavement had been learned when his mother died; grief had to be shut up in a closed compartment. Like all things personal, Norman kept his feelings for his father private and immersed himself in work. He had book contracts to fulfil. In July 1953 he had agreed to write a book about the early visitors to the Lake District, which he intended to call *The Lakers*. This title was taken from an 18th century comic opera, attributed to James Plumptre and never performed, which had been suggested to Norman as a suitable subject in a letter from one of his friends, who reported that it had been described as a 'lively burlesque on the fashionable propensity of lake visiting'. It had comic characters likely to appeal to Norman, such as Miss Beccabunga Veronica of Diandria Hall, who was a 'botanical aunt'. Veronica Beccabunga is the Latin name of a plant called brooklime and Diandria is a plant with two male parts (stamens). The real 'Lakers' included painters like William Gilpin, and Thomas Smith of Derby, the evangelical reformer John Wesley, and writers such as Anne Radcliffe in search of Gothic locations for her novels, Celia Fiennes – 'garrulous as a 17th century Gertrude Stein', Ruskin, De Quincey, Thomas Gray and Wordsworth himself. Norman stopped short of Hugh Walpole, but there were many readers who wished that he'd included Beatrix Potter.

The genesis of the book came from a radio programme that Norman had recorded for the BBC Home Service as far back as 1947, called 'The Discovery of the Lakes', subtitled 'A polite guide to the England Lake District' and compiled from the diaries and letters of 'early travellers and Gentlemen of Taste'. Norman was a regular broadcaster throughout the forties and fifties, recording programmes from the Manchester studio of the BBC and his scripts were often connected to work in progress, or part of the development of ideas. As early as 1950 the Barrow librarian had been supplying Norman with information and book titles for the project and he was hard at work on it all through 1954 for proposed publication in 1955.

Reviewing the book, Kathleen Raine commented that Norman had cast 'on three centuries of tourists the cold, humorous eye of the native'[8] and *The Lakers* is still a good read. It's stuffed full of odd characters, quirky travellers' tales, legends and supernatural events as well as local history, excerpts from journals and letters and poetry, much of which had fallen out of view by the second half of the twentieth century. Norman reminds the reader that the Lake District is not all Wordsworth and daffodils. But most importantly of all, by connecting these tales and anecdotes to their geographical location, *The Lakers* fulfils the important purpose of storying the landscape, creating a different kind of map, adding a new dimension to the picture postcard views, connecting the rocks and their human history.

At the end of the book, Norman repeated the environmental warning he had been sending, in his previous books and plays, in even more forceful terms. The greatest danger to mankind was through 'perverting the true order of nature'. Already the poet is aware of the growing threat. 'Everywhere we see the fertility being dried out of the soil like water from a de-hydrated egg. Valleys are dammed to generate electricity to work vacuum cleaners and hair-driers; acres of wood are ripped up to give a few thousand extra tons of open-cast coal ... Plough-land is gouged and bricked to site factories for tin-cans and imitation cheese and synthetic rubber'.[9] He draws our attention to the paradox of felling forests 'to make wood pulp to make plastic' as a substitute for wood. And then there is the perversion of the natural lives of animals – 'cows calve without knowing a

CHAPTER TWELVE

bull; hens, imprisoned in batteries, secrete eggs in their sleep as an oyster secretes a pearl'. The greatest threat of all, which was worrying millions of people in Britain during the fifties and sixties, was the threat of nuclear power. Norman, living within twenty miles of the nuclear reactor at Sellafield – then called Windscale – was deeply concerned about the effects of radiation and the possibility of a nuclear catastrophe. 'The earth itself is no longer safe ... The very flowering of matter, the creative fission by which all energy and life enters the material universe, even this has become our greatest and most terrible danger.'[10]

Norman repeats his view that he doesn't want the countryside preserved, like an outdoor museum – those who do so, he claims, are just as guilty of exploiting the countryside as the industrialists – one for pleasure, one for profit. He hates the sentimentalising of nature. 'No more coddling of the countryside; no more rambler-rose calendars pinned above the cocktail cabinet.' A balance must be struck between the organic and the inorganic, between 'corn and cows' and 'iron and electricity'. When that balance can be found, 'Man will once more be an integral part of his own environment. He will know the rhythm of the seas, the sun, and the seasons; he will eat, drink and breathe the natural vitality of the earth in food, water and air.' And if man can't find a balance between his own needs and those of nature, 'it is unlikely that he will be able to go on living at all'.[11]

The Pot Geranium, Norman's eagerly awaited new collection, the first for six years, was published by Faber in the summer of 1954 and became the first collection of poems to be recommended by the new Poetry Book Society. Philip Gardner thought that the collection represented 'a watershed in Nicholson's work', because he was no longer deliberately seeking universality, but content to write from 'provincial or personal experience'.[12] Norman had left the Way of the City and taken a deliberate, but controversial, stance that would be underlined in prose articles and radio broadcasts over the next three or four years, culminating in his 'fictional' memoir of Millom, *Provincial Pleasures* in 1959. The poet Vernon Watkins wrote to tell Norman that he was 'doing something unique'.[13] Poet and critic Robin Skelton also wrote to Norman telling him how much he had loved the collection. He hoped that the critics would see that Norman's 'poetic landscapes are important and not put them down as "regional" in such a way as to suggest that the word is synonymous with "parochialism" or "narrowness".' Robin felt that Norman's Millom was 'as universal a place as Eliot's Waste Land or Marvell's Holderness and a good deal more universal than [William Carlos] William's Paterson'.[14] But the direction Norman had chosen to take had a cost and Robin Skelton's fears were soon borne out. A *New Statesman* review of the *Chatto Book of Modern Poetry 1951-55*, which included Norman's work, referred to him and Roy Fuller as 'excellent and honest minor poets', and a minor poet was not what Norman wanted to be. There were signs that Norman's audience was getting a little weary of hearing about Millom. One reviewer noted that, 'Mr Nicholson's universe is not various enough. The geology becomes too much like a catalogue', and suggested that he was in danger of becoming 'the victim of his own formulas'.[15]

There was further trouble. John Lehmann gave *The Pot Geranium* to George Barker to review and George didn't spare any words on what he believed to be its weaknesses in a scathing review in *The London Magazine*. He observed that Norman was 'like a chip off the old Wordsworthian rock', in that he had given the exact measurements of the geranium pot, 'six inch deep by four across', just as Wordsworth had given the measurements of a pond. The 'spectacle of a man behaving like an inch worm when he is supposed to be entertaining an angel not unawares' is anathema to George Barker. In his opinion, Norman's poems 'report … they catalogue; they collect. But I am left wondering what to do with a book containing geological specimens, geraniums, clocks, Ravenglass Railway Station, fossils etc, but very few poems'.[16]

Norman, who was always badly affected by adverse criticism and rejection, wrote to the editor 'incensed'. He felt that John Lehmann should have known how George felt about his poetry and sent the book to another reviewer. John Lehmann wrote back apologetically, claiming haste and ignorance. There was nothing he could do about it now – George Barker was too big a literary figure to take issue with. 'Barker's review was sent in too late for me to get him to change more than one or two things in it of a minor sort. I could not treat him like a young poet in his twenties'. Norman asked for some form of retribution – perhaps a retraction or public apology, but John Lehmann couldn't promise anything, 'I am trying to do something about it …', and tried to smooth things over by suggesting that he publish a 'good poem' by Norman in the next issue.[17] In the end John Lehmann published a letter from Anne Ridler, giving a robust defence of Norman's work and suggesting that George Barker's review should be headed 'unfair comment'.

Anne also wrote to Norman, advising him to ignore the whole thing. 'I'm sure you won't be depressed for long by these reviews. If you had not

CHAPTER TWELVE

already won your place, they would not have been written.'[18] There were others who really liked *The Pot Geranium*. Spartaco Gamberini, a young Italian who had translated some of Norman's poetry into Italian, wrote; 'you are a European poet, free at last from the cosmopolitan provincialism of London' – a comment that pleased Norman very much.[19]

Norman's diary for 1954 is simply a botanical list. He was walking every day, when he could, making notes of the wild flowers that grew around the ironworks and in the lanes behind the allotments. His favourite place was the promontory beyond the iron workings, with its view of the estuary, and 'Devil's Hollow … a wild acreage' enclosed by the outer sea wall that had been built to protect the mine lodes that had been bored under the sea in a vain attempt to prevent leakage. It was a very personal landscape for Norman; his father had walked there regularly, and one of his uncles had been fatally injured in a roof fall in one of those seams. On the promontory there's the ruin of an old lighthouse, which Norman used for his novel *The Green Shore*, the remains of a derelict windmill, and a disused quarry. The Hollow, once washed by the tides, is now abandoned to nesting birds, 'like the crater of an exhausted volcano', loud with the warning calls of plovers, oyster-catchers and curlews; underfoot, 'larks go up like a flight of balloons at a country fair.' In the old quarry, the Bloody Cranesbill is in flagrant display; 'the flowers here are red and dark, as if the haematite were oozing through – ragged robin, lousewort, marsh cinquefoil and half a dozen different orchids. Farther inwards, where the mud gives place to water, the wild iris spreads a yellow mattress for the flies.'[20] Every week, perhaps planning these passages for *Provincial Pleasures*, he wrote down the species that were in evidence; in July it was sea lavender and wild parsnips, field poppies and red goosefoot; in October common camomile and butterbur.

But in Norman's private life, something else was taking root. The previous year a new vicar had come to Millom, Norman Darrall, with his wife Sybil and her best friend, Yvonne Gardner. Yvonne was thirty two in 1953 when she arrived in Millom, blonde, slim and very pretty. She came from a completely different background and had been born in London, where her father was a brilliant engineering draughtsman. Yvonne was one of four children – three girls and a boy. They were all very well educated. It was a typical, southern, middle class family and her sister Rosemary – her closest sibling – worked in a GP's surgery, lived in Barnes and was married to someone who worked in publishing. During the war, Yvonne had been a Wren and, when she was de-mobbed in 1945, she had chosen to go on one of the 'fast-track' training options offered to service personnel. It isn't known how she met Sybil Darrall, who was considerably older than herself, but it may have been during her first teaching placement. Yvonne qualified as a teacher of eleven to fifteen year olds in English, Religious Education, Physical Education and General Science and went on to take extra certificates in Swimming and Drama. Although her qualifications were slanted towards Physical Education, it was English and Drama that she really enjoyed teaching. Her first teaching appointments were in the south of England and it's not really clear what her motivations were for moving north with the Darralls, but her reasons may have been personal rather than anything to do with career development. Millom was just about to go through the upheaval of conversion to a three-tier comprehensive system and Yvonne took up a position teaching English and Drama in the middle school. Yvonne loved teaching and was quite ambitious. As a teacher she had a reputation for being very strict, but pupils who were part of her drama group loved the experience.

Initially, Norman and Yvonne met at church and knew each other superficially as part of the parish community of St George's under the spiritual guardianship of Norman Darrall. The two Norman's liked each other. Rev. Darrall was at the other end of the religious spectrum to the high-church George Every, and he was an ecumenical vicar – a friendly, open man who was very popular. Like Norman, he was an enthusiastic advocate of adult education. Through the Darralls Norman got to know Yvonne better. At the beginning of 1954, the Education Authority allowed her to go to London for three months to attend a full-time course in Drama and Theatre production which enabled her to become an Associate of the Drama Board. One of her tutors was E. Martin Browne, and it was part of the course requirement that she had to study the first act of a play. She chose one of Norman's verse dramas and, when she came back to Millom determined that her drama group should perform *The Old Man of the Mountains*. So, rather in awe of the 'famous local author', she came to the house to talk to Norman about the play. This was the beginning of a much closer friendship which began to develop over the next two years into something more serious.

Chapter Thirteen

By 1954, Norman's work was being so regularly anthologised that, when the PEN anthology was published without including a poem of his, the *Times Literary Supplement* commented on the omission. Editors now asked for contributions to their magazines rather than waiting for submissions. Tambimuttu had gone to New York to set up a new poetry publication and wrote to Norman asking for poems for the first edition of the magazine which was also going to feature Wallace Stevens and Marianne Moore. Norman was also being asked to do readings, though he turned down almost all but local requests on health grounds. In June, Whitehaven Public Library set up an exhibition of his books.

Norman's plays were doing well too. *The Old Man of the Mountains* had an open air production in Denmark in the summer of 1954, and *A Match for the Devil* was being produced locally at the Green Room Club in Carlisle. It was also about to get an American production. The department of Theatre Arts at Denison University, Granville Ohio, wrote to Norman in 1953 to say that five of their students had seen the play at the Edinburgh Festival and really liked it. Their review had noted that 'only occasionally did the language seem to be striving for poetical effects', and that one character's lines in particular 'seemed to be speaking poetry only and not the meaning behind the poetry'. The play contained more form than the Old Man and 'none of the pretentiousness of *Prophesy to the Wind*'. They also noted that there were 'seven well drawn characters and two dull ones'; the chief priest Amaziah was 'an obtuse bore'. The university offered Norman $115 in royalties for four performances at the university theatre.[1] It was salve to the ego, but even these successes didn't change Norman's feeling that he was finished with the theatre and he turned down a commission to write another full length drama for the Epworth Press.

He was becoming more interested in doing public battle in what he saw as the provincial versus metropolitan debate. Ever since he had heard the 'Abolish London' programme as a teenager, his ideas on the subject had been developing and it was rapidly becoming a philosophy articulated to justify his own life-choices. In the summer of 1954, Norman gave a talk on 'Being a Provincial' which was subsequently printed as an article in *The Listener*.

Norman defined a provincial as a man who lives in the place where he was born; the place where his parents live, and his friends and relatives; someone who has shared from childhood the culture of his native region – the way of life and the pattern of activities. Provincialism is something to be desired. He cites D.H. Lawrence as an example of someone who travelled all over the world seeking for a place to belong, without realising that he was searching for the 'rough, warm friendliness' of his home town.

Yet, in the broadcast, Norman admits that it's not from 'this sort of provincial background that we shall get our major works of art' – the writers he cited had all travelled, even if some of them had come back, which seems to undermine his argument. But 'the main contribution which the provinces can make to the culture of the nation is to remind us of that which is common to the lives of all of us, that which is ordinary and local … the permanence of the commonplace … that which does not change or only changes slowly'.

Norman's argument still wasn't fully worked out. This isn't Town Mouse versus Country Mouse; nor is it about 'Regionalism', this is London versus the Rest of England. Norman is identifying 'provincialism' as a rural thing – a small village or town thing – and the fact that people might find the same identification, the same sense of community in locations that are metropolitan – isn't considered. An east-ender may have a very strong sense of rootedness and fulfil all Norman's criteria, without being a provincial in Norman's sense. The universal 'common to the lives of all of us' is to be found in the gutters and back streets of the capital city as well as the streams and backwoods of Cumberland. You can't conflate provincialism with a sense of place.[2]

Just before the broadcast, Norman had signed a contract with Robert Hale for a book to be called 'Provincial Pleasures', to be brought out in hardback at fifteen shillings a copy. Norman got an advance of £150 and a twelve and a half percent royalty. It was to consist of a series of sketches of the fictional town of 'Odborough', recognisable to anyone who knew, as Millom. Around the same time, Robin Skelton wrote to say that he was editing a new quarterly magazine and intended to publish 'poetry, creative

CHAPTER THIRTEEN

prose, criticism and politico-sociological crit'. He asked Norman for an article on 'attitudes to regionalism' for a three-way debate on the subject. Norman was rapidly becoming an expert on the subject.

Norman's relationship with Yvonne Gardner had been growing more and more intimate. They shared a common interest in drama and poetry and a deep Christian faith. But more importantly, Yvonne – the Londoner – was prepared to stay in Millom and share Norman's 'provincial' life on his terms. In 1956 they decided to marry. Norman wrote to Sylvia Lubelsky to say that the wedding ceremony was going to be 'not so much quiet as inaudible' – a jokey reference to his days of whispering in the sanatorium. Only close family were going to be invited. Yvonne had bought a two piece woollen suit at Dickins and Jones in a shade of pink, 'midway between Ladies Smock and Honesty' with a matching hat. But although he describes the arrangements in some detail to Sylvia, Norman doesn't mention his feelings at all.[3] Despite the fact that most of their friends and family were not invited, a generous quantity of wedding presents began arriving at number fourteen. Josefina de Vasconcellos and Delmar Banner sent a bronze cast of a sculpture of Norman's head that Josefina had made. Helen Sutherland and Sylvia Lubelsky sent cheques, and there was the usual random mix of tablecloths and bed linen, china and casserole dishes. George Every, who must by now have realised that the Brotherhood had lost Norman to Charles Williams' Affirmative Way, sent one of his own books, which he dedicated to the couple. Contact between the two men was drastically reduced after the marriage.

When the day arrived, the Rev Darrall conducted the ceremony, Yvonne's father gave her away and her sister Rosemary was maid of honour. At Norman's side there was Rose. In the photographs, Rose can be seen, arm on hip, glowering into the camera. She looks formidable. After the ceremony at St George's, a small reception was held in the Vicarage and Norman and Yvonne left for a three day honeymoon at a Lake District pub called The Woolpack Inn near Boot in Eskdale, where their bed and breakfast, plus afternoon tea, cost £10.50.

Yvonne's family were rather taken aback when they discovered just what she had agreed upon in order to marry Norman. Her sister Rosemary commented that 'My sister had to accept that marriage with Norman meant no family – his health, pattern of life would not permit it'. This was a big sacrifice for a woman who liked children and had one day hoped for some of her own. Yvonne also had to agree that she would live at 14 St

George's Terrace with Norman and his step-mother. This meant that not only did she not have a home of her own – Rose would not allow her to cook or to move so much as a chair or an ornament – she would also not be able to share a bed with Norman. Rosemary was horrified by the fact that, until Rose died, Yvonne 'had to sleep in the library on a put-u-up whilst Norman occupied the front attic where he both worked and slept'.[4] Rose's wedding gift to the couple had been an eiderdown, which was ironic in view of the situation they faced. According to one of Norman's cousins, Rose had been scandalised when it was suggested that Norman and Yvonne might want to share a bed. Norman's room was only big enough for a single bed, and Rose was occupying the only double bedroom in the house, which she was not willing to vacate. The shop space on the ground floor could easily have been made into a sitting room, freeing the front upstairs room to create a bedroom for them, but the ground floor room was still rented out to provide an income for Rose. With Yvonne's teacher's salary now coming into the house, the small sum from the shop rental could easily have been foregone, but Rose had been in charge now for too many years to give way on anything. Besides, as Norman commented later, for Rose 'it was as if the shop were part of her own self, the front that she turned to the world'.[5]

Just over a year after the wedding, on 10th October, 1957, the environmental catastrophe that Norman had feared became a reality. The nuclear reactor at Windscale in Cumberland caught fire and burned out of control for three days creating the United Kingdom's most serious nuclear accident. Windscale was a gas-cooled reactor which had been built to provide weapons-grade plutonium to make bombs. It had a graphite core and air was blown through channels in the core to cool it, then vented at the back of the reactor through chimneys that released the air straight into the atmosphere, though they were fitted with 'scrubbers' in an attempt to limit the amount of radiation released. The cooling process was monitored by thermocouples. Unfortunately there was a flaw in the design – graphite proved to be far from ideal because it heated unevenly when bombarded by neutrons, leading to the build up of 'hot-spots'. These could be eliminated by the process of 'annealing' the core which entailed super-heating it and then allowing it to cool down again to release the built-up energy. The thermocouples were in the wrong places to monitor this process and allowed more hot-spots to form which could not be detected on the control panel and there was no reliable way to monitor the actual temperature across the

CHAPTER THIRTEEN

whole core. Subsequent events were described as 'an accident waiting to happen'.

Staff at Windscale had begun an annealing cycle on the 7th of October and, when it didn't appear to be working – due to a lower than normal temperature reading – they had begun another cycle of super-heating. All seemed to be normal on the temperature control dials during the second heating and it wasn't until the 10th October that anything unusual was noticed. Some of the thermocouples were registering higher than normal temperatures. By then the core was so hot that the uranium fuel had caught fire without the staff being aware of it. They increased the air-flow through the graphite in order to bring down the temperature, but this only fanned the blaze and increased the discharge of radiation through the chimneys. When the relevant dials were consulted, the reading was off the scale. An inspection plug was taken out and the fire was discovered. The fuel rods were white hot. By then the conflagration was threatening to destroy the concrete containment wall at the back of the building, which was glowing red.

A full emergency was declared. Personnel at Windscale tried to put out the fire, first by removing the rods, but the heat was so intense that some of the rods couldn't be pulled out. By the 11th October, eleven tons of uranium fuel were on fire and temperatures were estimated to have risen to 1300º. The senior manager, as a last resort, ordered water to be pumped into the reactor, though it was feared that this would cause a hydrogen explosion. Risking his own life to do so, he then shut down all the vents in order to prevent oxygen entering the reactor and fuelling the fire. The introduction of water caused another huge discharge of radiation from the chimneys but not the explosion they had feared.

The drastic measures worked, and one of the world's most serious nuclear accidents, graded at 5 out of 7 on the international scale, was prevented from becoming a much bigger environmental catastrophe. 'Scrubbers' in the chimneys contained some of the radiation given off in the smoke, but a significant quantity was still discharged into the atmosphere and carried off on the wind across a large area of northern Europe – detected in Norway, Belgium and Germany. Too little was known about how radiation dispersed and, instead of looking at wind plumes and temperature inversions, a cordon was drawn around the reactor based on distance from it, ignoring some of the worst affected, but more distant, areas. There was also a much heavier contamination – probably more than twice the figure that the government were willing to admit at the time. Milk was dumped into the

Irish Sea, from the surrounding area as a precaution, but only for a month. Although some animals were destroyed, most were still grazing in the fields and on the fells, absorbing radiation into the flesh that would eventually appear in the supermarkets. There was no evacuation plan for people living in the immediate area and children still played outside in contaminated dust which they breathed in with the air. Although there were no directly attributable deaths at the time of the accident, many feared that there would be a legacy of cancers and other radiation related diseases in the future. There was particular concern about the huge release of iodine-131 which affects the thyroid.

Norman, living only fifteen road miles from the reactor – much less as the crow flies – was among those most concerned by the disaster and his poem, Windscale, written at the time of the event, was published in the *New Statesman* on the 30th November.

> The toadstool towers infest the shore:
> Stink-horns that propagate and spore
> Wherever the wind blows.
> Scafell looks down from the bracken band,
> And sees hell in a grain of sand,
>   And feels the canker itch between his toes.
>
> This is a land where dirt is clean,
> And poison pasture, quick and green,
>   And storm sky, bright and bare;
> Where sewers flow with milk, and meat
> Is carved up for the fire to eat,
>   And children suffocate in God's fresh air.[6]

Windscale (now re-named Sellafield) remains one of the world's four biggest nuclear disasters alongside Chernobyl, Three Mile Island and Fukushima. The piles had to be shut down, the reactor chambers sealed and they won't be de-commissioned until 2037. A report on the incident, by Sir William Penney, was only released to the public in a severely censored form, since 'Prime Minister Harold Macmillan feared that Penney's original report would shake public confidence and harm Britain's nuclear pact with America, which was awaiting congressional approval. The government was equally tight-lipped about the radioactive fallout.'[7]

CHAPTER THIRTEEN

Maryport was one of the other coastal towns affected by the Windscale melt-down. Norman had run courses there for the WEA and during the war became involved with the Educational Settlement project. Maryport, like Millom, was small and had been badly affected by de-industrialisation. The Educational Settlement movement had been founded to provide hope for towns ravaged by unemployment. The movement had grown out of the Quaker adult schools, pioneered by the Yorkshire Rowntree family, and it aimed to provide free education and access to the arts in the belief that these would help unemployed men and women to find a way out of their situation. Norman had been involved with the Settlement at Maryport since the early nineteen forties and was sometimes referred to as 'our own poet'. In 1958, there was an anniversary celebration of twenty one years of the Settlement's work in Maryport and Norman was invited to read. He chose to give a lecture on 'The Provincial Poet', which was very well received. According to one who was there, Norman 'fascinated a large audience by the vigour of his outstanding personality, and left no doubt that the vitality of his poetry arises from an inspiration which is firmly rooted in the soil and people of Cumberland'.[8]

One of the people Norman made friends with through his Maryport Settlement involvement was a young local artist called Percy Kelly – a unique talent and a very eccentric individual. He came from a working class background, born in Workington, and was largely self-taught. When Norman met him he was working as a postman and struggling to gain recognition. They had first been introduced a year earlier in Edinburgh at an RSA art exhibition and Norman had admired Percy's work – a painting of cow parsley and teasels. In 1959 they met again at an exhibition of French etchers in Maryport and had coffee together. Percy confided to Norman that he was having difficulty in finding classes to develop his work – there were techniques that he wanted to learn, but the only courses available took place during the day and he couldn't attend without giving up his job. This was impractical because he had a wife to support. Norman gave Percy an introduction to Helen Sutherland by letter, and as a result Percy received an invitation to lunch. The painter arrived at Cockley Moor on a scooter, but the visit was a success. Percy was dazzled by her collection of paintings which he compared to a 'wonderland'. Helen, he wrote, 'uplifted my spirits and made me think with a new sense of purity'. She also paid for Percy to go to Art College to get some formal training – something that wouldn't have happened without Norman's intervention.

Yvonne was a drama specialist and, under her influence, Norman began to reconsider his decision to leave drama alone. When he was approached once again by Pamela Kiely to write another play for the Committee for Religious Drama in the North, this time he accepted. The play was intended to commemorate a particular occasion – the founding of the 'Community of the Resurrection' which was, and still is, an Anglican monastic brotherhood based at Mirfield in Yorkshire. They wanted a play which could 'be enjoyed by some three to four thousand folk of "bank holiday" texture.'[9] It was performed in the Quarry theatre at Mirfield on July 9th 1959 by a cast of theological students, directed by Pamela Kiely.

Birth by Drowning was written for a northern audience familiar with its dialects. It is based on the story of Elisha and Naaman in the Second Book of Kings. The historic conflict between Israel and Syria is transposed to the areas of medieval Cumberland ravaged by the Border Reivers and Norman gave it a Greek chorus of Fells who set the scene and often enliven the action with comedy.

At the end of the play, when Naaman, Elisha's enemy and an off-comer to the dale, comes to ask him for a cure for his leprosy, Elisha initially resists. Although the Fells have relayed a message that he must prepare to cure an unknown person, he expects that it will be someone local, believing that 'The echoes speak only for those who belong to the dale'.[10] When he realises that they are talking about Naaman, he begins to understand that God is asking him to enlarge his horizons. Naaman is 'the first man from beyond the bounds of the dale/That the echoes ever spoke for'.[11] Was Norman thinking about enlarging his own horizons? Did he sometimes feel the nudge of a broader landscape than Millom? Philip Gardner felt that 'The view expressed by Elisha' had 'great significance' for Norman 'himself, as a provincial writer aware of the dangers of provincialism'.

Birth by Drowning was virtually ignored by reviewers. Among the handful who gave it a mention, *The Church Times* approved its 'vigorous verse ... sturdy dialogue ... homely humour'.[12] The *TLS*, predictably, turned up its nose, observing that 'It would take a great deal of faith, one suspects, to make it live ... it is not a pulsatingly dramatic affair'.[13] Philip Gardner thought that 'in its limited way, it fulfilled the limited purpose for which it was conceived'.[14] Norman wasn't there to see it performed, but apparently there were 'exceptionally difficult' weather conditions at Mirfield on the Saturday night with 'too much wind and too many trains'.[15] The BBC sent Phoebe Hesketh to see it for their radio programme 'Christian Outlook', where it was discussed by a panel. Phoebe liked the humour

CHAPTER THIRTEEN

in the play, but there was little enthusiasm for it. *Birth by Drowning* had only four productions, partly because interest in religious verse drama was waning. England was approaching the nineteen sixties and people's tastes were changing. Society was becoming increasingly secular; Norman's faith was unwavering.

Provincial Pleasures was also published in 1959 and dedicated to Yvonne. It is a snapshot in time, a portrait of a small, provincial town, and has remained one of Norman's most popular books. 'Odborough', was the fictional name that Norman gave to Millom in his prose works, perhaps influenced by an early nineteenth century book he liked very much – Crabbe's *The Borough* – a series of verse letters celebrating the town of Aldborough, published in 1810. There is a long string of connections between the two. Norman had chosen On the Suffolk Coast, from *The Borough*, for an anthology he was asked to contribute to in 1949.[16] Crabbe's *Borough* was also the origin of Benjamin Britten's opera Peter Grimes, and the libretto had been written by Norman's friend and fellow Millom-ite Montague Slater. Norman had always felt that Montague, though ostensibly writing about Aldborough, was actually writing about Millom.

In *Provincial Pleasures* the narrative is divided into months, to tell the story of a whole year. It is written in lyrical, poetic prose. An old woman 'lies in a widowhood of candlelight'; daffodils unfurl their trumpets under the apple trees in 'a shudder of yellow'; old Mr Sprout stands at his door 'wheezing like a harmonium'; and on Sundays 'a long, dry, joyless yawn passes from mouth to mouth like an infection'. For all Norman's detestation of Dylan Thomas, the reader is reminded strongly of *Under Milkwood* – there's a certain cadence in the prose, and a humorous characterisation that borders on caricature, as well as similarities in its celebration of a particular place and time. *Under Milkwood* was first broadcast in 1954, a year after Dylan Thomas died, but Norman may have also heard its precursor – a short story called 'Quite Early One Morning', broadcast in 1945. Apart from *Under Milkwood* and *The Borough*, another major influence on the book may well have been Edgar Lee Masters' *Spoon River Anthology*, published in the USA in 1915 and popular on both sides of the Atlantic. It became a 20th century classic. *Spoon River* is the portrait of a small, provincial community in verse. Each poem is 'spoken' by a different person, once an inhabitant of the town, but all now buried in the cemetery. It is a community of the dead, reminiscing about their lives. The poems are interlinked, in that the characters tell stories about each other, so that at the end, we know them all as rounded characters.

Like *Under Milkwood*, and *Spoon River*, *Provincial Pleasures* is full of voices, a polyphony of dialogue and monologue, but it is also a personal reminiscence, and a political statement. 'In Odborough a man may seem a long way from the centre of things, but he is closer to the heart of things … He sees the soil, the hills, all about him. He knows the farms that his milk comes from. He can watch the potatoes from furrow to Tommy Dale's shop. He can trace his roofing slates back to the quarries, his drainpipes back to the ore, his table and chairs back to the trees … he has before him continual reminders of the rock out of which he grows. The fields and mines are next-door, the fells are on the horizon. He has no illusions of the self-sufficiency of man. He knows where he comes from; he knows what he is up against.'[17]

Much of the book is autobiographical and provides many insights into Norman's own personality and some of the reasons why he remained rooted in Millom. Not only is the inhabitant of Odborough secure in the awareness of his own origins, and the structures that support him, he is conscious of belonging to a tribe; 'each man remains closely integrated with his fellows whether he likes it or not. He may try to disassociate himself; he may try to pretend that he does not belong. He may become an anarchist, a heretic, or even a poet. But they will not be impressed. They knew him long before he put on such airs. They knew him at school; they knew his parents; they know where he was brought up. They may laugh at him and even despise him, but they will never disown him. He is still one of them, whatever he may feel about it, so long as he stays among them'.[18]

Provincial Pleasures is full of nostalgia for a time and a place that have already gone into the past. Even as he wrote it, Norman's ideal of belonging was being destroyed by de-industrialisation, the growth of consumerism, the advent of supermarkets and national chain stores, and the displacement of people caused by social change. Most of the young people Norman went to school with had left for southern destinations – one of his school friends wrote to Norman wondering why he had stayed, when they had all 'got up, got out and got on'.[19] Norman's own relatives were also dispersing in search of work – he had Cornthwaite and Nicholson cousins now in Yorkshire and County Durham and many had emigrated; his Aunt Lizzie had accompanied her husband to New Zealand, another cousin had gone to Canada, others to South Africa. When Norman's last-remaining uncle – Uncle Jim – died in 1959, he wrote to Philip Gardner that 'I am now the last one of the Nicholson family left in the town'.[20]

CHAPTER THIRTEEN

New people were arriving from elsewhere to fill new jobs. Norman's own wife was an 'off-comer'. In *Provincial Pleasures*, Odborough is 'one of the last, half-dead-in-the-bud shoots of a huge, decaying trunk. It belongs to a world soon to be as distant as that of Merrie England'.[21] One of the problems for Millom was the exodus of young people to university, from which they rarely returned. Norman regarded the drain of the brightest and the best youngsters from the community as a bad thing. They were replaced by educated people from outside who know little about how the community works, occupying senior positions as 'parsons, doctors, teachers, civil service and local government officials, managers, inspectors, technical advisers and all the rest'. This created a big gap in the social strata of the town and a sense of alienation – an 'us and them' attitude. Norman observed that this 'intellectual cleavage in our society – which is far more dangerous than the economic cleavage – is exaggerated in small towns because so many of the top stratum are strangers'.[22]

In the book, Norman reminisces about his childhood, when he and his classmates 'drowsed and snorted, half-choked by the smell of hot socks, sweat, unwashed hair, ink, chalk and stale disinfectant.' They were 'boys of an iron time in an iron town',[23] congregating in groups with names such as the Rotting Road Gang and the Slag Bank Rovers, to chase each other down back lanes and round allotment sheds, spurred on by 'distant spyings, recognitions, shouted challenges, and long races to the home base'.[24]

One of the most vivid sections, tells the story of the 'Odborough' Amateur Operatic Society. Norman's father, when he was courting Rose, had taken Norman as a young boy to see the matinees, leaving him in the stalls, under the supervision of a responsible person, to sit 'small, silent, and completely enchanted'.[25] When Norman's father married Rose, he had begun to take a more active part in the society's activities. There's a photograph of Rose dressed as one of the three little maids in *The Mikado*, and another of Norman dressed in costume for the chorus. When he came back from Linford and studied music theory, he was roped in to transpose and arrange some music for the orchestra. Yvonne's keen interest in drama meant that after his marriage he was again actively involved.

Norman's description of an amateur orchestra striking up the overture is particularly vivid. 'It is a strange, eerie wailing – the voice, maybe, of unknown creatures on a ghostly planet. Slowly the ear gropes for the note like a hand groping for a stone in muddy water'.[26] He takes the reader backstage where nerves are frayed, there are last minute panics over scripts and lost voices, costumes that don't fit, sprained ankles, scenery and the weather, until everyone goes 'on the stage smelling of cough lozenges, lung tonic, embrocation, and camphorated oil', and at the end they 'present one another with bunches of flowers – like Russian footballers' while the orchestra plays the national anthem. Norman makes the point that it has become a seasonal festival, involving the whole town – a modern ritual. The 'true significance' of the amateur operatic movement, he asserts, is that 'it is the descendant, in an urban society, of the primitive fertility cults'.[27]

There is a whole cast of characters, some of whom are cartoon caricatures, with names like a children's card game; the three Miss Snoots who are not on speaking terms with the rest of the population, Canon Olds – a lover of birds and books, Mr Sprout the greengrocer, P.C. Goosefoot, Councillor Quorum who watches courting couples through his binoculars, Mrs Makeweight the butcher's wife, and the ubiquitous Daphne Huggins, glimpsed through the narrative with various boys in doorways and, eventually, pushing a pram. The characters claim to be the author's invention, but Norman's father appears on the page as himself, and Norman explains in the disclaimer at the beginning of the book that 'I could not have invented [him] since he invented me'. The book is, in part, a tribute to Joe Nicholson. Norman, the narrator, the 'I' of the text, is an observer rather than a participant. He watches from the attic window, 'like a cave-dweller, half-way up a cliff ... the tidal movements of the street below'. We see Odborough through Norman's eyes and his memory, in a narrative permeated by his quirky sense of humour and his firmly held personal opinions.

The 'May' chapter of *Provincial Pleasures* puts forward what, at the time, was a very controversial view. 'I have often thought that the National Trust ought to preserve some typical examples of the landscape created and shaped by industry and then deserted'. He has in mind a variety of post-industrial sites – factories and warehouses, 'decayed ports and wharves ... old lead workings', clay pits, quarries, derelict collieries, 'abandoned ironworks and slag-banks'. It isn't just that they are in their own way, romantic and that they are a reminder of human hubris, 'it is rather that they give a glimpse beyond the scale of history; they set man in the greater perspective of biology and geology, of the pre-historic and post-historic processes of nature. Here, in the flashes among the slag-banks or in the rubble-heaps of collieries, we can see nature fighting back, re-colonising the former enemy-occupied territory. It is not a ruin, but a renaissance.'[28] Norman's viewpoint was prophetic. In Millom today, twenty six years after his death, Hodbarrow mines and the site of the ironworks are now a nature reserve, greening over with plant life and raucous with visiting birds.

Norman admitted that, in his writing, it was the industrial landscape that caught his imagination, a landscape that the Romantic poets had 'turned their backs on', even though 'it was spectacular; it was dramatic; it was charged with social significance'. The new industrial age that unfolded during the 19th century was 'strange, barbarous and rather frightening'. Poetry was used to drawing its imagery from nature, until the emergence of what Norman calls 'the Pylon Poets' of the 1930s.[29] For Norman 'it was the collision between industry and nature which excited me'. But he was also aware that he didn't fit in with the urban poets he admired, such as Auden and Eliot. 'I was … completely immersed in my own backyard … I was fascinated by the geology and natural history of that landscape – its rocks, stones, river, flowers, fungi, birds and so on … material … almost completely ignored by the poets I admired'.[30]

Provincial Pleasures got the kind of reception Norman was beginning to expect. 'The main book-buying public – which is the London and Home Counties public – remains solidly unconcerned about almost anything north of Oxford. The average Londoner is, in fact, more likely to have visited Italy than Scotland!!'[31] In letters to friends he feared that the book would be overwhelmed by 'the illiteracies of the Picture Press and the mass-produced mythology of advertising, television, gramophone and cinema'.[32] Reviewers sympathetic to his work, like Derek Stanford, were enthusiastic and thought that the 'language so puts a glitter on things that the common round in a small northern iron town takes on the appearance of a fairy-ring'. But the *New Statesman* called it 'a slight book of great charm'[33] and Geoffrey Grigson in *The Observer* thought the book 'a disappointment from a poet who might have given us, from his Cumberland town, if in prose, a "Spoon River Anthology",' and added that it was 'a poor book'.[34] Norman referred to this review as 'a violent attack'.

The publication of *Provincial Pleasures* gave Norman the opportunity to write articles and make radio broadcasts to expand his theories, particularly his fight against 'provincialism'. He admitted in one article that he resented the increasing centralisation, accelerated by the war, which caused places like Millom to decline from neglect, while London thrived. He maintained his view that London was 'a city of strangers … a herding together of people who do not belong'.[35] He argued, with more reason, that the 'stampede' from the country to the city created an unbalanced society. In an article in the *TLS* on 'The Provincial Tradition' he doesn't distinguish between 'regionalism' and 'provincialism', and vents his frustration that the term 'regional writer' is only given to poets and authors of minor status. 'When a poet is important ... people cease calling him "regional" however localised his material'. Thomas Hardy, Arnold Bennet and James Joyce are regional writers, yet they are considered universal.[36] Norman saw no reason why he should not be similarly regarded.

In later articles and interviews, Norman was careful to separate 'regional' and 'provincial'. 'By "Regional Poet" I mean simply one who draws his imagery, references, or subject matter from one particular geographical area. Often however, the term is used to imply that the poet's work is of minor importance, restricted in outlook, peripheral to the main stream. It is in this sense – perhaps justly – that I have often been called a regional poet, though I stubbornly go on hoping that I write not just about Millom and Cumberland, but about life, human relationships, human society, the physical world we live on and our relation to it.' He goes on to define a 'Provincial Poet' as one attached to a community rather than to a region, though the logic is convoluted.

Patrick Kavanagh's lyrical essay 'The Parish and the Universe', was published in his *Collected Prose* in 1967. It makes an interesting comparison with Norman's provincial essays. Kavanagh talks about the provincial and the parochial, rather than regional and provincial, which he defines as direct opposites. 'The provincial has no mind of his own; he does not trust what his eyes see until he has heard what the metropolis – towards which his eyes are turned – has to say on any subject. This runs through all activities.' The parochial mentality, on the other hand, 'is never in any doubt about the social and artistic validity of his parish. All great civilizations are based on parochialism'. It takes great courage, Kavanagh commented, to be parochial; 'a man needs the right kind of sensitive courage and the right kind of sensitive humility'. But he concludes, as Norman does, that 'Parochialism is universal; it deals with the fundamentals'.[37] The danger is that 'there is always that element of bravado which takes pleasure in the notion that the potato-patch is the ultimate'.

This criticism could be levelled at Norman's provincial essays. Unlike Patrick Kavanagh's lyrical exposition of the poetics of place, Norman's tone is defensive and there are too many generalisations for his argument to be given the serious attention he wanted to attract. He was (and is) not alone in feeling that writers who live outside London don't get the same opportunities as those who live there and network within the literary community of the metropolis. Most publishers and agents are still based there and a large number of literary events take place in London. Fifty

CHAPTER THIRTEEN

years ago this divide was much more marked, and Norman had a legitimate gripe. To live in a northern outpost like Millom, without the willingness to travel to the capital on a regular basis, meant that Norman was cut off from a lot of valuable contacts. He felt that his profile should be higher than it was and that he was being discriminated against because of his chosen location.

His feelings of insecurity and resentment became much more intense in the last years of the nineteen fifties, fuelled by another crisis in his life. Although Norman had obtained personal happiness with Yvonne, he had stopped writing poetry. 'For nearly 20 years I had been writing one poem a month', then, without warning, 'the flow dwindled to a trickle and in 1955, dried up altogether.' It was, he admitted later, a kind of mid-life crisis in 'a completely changed literary climate'. One of the reasons for it, he speculated, was that he had exhausted his material. 'I had made my point as well as I could'. Apart from Norman's verse play *Birth by Drowning* and occasional poems such as Windscale and Scree, he had written nothing he believed worth keeping since 1955 and it was the source of considerable anxiety that adversely affected his health. At the beginning of August 1960 Norman went on holiday with Yvonne but when he came back he had what was described as a 'semi-collapse'.[38] It would take him five years to find his voice again.

Yvonne Gardner as a Wren during World War II
Photo © the family of Yvonne Nicholson, with permission

Norman Nicholson at the time of his marriage to Yvonne
Photo © the family of Yvonne Nicholson, with permission

The wedding of Yvonne Gardner and Norman Nicholson.
L to R: Rev. Norman Darrall, Rose Nicholson, Norman, Yvonne, Marie Gardner and John Gardner (Yvonne's parents)
Photo © the family of Yvonne Nicholson, with permission

The Carlisle Green Room Club production of A Match for the Devil, Norman's verse play banned by the Religious Drama Society.
Reproduced by courtesy of the University Librarian and Director, The John Rylands Library, The University of Manchester

Norman filming for the Living Rock television programme.
Photo © the family of Yvonne Nicholson, with permission

Percy Kelly's illustrated letter to Norman about the closure of Millom Ironworks.
Photo reproduced by kind permission of Chris Wadsworth

Engine at Hodbarrow mine. Envelope of one of Percy Kelly's letters to Norman.
Photo reproduced by kind permission of Chris Wadsworth

Yvonne Nicholson in her fifties.
Photo © the family of Yvonne Nicholson, with permission

Doreen Cornthwaite
Photo © by kind permission

The living room at 14 St George's Terrace.
Photo © the family of Yvonne Nicholson, with permission

Enrica Garnier, Anne Ridler and Vivian Ridler on holiday.
Photo © Kate Wilson, with permission

Norman on a Lake District outing with Yvonne's nieces, Liz and Sarah
Photo © the family of Yvonne Nicholson, with permission

Norman and Yvonne outside Buckingham Palace, after Norman was presented with the Queen's Gold Medal for Poetry
Photo © the family of Yvonne Nicholson, with permission

A cartoon of the Queen presenting a rather deaf Norman with the medal. Drawn by Chris Kelly. The family of Yvonne Nicholson.
Photo © to, and reproduced by kind permission of, Michael Mills

"Sorry, Ma'am, I didn't quite catch that...?"

Norman at the unveiling of Joan Palmer's bronze sculpture in Millom Library, June 1984.
Reproduced by courtesy of the University Librarian and Director, The John Rylands Library, The University of Manchester

Norman being made a Freeman of the Borough of Copeland
Photo © the family of Yvonne Nicholson, with permission

Norman with Irvine Hunt
Photo © the Hunt family

Norman writing in the living room at No 14 St George's Terrace
Photo © Ray Troll, reproduced by courtesy of the University Librarian and Director, The John Rylands Library, The University of Manchester

Yvonne and Norman's grave in St George's graveyard, Millom
Photo © Kathleen Jones

The commemorative stained glass window in St George's Church, created by Christine Boyce. *Photo © Kathleen Jones and Neil Ferber*

PART FOUR

GIVING IT WIGAN

1960 - 1987

'As I huff and grate and fill my lungs, and eye
The once-for-all starting bell,
God grant me guts to die
Giving it Wigan.'

Norman Nicholson, 'At The Musical Festival'

'Keep giving it "Wigan",
Affectionately, brother Cumbrian'

Percy Kelly

Chapter Fourteen

Norman gave a talk for BBC radio called 'The Poets of the Fifties' in which he observed that 'there comes a time in the life of that younger poet when he is made aware of a generation of still younger poets who are not much aware of him. That's the state I'm in now. I find it quite a salutary state'.[1] The nineteen sixties was a difficult decade for Norman. Society and the way it looked at itself through the arts changed rapidly. Films, books, music and poetry were all 'grittier'. In the theatre and the cinema, people were watching the adaptations of Alan Sillitoe's fifties' novel *Saturday Night and Sunday Morning*, Nell Dunn's *Up the Junction* and *Poor Cow*, as well as plays by Harold Pinter, John Osborne and Tom Stoppard. On the radio the Beatles and the Rolling Stones competed with American rock. Society was visibly more secular, more urban. The sexual revolution, brought about by the birth control pill, altered most young people's lives and a sudden surge in post-war prosperity put money in their pockets. There was a youth culture in the arts as elsewhere – Norman, heading for fifty, felt as if his time was over. He was often classified as 'a poet of the nineteen forties', a label that troubled him, but one he couldn't quarrel with. The poetry of the forties was suddenly out of fashion. 'We were the babies ... who were thrown out with the bath water'.[2]

In 1956 Norman, already experiencing a significant slow-down in his output of poetry, had described himself as a poet who had 'lost his first wind' but was 'not yet sure of his second'.[3] He had consoled himself with the thought that this 'pause' could be explained by the amount of creative energy taken up by his verse play *Birth by Drowning* and his prose memoir *Provincial Pleasures*. Between 1955 and 1960 he wrote a handful of poems, of which only two or three were worth keeping, but in 1959, after the publication of *Provincial Pleasures*, the well dried up completely.

Between 1960 and 1965, Norman wrote very little creatively – either poetry or prose. Most of his published work in the nineteen sixties came under the heading of 'non-fiction' – reviews, articles, radio broadcasts and re-workings of previously published books. He wrote a shortened version of his Cowper biography for the British Council, and *Cumberland and Westmorland* was re-written as *Portrait of the Lakes*, and then again as *Greater Lakeland*. Poetry had vanished altogether 'in a bang and a flap' and he had begun to believe that the gift had left him. He told interviewers later that, in his opinion, the seam had been exhausted – he had written Millom out, and he also believed that the public were tired of his tub-thumping on the subject of the environment.

Things had changed at Faber. Geoffrey Faber died in 1961 and in 1965 T.S. Eliot also died. He had been not only an enormous influence on Norman, but had also offered him his greatest opportunity by bringing him into the Faber stable. Norman was probably unaware that Eliot had eventually confided to the young poet Matt Simpson that Norman had disappointed him, by never fulfilling his early promise. Eliot had been replaced at Faber by Charles Monteith, who became Norman's editor for sixteen years, before he too was replaced by Craig Raine, whose attitude was less sympathetic. In the late nineteen fifties Faber had begun to encourage a new generation of poets – Philip Larkin, who was eventually to become a thorn in Norman's side, and in 1957 Faber published *The Hawk in the Rain* by Ted Hughes. Norman had been one of the first people to see Ted Hughes' poetry. His old school friend, John 'Ted' Fisher, now a school master in Yorkshire, had sent him a selection of poems by Ted Hughes, who was one of his pupils, and asked Norman's opinion of them. Norman responded enthusiastically, but with a warning that Ted Hughes should 'keep away from that Dylan Thomas'.[4] Norman did what he could to promote the young poet's work and Ted Hughes was always grateful for this early support. In 1960, after the publication of Ted's second collection *Lupercal*, A.E. Dyson, editor of *Critical Quarterly*, asked Norman if he still rated Ted Hughes highly. Dyson thought that the older generation was unconvinced by new developments in poetry. 'I find that some readers remain unimpressed, feeling a lack of rhythm and a certain monotony of theme.' Dyson had known Ted Hughes at university, and had found him a very private person. 'I had no idea he wrote poetry. As far as I know, he talked little of this.'[5] Norman was able to reassure Dyson that he was one of those who recognised Ted Hughes 'exceptional gifts' and that he was staunchly behind this strong, northern voice. There was a rapport between the two poets that lasted for the rest of their lives.

CHAPTER FOURTEEN

The nineteen fifties had been dominated by the poets of The Movement – anti-romantic and advocates of regular literary form. Norman's opinion was that 'the poets of the Movement, as it is often called, do not speak for a generation. They only speak for part of it.'[6] But the late fifties saw the publication of an anthology called *New Lines*, which included many of the poets whose work would influence literary fashions in the nineteen sixties; Kingsley Amis, Robert Conquest, Donald Davie, D. J. Enright, Thom Gunn, John Holloway, Elizabeth Jennings, Philip Larkin, and John Wain. Elsewhere, there was a lively interest in concrete poetry (which Norman detested) and sound poetry. There was also a reaction to the conservatism of The Movement, called the New British Revival, which looked back to the Modernist poetry of William Carlos Williams and Ezra Pound for their influences as well as to their British disciples, many of whom were personally known to Norman, including David Jones. These new modernists included Roy Fisher, Elaine Feinstein, Bob Cobbing, Michael Horowitz, Peter Finch and Edwin Morgan. Michael Horowitz also edited an influential magazine, *New Departures*. Like much that happened in the nineteen sixties, it was all very London centred and quite alien to Norman's natural inclinations. Norman had dabbled with Modernism during the forties, but found that it wasn't for him, 'I was never a Modernist', he said in an interview,[7] and he had little rapport with Movement poets such as Kingsley Amis and Philip Larkin. What was happening on the literary scene emphasised his feeling that his time was over.

In 1965 another link with the past was broken. Helen Sutherland died and Cockley Moor was put up for sale. Shortly before she became ill, Helen had written to Norman reminiscing about the old days, during the war, when Kathleen Raine had been a frequent visitor, and T.S. Eliot had stayed at Cockley Moor. She told him that she missed Eliot, who had died in January 1965 from lung disease – the result of heavy smoking. Helen's handwriting was shaky and she sounded lonely, begging Norman to come and stay the night with 'your Yvonne, who I sh'd so like to see again'.[8] Norman's papers don't record whether the invitation was ever taken up.

Norman's home life was generally very happy. Life with Yvonne suited him well. It was extremely lucky that he had found a wife with a temperament capable of tolerating Rose's absolute dominance in the home, and willing to give Norman the devotion he simply accepted as his due, though not, in Anne Ridler's words, without some 'friendly teasing'. In the words of the old saying, Yvonne 'waited on him hand and foot'. She made him rest, she folded his clothes, she washed his hair for him – one of the few tasks that Rose was prepared to relinquish – and she organised his poetry readings. Yvonne's sister Rosemary wrote, 'I cannot emphasise just how much of her life was devoted to Norman – he had to be cared for in every way'.[9] Yvonne was uncomplaining – she admitted in an interview that she liked being the wife of a poet, but she was also working full time as a teacher, now head of the middle school, and the job was quite demanding. The biggest change to Norman's life came when Yvonne bought a car – one of the new Morris Minor 1000s – and learned to drive. She was, Norman admitted to a friend 'not a compulsive driver'. According to local sources she was quite terrifying, driving the wrong way on roundabouts, and there were a number of bumps and scrapes. But she was courageous and Norman suddenly had a new found freedom, being able to go around the Lake District to places inaccessible by public transport. According to friends, 'Yvonne restored to him the freedom of Cumbria; for without her help, much of his local writing could not have appeared'.[10] Norman regarded these outings as 'very precious', but they had to be shared. Rose invariably accompanied them, sitting in the back of the car. There are a succession of photographs, taken by Yvonne, of Norman and Rose beside the car with the Lake District landscape in the background.

There were new friends. In April 1961, Norman went to the first big northern exhibition of a young Cumbrian artist, Sheila Fell. Sheila had been born in the small west coast town of Aspatria, and gone to London to study art, where she had been lucky enough to be noticed by L.S. Lowry. She became his protégé. Her exhibition was a huge success and more than two thousand people visited in one week. She sold quite a number of paintings and wrote to Norman afterwards to thank him for coming, commenting that 'a farmer who between buying sheep in Cockermouth and rushing home to milk the cows bought one of the dark, early ones' that she had never expected to appeal locally. Norman sent her a copy of his new book *Portrait of the Lakes* and later bought one of her drawings.[11]

Norman had also come to know the painter Delmar Banner and his wife, the gifted, half Brazilian, sculptor Josefina de Vasconcellos, who lived in Little Langdale. They were a very unusual couple who had met at the Royal Academy in London and become friends. Delmar was homosexual and their marriage was very much one of convenience. They were both committed Christians. Norman bought one of Delmar's paintings and Josefina sculpted Norman's head. Delmar and Josefina had a holiday cottage next to their house and Anne Ridler stayed there with her husband Vivian and the children when they came to visit Norman.

CHAPTER FOURTEEN

Anne liked Yvonne, but was secretly 'resentful for Enrica' who had remained a close friend. Anne found it incredible that Yvonne should have been preferred to her more artistic and refined predecessor. Anne was quietly humorous on Norman's solipsism, which was increasing as he grew older. The teenager who had advised Sylvia Lubelsky to be selfish in the cause of self-preservation had remained very self-involved. In her autobiography, Anne Ridler remarked that 'conversation on general topics was rather one-sided, for Vivian and I never felt he was interested in matters outside his own concerns.' This was particularly apparent when Norman and Yvonne went to stay with the Ridlers in Oxford. He wasn't interested in their family, or their lives. Even Vivian's printing press 'did not provoke a spark of attention'.[12] But Norman was otherwise so charming and endearing that his less attractive traits were quickly overlooked.

Norman's habit of seeing the world only from his own perspective had other consequences. A funny incident occurred when Norman was staying overnight with friends for a poetry reading. They had thoughtfully laid out some illustrated books of the area for him to look at, knowing that he was a topographer and thinking that it might interest him to know something of the countryside around them. Norman assumed, without checking, that the books were a gift, and popped them into his suitcase when he left. Nothing was ever said. Fortunately his friends were more amused than offended. Others occasionally joked about his ego. Norman's handwriting was so illegible, he had begun to use an old typewriter to type his letters. One friend sent a jokey note, which said, 'I have typed this letter myself to show you how greatly the letter i on your typewriter needs attention!' Norman's letter 'I' – always capitalised – had a habit of jumping above the line, giving it a quirky prominence in his correspondence.[13]

After the break-up of his relationship with Enrica Garnier, Norman needed to find someone to type his manuscripts. Few people could decipher his handwriting. Norman was eventually lucky enough to find a single lady, Miss Mullins, in Berwick on Tweed, who seemed to have the knack. The one drawback was that she insisted, because of the difficulty, on being paid by the hour rather than the page. Norman agreed, and manuscripts and typescripts were posted backwards and forwards across the north of England.

In April 1963, the University of Kentucky wrote to ask for one of Norman's hand-written manuscripts and Norman made the shocking admission that he didn't keep them. His poems were all written on the backs of the letters he received; 'no letters, no poems' he joked. But he hadn't kept any of the prose work either. Once Miss Mullins had typed the manuscript he didn't keep the originals. 'I am afraid that practically the whole of my manuscripts have been destroyed. It did not occur to me that anybody would be interested in them.' However he did still have the typescript of his latest book *Portrait of the Lakes* and he offered that instead. But the university wanted only hand-written manuscripts and in the end Norman copied out three of his poems and sent them.

Portrait of the Lakes, published in 1963, was basically a re-writing of *Cumberland and Westmorland*, updated to include the new material and the corrections suggested by Mary Fair. It was dedicated, like its predecessor, to Walter Wilson, Norman's old headmaster, and he wrote to congratulate Norman on the way that he had re-worked the book to appear new. *Portrait of the Lakes* was reviewed favourably with comments such as, 'The smell and the feel of the place [are] magically distilled into words,' and it was widely thought to confirm Norman's reputation as a brilliant topographical writer.[14] Norman himself admitted in an interview that he now thought of himself as a poet who earned his living from topography. But the genre was becoming fashionable as the tourist industry boomed in the nineteen sixties and Norman was up against a great deal of competition. *Portrait of the Lakes* was published at the same time as Harry Griffin's *In Mountain Lakeland* and Molly Lefebure's *The English Lake District*. Wainwright was also on the horizon.

Yvonne's car meant that Norman could accept poetry readings further from home, though he still read mainly in the northern counties and their bigger cities, what Norman described as 'a Feature Writer's tour of the Industrial North'.[15] He took his readings seriously and Yvonne was responsible for coaching Norman in better performance. According to Yvonne's sister, Norman's readings 'owed much to her for the presentation, appearance, timing and to be perfectly honest, acting!'[16] Norman spent a lot of time deliberating how much to charge for a reading, but eventually settled on the sum of fifteen guineas plus expenses. It could have provided a comfortable income, but Norman never gave as many readings as he might have done. It was rare for him to venture into the south of England, though he travelled to London for special events. Local readings were also circumscribed by the fact that he often asked for two nights in a bed and breakfast, rather than the usual one, and he refused to stay with the promoter – it was common for the person organising the reading to provide a bed for

CHAPTER FOURTEEN

the poet to save money. Norman insisted that it was important for him to arrive the day before so that he could rest properly before the reading, and it always had to be a double room because Yvonne had to accompany him. This was an added cost for poetry promoters who were usually working with tiny budgets.

Norman was also getting quite a lot of radio work. Apart from his regular features, he contributed a series of five minute talks to the Home Service's regular slot, 'Lift Up Your Hearts', and in June 1961 he read excerpts from Wordsworth's *Prelude* on the Third Programme, much to the delight of the poet's descendant Christopher Wordsworth who wrote to congratulate Norman and ask why he and his wife had never accepted any of his invitations to tea.

Television work also became a regular thing for Norman during the nineteen sixties. He remained a good-looking man in middle age – thin, with a handsome face, laughing eyes and thick, wavy hair. Norman was one of those whose personality beams through the camera – he had that elusive quality known as charisma. His first television appearance was a short interview about his work, on the regional programme 'Points North', in November 1960. Then, in August 1962, he was commissioned to do a Christmas special, to be broadcast in December 1963, called 'No Star on the Way Back', for which he was paid a hundred pounds. It was described as 'an allegory in verse, music and narration', putting the story of the Three Wise Men into a contemporary context. For Norman it was 'hack work', drawing on his biblical knowledge and ability to put together a ballad. The lyrics seem rather pedestrian now, but it was written for a mass audience, to be chanted and sung, and includes carols for the wise men, and the shepherds present at the nativity. The music was written by a woman – the Scottish-American composer Thea Musgrave. The film crew spent a week with Norman, translating – as he put it – 'the basic imagery and analogies of my work into visual terms'.[17] It was generally successful. Programme controller Patrick Campbell thought it was 'one of the rare occasions where 'author, composer, designer, producer, director and actors all find themselves working inevitably towards the same end'.[18]

But Norman could be awkward at times, as some producers found. He had signed a contract with Border TV to make a programme that entailed going to Cardiff, but when the time came, Norman refused, saying that he was too tired. 'I'll be very unpopular in Carlisle,' he wrote to a friend, 'but I really feel this is far too much to ask'. Border TV was understandably annoyed.[19] On another occasion, the Lake District Planning Board thought that it would be a good idea to have some recordings made by writers and poets living in the area for their new visitor centre at Brockhole. It was arranged for a technician to go to Norman's home to record a poem for this project, but when the sound recordist arrived, Norman 'turned a bit mulish' and refused to record the poem unless they also recorded Yvonne reading Southey's 'Three Bears'. Fortunately, the archive was glad to have both.[20]

Norman's days were lived to a strict timetable. He worked every morning from 10am until lunch, slept in the afternoon and then did an hour or so's more work, either writing or reading. If it was fine, he might go for a walk. In the evenings there were letters to write and proofs to correct. He often wrote in bed in his little attic with views of Black Combe and Coniston Old Man. Norman wrote slowly, about five hundred words a day and, when he was writing poetry, a poem could take months to finish. He often started with one line, perhaps the first or the last and sometimes it would be a year before the poem was complete.

The quiet routines of Norman and Yvonne's life together were painfully disrupted in 1965 when Yvonne was diagnosed with breast cancer. She was only forty three. This would be terrifying for any woman today, but fifty years ago, without modern drugs and contemporary surgical techniques, it was a much more serious illness with a much poorer prognosis. Both Norman and Yvonne were devastated. Norman immediately blamed the Windscale disaster for Yvonne's cancer. Many people, including Anne Ridler, agreed with him, and a local campaign cited a cluster of cases, particularly of childhood leukaemia, in the area. Yvonne's relatives pointed to other members of the family who had suffered from cancer without being anywhere near the nuclear disaster. Yvonne's older sister and brother both had cancer, as well as one of her nieces. Her sister Rosemary was later put on a preventative drug trial because of the family connection.

But wherever the roots of Yvonne's illness lay, it created immediate practical problems. Yvonne had to take sick-leave from her job, and it was decided that Rose would have to go into a nursing home while Yvonne was in hospital. Rose was understandably reluctant but acknowledged that it would be impossible for Norman to cope without Yvonne. Rose, now approaching eighty, had become much more frail and unable to look after him or manage the household properly. She had recently broken her ankle and had had to spend a few days in hospital herself. So Rose went into a local nursing home for respite care and Norman went to stay with the

CHAPTER FOURTEEN

Darralls at St George's vicarage while Yvonne had her operation. When she was discharged, they went to other friends at Wreay vicarage, just outside Carlisle, while Yvonne convalesced. It was a month before they returned to St George's Terrace.

Yvonne's subsequent recovery was slowed by worries about Norman. He was thought to be suffering from a gastric ulcer and admitted to hospital for tests. Stress had always seemed to manifest itself in Norman's stomach. To the Nicholsons' relief, his gastric bleeding and pain were found to be caused by the consumption of aspirin, which was the commonest pain-killer available until the introduction of paracetamol. The hospital took the opportunity to x-ray Norman's chest at the same time and pronounced it to be clear, but Norman's health was a source of constant anxiety for Yvonne. She was also very distressed when the Rev Darrall died suddenly in his sleep at the vicarage, shortly after she was discharged from hospital. In the end Rose spent six months in the nursing home before Yvonne felt well enough to have her back. When Rose returned to 14 St George's Terrace it seemed as though the displacement had broken her spirit. Norman wrote to Sylvia Lubelsky that Rose was suddenly very happy 'to let Yvonne take over the running of the home (at last!) … To our surprise and relief'.[21]

The North/South divide continued to annoy Norman. In 1967 there was a bitter and undignified spat with the historian and poet A.L. Rowse. Rowse came from a similar working class background, but had won a scholarship to Oxford where he obtained first class honours and where he remained, occupying a number of distinguished academic positions. He had a reputation for being irascible and intellectually arrogant.[22] Norman had reviewed Rowse's new volume of poetry and confessed that it was not to his own personal taste. Always colloquial and direct, he used the word 'jell'. A.L. Rowse was quick to respond. 'Fancy a poet using such a journalistic word as "jell". Ugh! My poetry may not "jell" for you, but it does for better poets'. He cites Betjeman and Blunden whose 'inspiration and sensibilities have not become atrophied'. Just to plunge the knife in deeper, Rowse comments on Norman's own dearth of publications; 'I used to admire your poetry in earlier years. Are you still writing? I never see any evidences. And, to judge from your review of my book, I should imagine not; your sensibility must have dried up.' A.L. Rowse states that he doesn't expect Norman to like his work, 'since it is obvious that you are a more normal, conventional, commonplace man'. And he ends, 'Best wishes for a thawing of your (always somewhat knotted) arteries'.[23]

NORMAN NICHOLSON

This letter cut to the quick. But, unknown to A.L. Rowse, Norman was writing poetry again, although very slowly. Changes had been taking place, and Norman was no longer an isolated voice in the north. Basil Bunting was fourteen years older than Norman, also a northerner, born in Northumberland but educated at a Quaker school in the south. Between the wars he lived in France and Italy and was a friend of Ezra Pound, before being posted to Persia by military intelligence during World War II. He had struggled all his life to gain recognition for his poetry, which often appeared in obscure Modernist journals. In the nineteen fifties, he returned to live in Newcastle and a significant number of young poets began to gather round him. Jon Silkin was among those who moved to Newcastle, bringing with him the cutting edge poetry magazine, *Stand*, which he had started in 1952, and which became one of the most respected periodicals in Britain, publishing established poets alongside many new northern voices. One of these was Tom Pickard who lived in Newcastle and became first a fan and then a friend of Basil Bunting. Pickard and his wife Connie opened a bookshop at Morden Tower, a medieval building on the city walls, aiming to provide international magazines and poetry not available through mainstream bookstores, and they began to organise a series of poetry readings. Basil Bunting was the first poet to read there, but later programmes would include Ginsberg and Ferlinghetti. Norman, too, was asked to read, and it is obvious from his letters that he enjoyed feeling that he was part of a northern-centred scene. He was often published in *Stand* and identified strongly with northern writers such as Yorkshire-born Ted Hughes, Donald Davie from Barnsley, Sid Chaplin in Durham, and James Kirkup, who lived in South Shields. Norman preferred James Kirkup's account of his childhood in the north east, *Sorrows, Passions and Alarms*, to Laurie Lee's *Cider with Rosie*.

Sid Chaplin was one of the emerging northern writers closest to Norman. He was a working pitman at one of the Durham collieries, struggling to support a wife and two young children and still find time to write. Norman had read one of his poems, 'A Widow Wept', featured in *Penguin New Writing* in 1946. The two men had first met at the house of Norman's friends Bessie and Leonard Schiff just after the war. At the time Leonard was vicar of a parish at Spennymoor in County Durham and he and Bessie, like Norman, were keen supporters of the Educational Settlement programme. Sid had studied economics through the Educational Settlement in the nineteen thirties, before the war returned him to the pits. The Schiffs wanted to promote his writing and hoped that Norman would be able to help. Sid

CHAPTER FOURTEEN

came straight from his shift at Ferryhill, 'rather diffident even rather gawky, but clearly and determinedly convinced of his ability to record and interpret the life of colliery County Durham as no one had quite done before'. According to Norman they shared the same background. 'Both of us were northerners, at a time when there were not so many north-country writers about. Each came from a mining area – in his case, coal-mining, and in mine, iron-ore. We also shared a non-conformist upbringing – his, I fancy, being that of the Primitive Methodists, who were strong in the north-east while I belonged to the rather more consciously respectable Wesleyans'. Norman thought very highly of Sid as a person and as a writer, admiring his 'immense enjoyment, his sense of fun, his compassion, his modesty, his moral strength'.[24] Norman's approval and encouragement meant a great deal to Sid. His wife Rene always remembered how he had come home that night filled with enthusiasm and the energy to go on writing; 'to find another writer-poet who he could talk to was absolute joy for him'.[25] Sid got an arts council grant, with Norman's backing, to write a collection of stories, *The Leaping Lad*, and went on to write one of the North-east's most important literary novels – *The Thin Seam* – an account of a day at the coal face. The friendship between the two men was important for the careers of both, since both were fighting the same battle against regional prejudice.

In 1966 Fulcrum press published Basil Bunting's *Briggflatts*. Norman read it and declared that it was a masterpiece, as well as being 'the most aggressively "regional" poem of the second half of this century'.[26] *Briggflatts* is named for a Quaker meeting house in Cumbria, and it is an autobiography in poetry. It had a big influence on Norman's work. He was struck by Basil Bunting's sense of being rooted in a landscape; his use of Viking words, Northumbrian dialect, and all aspects of oral poetry, particularly the musical aspects of language. Poetry, Bunting wrote, was not just written text, it was 'sounded speech'. But *Briggflatts* is a personal landscape and it was this aspect of it that was particularly important for Norman. A new, confessional, more personal poetics had been evolving in America, from the poetry of Walt Whitman, and the effect of this was being felt in Britain. Robert Lowell had published his seminal collection *Life Studies* in 1959, and the following year in England John Betjeman brought out his autobiography in blank verse, *Summoned by Bells*. Anne Sexton's *To Bedlam and Part Way Back* and Sylvia Plath's *Ariel* were also part of this new movement. Norman read them all. Eliot's maxims were put aside; it was suddenly possible to write directly of the personal and the private. Somewhere around the years 1965 to 1966, Norman had a kind of epiphany. He later told a friend that, although he was 'not sympathetic to confessional poetry', Lowell had opened up 'a whole new area' for him. He had previously written about the landscape, but now Norman began to think about the people of Millom he had humorously depicted in *Provincial Pleasures*, and the deceased members of his own family, who might have stories to tell. In the mid-nineteen sixties, inspired by Robert Lowell's biographical poetry, Norman wrote a poem about the Nicholson family called The Seventeenth of That Name.[27]

It's the story of his grandmother Maria's arrival in Millom, with her baby son in a basket 'Bundled in with the eggs and the luggage', and how, when she saw 'the black marsh' and the chimneys of the ironworks, she ordered the carter to turn round. Her sons are all described in the poem. Uncle Jack who 'played full back/for the Northern Union', as well as cricket, and who died down in the mine, his back broken in a rock fall. Uncle Tom the cobbler at the Co-op where Norman's Uncle Jim sold shoes – 'He, best-loved uncle/And my father's friend'. Uncle George and Uncle Fred moved away from Millom and went to work in a Durham pit. Uncle Bob was 'a tom-thumb tailor' who went to stay with his brothers in Durham, 'drove out on a motor-bike and rode back in a hearse'. Arnold the youngest, was a painter and decorator, another brother Harry was a waiter, Richard the epileptic had died as a young man and there were three other brothers who had died in infancy. And then Norman comes to his father;

> One other brother
> Left me what an uncle couldn't: – a face, a place, a root
> That drives down deep
> As St George's Steeple

Norman himself is 'the seventeenth of that name' and, since he has no children, the last of that line. Talking about the poem in an interview, he said that it was 'a rebuke'.[28] In the final stanza, the lead lettering on his father's tombstone seems to accuse him, spelling out –

> Its what-are-you-going-to-do-about-it
> Memorandum. As once when a boy I see it scratched
> On backstreet slates and schoolyard gates. Step on the gravel and the
>   stones squeak out
> Nicholson, Nicholson...
> And I, in their great-grand-childless streets, rake up for my reply

CHAPTER FOURTEEN

Damn all but hem
And haw about them.[29]

Chapter Fifteen

On Friday 13th September 1968 a procession of dejected men, in flat caps and tattered clothes, carried a coffin through Millom as a defiant symbol of the death of their working lives. Millom Ironworks was now closed and they were all redundant; 'five hundred men/At one stroke out of work'.[1] In only a hundred years, Millom had grown from a beautiful coastal village into a booming iron town – one of the most productive in Europe – and then declined into an industrial ruin. From an environmental point of view the end to pollution was a benefit to the town's inhabitants, but economically the closure of the town's main employer was disastrous, as Norman recorded in his poem On the Closing of Millom Ironworks;

> It's beautiful to breathe the sharp night air.
> But, morning after morning, there
> They stand, by the churchyard gate,
> Hands in pockets, shoulders to the slag,
> The men whose fathers stood there back in '28,
> When their sons were at school with me.
> The town
> Rolls round the century's bleak orbit.
> Down
> On the ebb-tide sands, the five-funnelled
> Battleship of the furnace lies beached and rusting:
> Run aground, not foundered;
> Not a crack in her hull;
> Lacking but a loan to float her off.[2]

Millom was filled with fear for the future. Most people there remembered the deprivations of the twenties and thirties and there were big public

CHAPTER FIFTEEN

meetings in St George's Hall. Norman didn't feel able to go because of the fear of infection, but Yvonne went to them and reported back on what had been said.[3] The poems that Norman was writing at this period were more transparently political, perhaps influenced by north-eastern writers such as Sid Chaplin and Tom Pickard. Having opened his mind to writing about people rather than just landscape, Norman also recorded their concerns. When he wrote about his grandmother, Maria, in The Tune The Old Cow Died Of, he wrote of the poverty she had been brought up in before the days of the welfare state, when people euphemistically 'went without'. In the poem Norman makes an analogy with the millions of starving people in the modern world. 1968 was the year that the Biafran crisis began making news headlines, as well as the severe drought and famine in the Sahel region of Africa.

> When she was a girl
> There was nothing funny,
> My grandmother said,
> About the death of a cow,
> And it isn't funny now
> To millions hungrier even than she was then.[4]

When it was clear that there was going to be no reprieve for the ironworks, the demolition began and the town was rocked by explosions and earth tremors as the structure was blown up and carried away for scrap metal. Norman recorded the process in a highly political poem, On the Dismantling of Millom Ironworks, which addresses not only the environmental issues but also the human cost. 'They cut up the carcass of the old ironworks/Like a fat beast in a slaughter house,' until 'one last core of clinker, like the stump of a dead volcano,/Juts up jagged and unblastable'. Auxiliary buildings and slag heaps were also flattened. The industrial horizon was gone. In common with most of his contemporaries in the town, Norman watched his childhood being 'shovelled' onto 'the rubbish heap'. Now, old people's bungalows creep up the hillside and 'An age/Is pensioned off – its hopes, gains, profits, desperations/Put into mothballs'.

But Norman observes nature staging a revival. The Duddon river is able to rediscover its old course, 'Shelduck fly low from feeding-ground to feeding-ground . . . and shunting-yards succumb/To a yellow encroachment of ragwort'.[5] Grass began to grow over the iron lodes at Hodbarrow and fresh water gradually filled in the area behind the sea walls that had protected the mines from inundation, creating a lagoon frequented by wild life. 'Where once the shafts struck down through yielding limestone/Black coot and moorhen /Lay snail-wakes on the water.' Norman found bee orchids growing in the limestone grit at Hodbarrow, 'Decoy queens,/Honeyed and furred'. Nature was regenerating everywhere.

Towards the end of 1968 a chance meeting brought a new member of the family into Norman's life. His second cousin Doreen Cornthwaite, born in South Africa, had returned to England and was working for Border Television in Carlisle. Her grandfather and Norman's Cornthwaite grandfather had been brothers, but there had been little contact between the two branches of the family since one of the brothers had emigrated to South Africa. Doreen was in touch with her Cornthwaite cousins, who still lived near Millom, through her parents, who had also returned, and were living in nearby Gosforth. It was on one of her visits to them that Norman was pointed out to her, while they were walking along the sea wall at Haverigg. Introductions were made and Norman immediately liked her. He wrote to Doreen in November, addressing her as 'My charming cousin' and making an apology. 'I'm sorry if the beginning of this letter sounds like something out of a Henry James novel, but the ridiculous thing is that I don't know your Christian name!'[6] He didn't know her address either, so the letter was sent to Border TV. Soon he was writing to 'My favourite cousin' and then to 'My dear, sweet Doreen'. It was the beginning of a lively (and sometimes flirtatious) correspondence and an enduring friendship.

In May 1969 Rose was 82, but she was already terminally ill with cancer of the colon and her kidneys were failing. A few weeks later, on the 17th of June she contracted pneumonia and died in her bed at home. Rose was the last member of Norman's close family, a dominant woman whose character had probably been the most important influence on Norman's personality as he was growing up. She was buried with Norman's father in the cemetery behind St George's church; 'Safe in the glowing graveyard/ Another generation is put to bed'. Norman's poem One Minute, recalling Rose's death and perhaps his father's, is a hymn of praise to Yvonne, remembering how, one bitter 'hibernating February' in the early days of their relationship, she had pointed optimistically to 'the small/Re-kindling of the dead end of the day' and directed him towards the brighter future beyond the horizon. The metaphor is hackneyed, but the poem is a heartfelt tribute to the fifteen years of their life together. For Yvonne, Norman's total dependence on her was sometimes difficult. Her own mother was suffering

CHAPTER FIFTEEN

from dementia in the south of England and had been admitted to a home, where she died at the end of 1969. Yvonne's father, now over ninety, was struggling to remain in his own home. It was hard for Yvonne to visit for any length of time, though she tried to travel south four times a year. The stress of teaching, running a household and looking after Norman, seems to have affected Yvonne's health and she suffered from pain in her neck and back, for which she had physiotherapy, and from colitis.

Perhaps inevitably, given the bereavements of 1969, Norman's thoughts went back to the death of his father and he wrote a poem, The Cock's Nest, which expresses his feelings using an image of male abandonment.

> The spring my father died – it was winter, really,
> February fill-grave, but March was in
> Before we felt the bruise of it and knew
> How empty the rooms were . . .

A cock wren had flown into their back yard and begun to build a nest behind the bathroom drainpipe, high up on the wall of the extension, flying in and out laden with nesting material, 'Three times a minute, hour after hour,/Backward and forward to the backyard wall'. Wrens apparently build several nests and it's up to the female to choose which one she will lay her eggs in. Norman records sadly that, 'she didn't choose our yard', and as the spring unfolds into summer, the two events of loss become one in his memory:

> The cock's nest with never an egg in,
> And my father dead.[7]

Other poems surfaced about Norman's father, including the humorous anecdote about the afternoon that Edward VIII, then the Prince of Wales, had visited the town. 'I gave him an – err,' my father said, meaning/ Masonic handshake: holding his fingers/As if they still were sticky from the royal touch'.[8] It was a story that Joe Nicholson had often told.

After Rose's death, days out became private excursions for Norman and Yvonne. It was also possible to go on holiday without being obliged to take Rose with them, or worrying about arranging respite care. Norman was very frugal and they often made short trips based around poetry readings, knowing that two nights' accommodation was already paid for. Planning their annual holiday was one of the Nicholsons' great pleasures. They loved northern Scotland, particularly the Orkneys and Shetlands. In 1965 they had gone further afield with a brief visit to Norway and Norman had ambitions to go back again to pursue his Viking heritage. Another benefit of their new-found freedom was that Yvonne could at last have a bedroom of her own. Norman remained in his attic, though they do seem to have shared a room when they had visitors, or when staying in hotels. When Norman was ill he moved down into the sitting room on the first floor, to sleep on the guest bed, in order to save Yvonne climbing up two flights of stairs with food and drink. Although Norman's living arrangements remained the same, there were other, subtle changes, funded by a small legacy from Rose. They made a garden in the narrow, dark back-yard – a canyon of lush greenery and climbing plants that astonished visitors. Inside, the old gas boiler was replaced and a heater purchased for Norman's attic. Yvonne began to decorate the house and alter the rooms to suit their way of life. Norman hated having workmen in the house, so Yvonne learned to hang wallpaper, lay carpets and even do simple plumbing so that his routines would not be disturbed. If bigger work had to be done, Yvonne tried to arrange it while Norman was out, or they were away on holiday. At the end of the summer term in 1971, Yvonne retired from teaching. She had been working only part-time because of her health problems and family responsibilities and was delighted to find that she received more in pension than she had been earning in a part-time post. Norman was glad of the increased flexibility. He could now accept more poetry readings during the week and outings needn't be confined to the weekends.

Norman's poetry had earned him several honours. As far back as July 1959 he had been awarded an honorary MA from Manchester University – something he was very proud of. His work was also beginning to be recognised in other countries, particularly Italy. Professor Giorgio Melchiori had written a long essay about Norman's poetry, making a connection between him and the Italian poet Eugenio Montale – regionalism, for Melchiori, was no bar to international understanding.[9] In 1961 a translation of Norman's poem On My 35th Birthday, by Italian scholar Robert Saveri, had been published in *La Corriere d'Informazione* as an example of 'a good translation of a good English Poem' and, in the late sixties, the first academic study of Norman's work was undertaken by another Italian, Joseph Carnelli. Norman's plays had been translated into Danish, Dutch and Welsh; performed in Scandanavia, Holland and the USA. Then in 1965 Norman had the odd privilege of a piece on the Lake

CHAPTER FIFTEEN

District in *Anglia*, a Russian language magazine about life in Britain today, Cold War propaganda from the Foreign Office, published by the Central Office of Information.

In 1967, alongside Seamus Heaney and Brian Jones, he was a recipient of the much coveted Cholmondeley Award. The award was administered by the Society of Authors and had been set up the previous year by the Dowager Marchioness of Cholmondeley to honour distinguished poets and provide a sum of money for their support. It was a very valuable prize – almost £400. The Dowager's daughter-in-law, Sybil, wrote to Norman to congratulate him and extend an invitation to Houghton Hall in Norfolk – gratefully accepted in principle by Norman, but never taken up. Norman was disappointed that the local press gave little attention to this important award – 'nobody seemed even to hear of it!'[10] This was one of the problems of having a publisher whose publicity machine was in the south, but also an example of the old saying about prophets in their own country. When Seamus Heaney became a Nobel Laureate, one of the Irish papers ran the headline 'Local Poet wins Prize'. It was very lucky for Norman that Doreen Cornthwaite was soon to be promoted at Border television and she was able to give Norman helpful feedback through her media contacts. If he had won an award, he always told Doreen first.

In the nineteen sixties a young academic currently teaching in Japan, Philip Gardner (no relation to Yvonne) approached Norman with a view to writing his doctoral thesis on Norman's poetry, under a supervisor at Liverpool University. The two men met and got on very well, so the project was approved. Gardner intended to confine his study to the poetry and the verse dramas, though in the end he also wrote a separately published essay on the two novels. This gave him a broad view of Norman's work and deservedly earned him his doctorate. Subsequently, Philip Gardner accepted an academic position at Newfoundland and moved across the Atlantic where he began to establish a reputation for himself in Canada. His thesis was published in the USA by Twayne Publishers Inc. in 1973, as part of their 'English Authors' series, and was the first full-length critical study of Norman's work, adding considerably to his standing. The book jacket refers to the ups and downs of Norman's reputation – a poet 'undeservedly neglected'. Philip Gardner – who was a poet himself – admitted that, 'Nicholson has never been a fashionable writer'. But the jacket of the book suggested that 'the recent shift of emphasis away from a London-centered literature to a wider understanding of regionally-based writing seems to be bringing Nicholson's work, especially his more recent poetry, back into more favourable notice.' He was, Gardner insisted, 'unique in contemporary British literature'. Sadly, few of the letters that were exchanged between the two men are available, since they would have provided a great deal of insight into Norman's working methods and the thinking behind many of the poems. However, some of the information that Philip Gardner obtained from Norman is included in the text and he was able to talk to George Every, who allowed him to read their correspondence, as well as Anne Ridler, who showed him an important letter from T.S. Eliot, and he was able to read letters and manuscripts that Norman had sent to Bessie Schiff. This is invaluable for any subsequent student of Norman's work.

Philip Gardner's study was completed before the publication of *A Local Habitation,* Norman's first new poetry collection since *The Pot Geranium* in 1954 – an interval of seventeen years – though some of the poems Norman had written for it were included. The critical study covers Norman's first three collections and all the plays. Gardner was enthusiastic about the poetry, but less convinced by the verse dramas. He placed Norman's work within the 'conservative tradition' of twentieth century poetry, distinctively regional, avoiding 'technical experiment for its own sake', and using 'conversational directness in words and rhythm'. Gardner felt that Norman managed to transcend the provincial issue in his poetry, but not in his verse plays. He made a comment about them which could equally apply to Norman's work as a whole: 'By writing for a certain kind of audience, Nicholson has opted for a necessarily restricted kind of success'.[11] Norman's poetry divided the critics during his lifetime and would continue to divide them – vigorously – even after his death.

Philip Gardner, in his conclusion, addressed the 'disparity between what seems to be [Norman Nicholson's] importance and his critical reputation'. He thought that Norman's neglect was due in part to his 'Christian attitudes' which were no longer fashionable after the war; and also to the fact that Norman was a 'neo-romantic' at a time when the critics were sternly modernist. But he also gives great weight to the 'influence of a sort of literary orthodoxy which forms part of the general metropolitan sense of superiority'.[12] Regionalism, Gardner adds in his summing up, 'is an ingredient of the poetry, not a disadvantage under which it labors', and – if there are more people in the world who are provincial rather than metropolitan – then Norman's poetry should actually be more universal, 'common to the lives of all of us'. The problem, Gardner asserts, lies with the critics who are not 'willing to admit to themselves their own basic likeness to their fellows'.[13]

CHAPTER FIFTEEN

By the time Philip Gardner's book was published the effects of the closure of Millom Ironworks were being felt everywhere. Several shops closed in the street and Norman's tenant gave notice. Fearing that they might not be able to lease the shop again easily, the Nicholsons decided to turn their entire house into a home. Having lived 'above the shop' all his life Norman found it odd at first; 'I was conscious of a strange quietness'. But Yvonne enjoyed the domestic challenge. She loved interior decorating. Norman wrote, with characteristic humour, to her niece Liz to tell her that she would no longer have to fight through crowds of customers to get to the dining room, as the shop has been turned into a hallway. 'We've curtained off the glass door, dropped Venetian blinds up to eye height and blocked off all the back of the window with a great forest of pickled beech leaves, spruce, dried grasses and oats and teasels. If anyone bangs on the door the air is filled with chaff'.[14]

It was also easier, without Rose, to invite friends and relatives to the house. Doreen Cornthwaite was a regular visitor, as she often stayed the weekend with her parents, half an hour up the coast at Gosforth. Yvonne's nieces Liz and Sarah, the teenage daughters of her sister Rosemary, came up from London to stay for holidays and had very happy memories of days on the beach, and trips up into the fells with Norman and Yvonne. He was fond of them both, but Liz, Norman's god-daughter, was his particular favourite and his most regular correspondent. For the Nicholsons, Liz and Sarah became the children they could never have.

There were other visitors. Norman had been corresponding intermittently with the painter Percy Kelly during the nineteen sixties, but in 1971 Percy and his second wife Chris moved to a cottage in Levens Park near Kendal. Yvonne and Chris liked each other and the acquaintance suddenly flourished. Norman became one of the privileged who received the beautiful 'painted letters' – both envelope and its enclosure decorated with ink drawings and watercolours. Norman wasn't good at keeping correspondence, but he kept almost all of Percy's letters and bought one of his ink wash drawings, a picture of Dockray, the village near Helen Sutherland's home at Cockley Moor. Another painter who sold Norman a canvas was fascinated to discover, when he delivered it, that Norman's home was full of paintings and sketches in black and white. Professor Alan Beattie believes that the fact that Norman bought drawings and paintings in monochrome, demonstrated his love of form and structure rather than colour and decoration – perhaps as a result of his encounter with the modernist paintings owned by Helen Sutherland.[15] Percy too, was a lover of form and was often criticised for his lack of colour. When Norman first knew him his work was mainly charcoal drawings, sketches in watercolour and ink, and black and white etchings. Later, his work became more colourful, but it was never about pigment – the structure was always the most important element, which is perhaps why his paintings – like Norman's early poems – are devoid of people.

Both the painter and the poet thought along similar lines. David Cross, in his book *Cumbrian Brothers*, states that it was 'remarkable how many themes they had in common, both in their correspondence and in their creative work'.[16] Percy believed that 'the true artist, whether figurative or abstract has to be part poet'. Norman often wrote with a painter's eye 'playing at poet with a box of colours'.[17] Percy and Norman came from similar working class backgrounds and Percy's parents were also Methodists. After his studies at Art College – which in retrospect Percy thought had been a mistake – he often depicted industrial scenes, including Millom. Percy spent days, just before the closure of the ironworks, taking photographs and making sketches, before creating a painting in haematite red ('Millom, Cumberland') to commemorate the event, just as Norman had recorded it in poetry. Both painter and poet loved wild flowers and birds and the Cumbrian landscape. Like Norman, Percy was rather reclusive and had a distrust of the commercial world of critics and art dealing, that would soon escalate into phobia. He approved of Norman's 'provincial' crusade, writing that 'it is great news that you carry on the good fight'. He sold very few paintings in his life time, and those went mainly to friends, though he dreaded work leaving his studio and had been known to ask for his paintings back. 'I cannot paint for monetary gain,' Percy wrote. 'I would rather starve than sell one piece of my work, but I know that when I depart this world people will stop and wonder at the beauty and truth that I have endeavoured to portray.'[18] He had a complex personality, bordering on insanity, and suffered from hypochondria and paranoia. Unknown to his friends, he often dressed as a woman and towards the end of his life changed his name by deed poll to 'Roberta Penelope', began HRT treatment and painted himself in a red skirt and red hat.

In June 1971 Percy invited Norman and Yvonne to visit his new home and this seems to have been a success as the Kellys were invited back to St George's Terrace. Percy was very enthusiastic about Norman's poetry and wrote 'One day we must fuse our work for the whole world to see and read!'[19] In the letters he talks about illustrating one of Norman's poems. This may have been On the Dismantling of Millom Ironworks,

CHAPTER FIFTEEN

but the project was never realised. There were more reciprocal visits and the two men continued to correspond until 1985, when something in one of Norman's letters, or perhaps the fact that Norman was slow to respond, irritated Percy and he ceased to write to him.

In 1972 Norman published his first collection of poetry for eighteen years. Because of the long gap, *A Local Habitation*, named from a Shakespeare quotation, attracted a lot of attention and was a Poetry Book Club choice. The first poem in the collection, The Dumb Spirit, recalls the fear that Norman had felt at being 'struck dumb', with a glancing reference to the biblical parable where Christ heals a man dumb from birth by mixing his spittle with the earth and placing it on his tongue.

> Cast out the dumb,
> Lord.
> Touch ears.
> Let spittle un-numb the tongue.
> Let there be no impediment on lung or larynx,
> And let the breath
> Speak plain again.[20]

Norman makes an analogy between this creative silence and the enforced silence of the sanatorium, where he was made to whisper for nearly two years. In the poem The Whisperer, Norman is still struggling to be heard, while 'Life roars round me like/A dynamo'. He cries out for 'You or you,/ Anyone who/Can lip-read the words of my whisper as clear as the clang of a bell'. Norman was always a poet who needed an audience. The collection contains the handful of poems he had written between 1954 and 1959, Scree, Windscale, Bond Street, and September on the Mosses, as well as the recent poetry he had written about his family. Norman's sense of humour is more evident in this collection – as though he now has enough confidence to include the lighter poems. A typical example is Nicholson, Suddenly which was a kind of family joke between Norman and his wife and which made Yvonne groan every time he mentioned it. 'Here comes the dumb blonde poem,' she used to remark. One evening, browsing through the *North West Evening Mail*, she had read out an item about the death of Norman Nicholson – Norman's Millom namesake – and then said with complete seriousness, 'That'll be the other Norman Nicholson'. Norman told the joke every time he read the poem.

There are also a number of overtly political poems, among them The Elm Decline, which may have been inspired by the spread of Dutch elm disease, which was rampant in England by the early nineteen seventies. The poem addresses the effect that de-forestation has had on the landscape that 'man/helped nature make'. There is an implication that we are the architects of our own destruction. One day, the poem concludes, 'no human eye' will remain to see the devastated landscape it has created. In the poem, the decline of the elm tree is an indicator that something is terribly wrong – a precursor of 'a perpetual/sour October', caused by human activity.

> Today
> electric landslips
> crack the rock;
> drills tunnel it;
> valleys go under the tap.
> Dynamited runnels
> channel a poisoned rain,
> and the fractured ledges
> are scoured and emery'd
> by wind-to-wind rubbings
> of nuclear dust.[21]

The *Times Literary Supplement* reviewer disliked the mix of poems and thought the collection 'uneven' and sometimes 'scrappily anecdotal'. Another reviewer made the perceptive comment that Norman was 'widening, not deepening' his territory.[22] But Seamus Heaney in *The Listener* thought that it contained 'poetry that is sometimes as elegiac and patient as the processes of geology'. Norman Nicholson, he went on, was a 'fathering voice' and there was also 'a filial link with that other old man at Rydal Mount'.[23] Alan Brownjohn wrote in the *New Statesman* of 'earthy simplicity . . . The strength of Norman Nicholson's verse is its patient rootedness in one place, his quick and compassionate eye for its changing appearances and the sheer interest of the ordinary people living, and enduring, in it.'[24] Anne Ridler sent Norman a long, encouraging letter about the collection. She liked Bee Orchid at Hodbarrow and the autobiographical poems. 'It seems to me that in these and The Cock's Nest for instance, you have mastered a new informal style; and these subjects and treatment have helped you over that awkward dry ditch of middle-age, so that one sees this book as the beginning of a new flow, rather than the end of an old one.'[25]

CHAPTER FIFTEEN

Norman was pleased with the reception of *A Local Habitation*, but then, at the end of 1972, he was sent the *Oxford Book of Twentieth Century English Verse*, edited by Philip Larkin, for review, and discovered that he had been omitted from it. This seemed a deliberate slight and Norman was ill with the emotional stress. The book was sent back, explaining that he could not review it objectively. Then, urged by Yvonne, he wrote to Philip Larkin. 'I have been thrown into such depression and tension that my wife begs me to write to you to lance the absecse [sic] before I make myself ill. Because, after all, it's not just exclusion from an anthology of 50 or 100 poets, but of over nearly 250 and – except for Anne Ridler, whose work I admire, but who is not everybody's choice – I think I am just about the only poet of my generation who might have expected to have been included and isn't ... certainly when I look at the enormous number of names which are included, I ask myself, incredibly, can anybody think I haven't written one poem up to that standard . . . ?' The Oxford anthology was regarded by many as a guide to the best poets of the century and read by people who wouldn't normally buy individual collections. Norman was particularly upset by the thought that he had lost the chance 'of being able to hope that one little poem of mine will go down for a few more decades, at least'.[26]

Philip Larkin wrote back at length and one can sense him trying to put the best gloss on the situation that he could. He told Norman that if *A Local Habitation* had been published before he made the selection, then it might have been a different matter and reassured Norman that he regarded him as a 'distinguished poet', referring to his honorary degree from Manchester University and his status as a Fellow of the Royal Society. He then went on to explain that he hadn't made selections for the book to produce 'a list of the best 250 poets of our time', but a mix as 'a work of entertainment'. He was afraid that Norman's complaint was only the courteous forerunner of 'a howling and abusive horde'.[27] Larkin was right. His anthology – which reflected his own personal tastes – proved to be very controversial and is still described as 'quirky and idiosyncratic'. But, despite the fact that Larkin was based in Hull, it confirmed Norman in his belief that the poetry establishment, rooted in the south, was determined to ignore him.

Chapter Sixteen

In the aftermath of *A Local Habitation*, the BBC expressed interest in some more autobiographical contributions from Norman. Radio Producer Tony Gould, who was also the literary editor of *New Society*, suggested that Norman should keep a writer's journal for a year and then read edited sections of it for a radio programme. It sometimes surprises people that a poet and author like Norman didn't already keep a journal or notebook, but it seems to have been quite foreign to the way he worked. He made notes on scraps of paper; poetry was written on the backs of old letters. Nothing personal was recorded at all. Introspection, the great interrogation of the soul, was not something Norman wanted to share with the outside world. However, Norman allowed himself to be persuaded by Tony, but in the end he didn't write the journal. Instead, he wrote letters about his daily life and what was happening in Millom, addressed to his niece Liz and his old friend Ted Fisher. They were chatty, humorous, and full of life, but they were curiously impersonal. The resulting broadcast, on Radio Three, was adequate, but not ground-breaking, and it was subsequently published in *The Listener* in April 1974 as a 'Letter from Cumberland'.

The main topic of conversation in the letters was the changing nature of Millom. The clean-up of Hodbarrow was continuing and 'acres and acres [were] now a horrible mass of churned up mud and clay and smashed concrete'. Most of the wild regeneration had been scraped away – even the bee orchids had been trampled.[1] The speed of the changes left Norman amazed. 'What really staggers me about all this is the way in which a living industry and a whole community based on it can so quickly pass into ancient history'.[2]

There were plans to create an industrial estate and a holiday village on the site and a management consultant came to visit Norman while surveying for the English Tourist Board. He seemed very optimistic that

CHAPTER SIXTEEN

the plan could succeed and Norman broadly approved of the idea. The main source of income in the town was now a K's Shoe factory, providing employment for the women, but the men were reliant on the Sealand Hovercraft Factory – a relatively new industry. In December 1972, this too began to collapse; there was no money to pay the workers and they were all made redundant. Norman was full of admiration when the men staged a 'work in' – refusing to leave and working for no pay until a buyer could be found for the factory. He and Yvonne went down to visit the Hovercraft plant to talk to the workers and find out what was happening, so that he could tell their story for the BBC programme. Christmas and New Year were bleak. In the next few weeks various plans were put forward – investors would agree to support them and then walk away at the last moment. There were weeks when the men got paid and hopes were high and then it would all fall through and they worked for nothing again. It couldn't go on, but Norman was impressed by their courage and tenacity.

There's a mention in the letters to Liz of one of Norman's major television appearances. In January 1973, the BBC broadcast 'The Whispering Poet' as one of its *Look Stranger* series that featured people and places around Britain. Most people in Millom watched it and Norman found himself suddenly famous in a different way – television reached ordinary people who didn't read books: 'I've hardly dared put my head out of the house … it makes me ridiculously self-conscious'.[3]

Much of his time during the spring of 1973 was taken up with sorting out family problems. He and Yvonne had been looking after Annie Brennan, the illegitimate cousin who had helped his grandmother Maria Nicholson after she was crippled in a fall. Annie had always been fiercely independent – not even drawing the full old age pension she was entitled to and turning down all offers of help. Yvonne was one of the few people she would accept when her health began to fail over the winter. Annie became ill with digestive problems over Christmas and New Year – an infection which also prostrated Yvonne – and shortly afterwards she died, single and intestate – the last of the older generation. The Nicholson family home had been left to her by Maria because she had promised to stay on and look after Norman's bachelor uncles. But they were all dead now and Annie had inherited everything. Because she was illegitimate the family knew very little about Annie's relatives. On the Nicholson side they were all believed to be dead, but no one was sure. Her father was unknown. Norman was one of a network of first cousins, and thought that there were probably half siblings somewhere in the country, but didn't know how to trace them. 'I know of ten relatives whose claim is the equal of mine, and there could very well be 20 or 30 more of whom we know nothing. In fact, the entire estate will almost certainly disappear in search fees'.[4] In the end Norman was registered as next of kin and given permission to wind up her estate. It was up to Norman and Yvonne to sell her house and dispose of her possessions – Norman kept those that had important memories, cramming them into number fourteen.

He was thinking a great deal about the past, his childhood and the inhabitants of Millom who had become names on tombstones – gone into oblivion like the mines and the ironworks, leaving no traces. Ordinary people and their lives rarely get written into the history books. Norman began listening to oral history recordings and writing down scraps of autobiography. When the creation of a 'folk' museum in Millom was proposed, Norman was one of its keenest supporters. The idea had been generated when a farmer in the nearby hamlet of Silecroft decided to throw out an 'old hand-driven wooden threshing-machine' which had been used as a 'rustic percussion' instrument in a local folk band.

It was realised that Millom's unique history was in danger of disappearing forever. There was a scramble to salvage what could still be saved before it went to the scrap dealers. 'The shaft and two drifts of the old Moorbank mine at Hodbarrow (opened in 1928, closed in 1968), with the cage, the bogies, overhead beams, picks, miners' lamps and underground telephone, and even the printed notices of signals and danger warnings' were rescued and reconstructed in the museum. The recorded sound of the descending cage on the next but last shift was also preserved. For the first visitors the effect was so real it was almost unnerving.[5]

Norman formally opened the museum on the 21st July 1973, commenting that it was 'a ceremony which had a special meaning for me'. The museum was housed in the downstairs classroom of the old secondary school where Norman and his contemporaries had spent two years being 'drilled into shape for matric'. The displays were put together on a tiny budget. Norman was amused to find that the commemorative plaque which he unveiled, 'was, in fact, originally the brass plate of an insurance firm's office, and had been unscrewed from the door, reversed and suitably inscribed for the occasion'.[6]

In February 1973 Norman was awarded a Society of Authors' travel grant of £500. He was undecided about whether to accept it, since he would have to find another £500 for Yvonne's travel, and he still hadn't

CHAPTER SIXTEEN

made up his mind whether to go to Canada – where Philip Gardner wanted him to give some lectures – or to Scandinavia. But quite quickly the pull of the Viking north decided the matter. Norman resigned as a *TLS* reviewer, telling them that he intended to visit Norway and Finland which, he wrote, had 'the best stocked bookshop anywhere in the world'. It was hoped that the grant would provide material for important new work. To cover the cost of the proposed itinerary, Norman sold the typed manuscript of one of his early verse plays to Northern Arts. Finding extra funding delayed their departure and it wasn't until the beginning of June 1974 that the Nicholsons left by ferry, crossing the North Sea from Newcastle to Stavanger. Norman remarked to a friend that 'the landscape seemed very like a larger and starker version of the Cumbrian fells and dales; but it was more because I felt I was returning to the Scandinavian ancestry of the Cumbrian people'.[7]

Norman was a little more forthcoming to his cousin Doreen, writing a long, lyrical letter about his 'never to be forgotten' four weeks in Norway. They stayed in modest bed and breakfasts 'booked for us by the Norwegian State Railways'. The weather was 'brilliant, serene' and warm – hot down in the valleys, cooler in the uplands, but even there old and young were stripping off to sunbathe. Norman was fascinated by the compulsion to expose flesh to the sun. 'Nobody under sixty, in Norway, wears anything but a bikini'. Norman and Yvonne spent five days on the coast of the Skaggerak – 'a maze of fiords, with thousands of small islands and skerries' which they explored by boat. Several days were spent at Settersdal, two and a half thousand feet up, on the edge of the alpine region, 'with a famous wooden church, old wooden houses, and a fir tree just outside our bedroom window'. But the highlight of the trip was the ten days they spent in the mountains of Telemark, on the snow-line. It was marred only by Yvonne jarring her spine as she jumped from a ski-lift. The food caused a few problems, since Yvonne had to avoid dairy and eggs and neither of them liked the cold fish which is a staple of Scandinavian cuisine. Norman thrived on boiled eggs and goat's cheese, which he was amused to find was pronounced 'gay-toast', he told Doreen that it sounded 'like Welsh rarebit for homos!'[8]

Apart from these paragraphs to Doreen, Norman was curiously silent, in other letters and articles, about this much anticipated and planned for expedition. It left few traces. There are a series of 'happy snaps' of Norman standing beside the rails of the ship – but hardly any of Yvonne, since she was the one holding the camera. Norman kept the certificate that commemorated the fact that he had crossed the Arctic Circle. Only two poems were written out of the journey, Fjord, and Glacier, though it's possible that Plankton was also influenced by the trip. Norman (and his funders) had probably hoped for more. The 1965 holiday in Norway had produced Tromso, and another in 1979, barely mentioned by Norman, produced Midsummer Fires at Sognefjord. The Vikings in Scandinavia proved less inspirational than the Vikings at home.

So far in his career, Norman had concentrated his thoughts on the history and landscape of Millom and of his family, but there was one subject that Norman still hadn't tackled. Himself. After the success of *Provincial Pleasures*, at the suggestion of his agent David Higham and the BBC producer Tony Gould, Norman had begun to think about the subject of a full length autobiography. Could it be done? Encouraged by his agent, Norman signed a contract for an untitled book of 80,000 words in August 1972, but the writing of it proceeded very slowly. By January 1974 he had written about 60,000 words of the 90,000 he intended to write, before editing it down. There was a need to have it finished before his trip to Scandinavia in June. Norman was sixty in January and he admitted that he 'felt quite ancient for a few hours, but I'm really full of thanks and amazement that I should ever have reached that age at all!'[9] It was a time for looking back.

The book forced Norman to think about the most painful parts of his childhood – the death of his mother, his early schooling, and then his relationship with his father's second wife Rose. His large and colourful family flooded onto the pages without any encouragement, but personal anecdote was harder to compose. There were certain set-pieces – the stories that Norman always told about his childhood; the grand moment when he had been asked to be Chairman of the children's concert; the prize-winning recitation; the award of the George Moore scholarship. There was nothing controversial in Norman's memoir, early relationships were disguised by name changes and his love affair with Sylvia Lubelsky was hidden altogether. What was surprising in the book was his attitude towards his step-mother, Rose. During her life time he had seemed devoted to her. But what he wrote after her death, in *Wednesday Early Closing*, was often critical. It is hard to ignore the accusation in the statement that she had 'dug his grave with a bread knife', or that, when the house was converted before her marriage to Norman's father and he had to sleep in the attic bedroom, they had 'taken a step up the social scale and I had taken a step down into chronic ill-health'. These statements imply an element of blame.

Norman's whole relationship with Rose provides fascinating material for a psychologist. He had found her very attractive, before his father married her; 'she was still young, lively, laughing, welcoming. She even seemed, as I thought, fashionable in her V-neck blouses and long strings of wooden beads – a complete contrast to all the other women I came in contact with. The contrast intrigued me'. Norman had been desperately looking for a mother. But after his father's marriage Norman appears to have suffered from Rose's dominant character. There was no doubt about who was in charge at number fourteen, though Norman's father did, occasionally, put his foot down – particularly over the subject of Norman's education. Appearances meant a good deal to Rose. She was a strict parent when it came to the observance of social rules; 'there was the matter of table manners to begin with. I had to learn to say "Please" and "Thank you" more often than it had been necessary before … it was repeatedly drummed into me, moreover, that whatever I did outside the home reflected directly on my mother. If I was ill-mannered, she would be blamed for not teaching me better'. On one occasion Norman was forced to eat ice-cream, which he hated, 'with tears dribbling down to the corners of my mouth' because Rose insisted that it would have been rude to refuse. Then there were the protocols; '"Ladies first" – which meant in practice, "Mother first"', and other stipulations, which were so strong they stayed with Norman for life. 'Even today when I am laying the table for a meal, I feel slightly guilty if I accidentally lay my own place before that of my wife, or any woman guest.'

There are a number of unanswerable questions. Rose had no children of her own – did this make her more possessive of her step-son? And how much influence did her prudish, nineteenth century attitude to sex have on Norman? It has also been suggested that Norman was thinking of himself and Rose when he wrote that Cowper's sexual inhibitions were caused by a feeling that the women he loved were mother-substitutes, and this 'led him to shy away from the sort of intimacy which led to marriage'.[10]

Wednesday Early Closing deals only with Norman's life up to the age of nineteen. It ends with his return to Millom from the sanatorium, to be re-instated in his unhealthy attic bedroom, leaving the reader with the ambiguous feeling that it was to become either 'womb or tomb'.[11] Eventually it proved to be both. But Norman professed to have no regrets: 'Forty years later,' he wrote, 'in that same attic room, I thank God for a lifetime spent in that same town'.[12]

The autobiography was published in 1975, and, unusually, Faber didn't allow any photographs, which many felt was a serious flaw in a memoir. Even if they had been included, there were some photographs that Norman simply didn't have. He wrote at the beginning of the book that 'I have no photograph of [my mother]; no visual image whatever'. Norman's cousin Doreen was horrified when she read that and immediately sent him a photograph of his mother. Norman was grateful, but he commented that he was glad he hadn't seen it before he wrote the book because the narrative rested heavily on the fact that he couldn't remember what she looked like at all.

Norman was sad that *Wednesday Early Closing* was only being brought out in hardback because that made it unaffordable for the very people who might want to read it. There were many who lamented the absence of photographs too. Faber and Faber didn't seem to be enthusiastically behind the book. Craig Raine, who was now in charge, told the poet Matt Simpson that he thought the book was '"charming" – but not commercial'.[13] Reviews were mixed. Ronald Blythe liked it, but the Sheffield University students' magazine thought it was 'a very ordinary life indeed' and boring to the young. The *TLS* called it 'a minor classic' and *The Observer* commented that is was as 'craggy, quizzical and minutely observant as [Norman Nicholson's] poetry'.[14] There were many personal letters of approval. Anne Ridler found the memoir illuminating and wrote that she hadn't realised until she read it, what a struggle Norman had had to fit himself back into his Millom surroundings after his stay in the sanatorium. Anne added that it 'was a book that Dickens would have liked' and she thought Norman's father was rather like Daniel Doyce in *Little Dorrit*. Norman wrote back explaining that he had been thinking about Dickens when he had written the book. He had seen many similarities between the young Pip in *Great Expectations* and the young Norman Nicholson, and he had written the memoir with that in mind. This partly explains the objective, humorous, rather distant approach to the narrative, almost as if Norman was inventing himself as a fictional character. The poet Glyn Hughes wrote to Norman to say that he loved the autobiography, which had taken him back to his own childhood. But he added (what many people privately thought) that it would have been better with less detail of the relationships between all the myriad people of Millom and more on Norman's own changing psychology as he grew up.[15] But Norman declined to look at himself, although he admitted in an interview that 'a certain amount of introspection always goes on'.[16] David Higham wanted to know what Norman's thoughts were

CHAPTER SIXTEEN

on a second volume, but Norman would not be drawn. Kathleen Raine had recently published the first two volumes of her autobiography, detailing her own anguished journey, and they were selling well. Norman was not going to follow this path. Confessional prose was no more acceptable to him than confessional poetry. You don't go to *Wednesday Early Closing* to 'find' Norman Nicholson.

At the end of 1975 Yvonne's car, with Norman as passenger, had a serious accident, colliding with the local *North West Evening Mail* delivery van. It left them both in a state of shock, stiff and bruised. Yvonne tore a ligament attached to one of her ribs, bumped her knees and Norman sprained his foot. He commented ironically that the newspaper was currently in negotiations with his agent to serialise *Wednesday Early Closing*. Weeks later he was still suffering aches and pains, limping and unable to type because his back ached. They had to buy a new car and eventually Yvonne was fined £25, but the *North West Evening Mail* paid handsomely for the serialisation, so there was some recompense.

During this period Norman published two important pamphlets, both in the North East. *Stitch and Stone* was a collaboration between Norman and Kenneth Dow Barker, a working man who designed and embroidered landscape tapestries in his spare time. Barker lived in Ingleton, a small community in North Yorkshire. He was a 'roadman'. In the years just after the Second World War the roadman's hut, with his bicycle propped outside, was a common sight on minor roads in rural areas. They cut the grass on the verges, kept the ditches clear, trimmed the hedges, and did minor repairs. It was a poorly paid manual job, but Barker's tapestries were very talented, though he earned little from them. *Stitch and Stone* was the first real recognition of his work. Norman contributed the poem Wall as well as six other recently written poems, including Scafell Pike and Nobbut God. There was an exhibition in Sunderland Arts Centre to coincide with publication by Ceolfrith Press. Since then, Kenneth Dow Barker's intricately embroidered landscapes have completely disappeared.[17]

Pamphlet publication was a new departure for Norman and suited the slow pace of his production. A second pamphlet, called *Cloud over Black Combe* was published by Pig Press for a reading at the Colpitts Hotel, Durham in 1976. It contained just a single poem and was a forerunner of *The Shadow of Black Combe*, a longer pamphlet that contained the whole series of Black Combe poems, as well as other new work, all of which was later included in the collection *Sea to the West*. Sid Chaplin wrote to say that he carried the poems with him everywhere and that he was teaching them to his creative writing students to extol 'the virtues of metrical verse ... I literally give them Wigan (my favourite poem)'.[18] *The Shadow of Black Combe* was favourably reviewed in the Poetry Society magazine; 'Nicholson's strength lies in his special combination of the easy-breathing voice and the interplay of rhythmic and aural devices.' The reviewer commented on Norman's 'intimate and resonant metaphors that reach out far beyond their geographical regions'. The same edition of the *Poetry Review* contained Norman's Edward Thomas poem Adlestrop – it was obvious that he was going in a new direction and the public reaction was very encouraging.[19]

At sixty-one Norman was still very slim and always immaculately turned out. His hair had turned grey but remained thick and wavy. The only difference in his appearance was the growth of abundant side-whiskers, which gave him an eccentric character and made him immediately recognisable. Yvonne teased Norman about them and used to say that he liked them because it made him look like Matthew Arnold. Norman was generally in good health, due to a flu injection every winter which radically decreased the number of colds and bronchial attacks he'd been subject to. He had an enlarged prostate, but was told that it was nothing to worry about, and had also become very deaf in his late fifties. This was a great sadness because it inhibited all the things that Norman liked – social discourse, listening to music and, most important of all, the sound of his own poetry, which he often composed aloud. Now

> Unspeaking faces
> Gape blankly about me.
> Night ties
> Bandages round my ears:
> Turns verbs
> To Blind Man's Buff;
> Sends me to black
> Coventry in my own skull,
> Where not one crack
> Of light breaks in
> From the town's genial hubbub.[20]

Norman struggled for a while with a National Health hearing aid, but after his sixtieth birthday, Yvonne persuaded him to buy a more sophisticated

CHAPTER SIXTEEN

device. The new aid had a switch that blocked off lower frequencies, that Norman could use when there was too much background noise. This made all the difference to Norman's ability to take part in discussions, as well as listening to the radio and talking on the telephone, which had recently been installed.

Another symbol of their increasing affluence was the purchase of a new typewriter, though it was hardly guaranteed to help the readers of his letters. Norman explained to his correspondents that it had been a bargain deal because it was a cancelled export order and had a foreign keyboard, without apostrophes (Norman used the French acute accent instead) or the exclamation marks he peppered his letters with. Since it had a variety of foreign characters, particularly eastern European letters, Norman's typos became even more exotic.

Norman was suddenly being showered with honours. In January 1975 he was awarded another honorary MA, this time from the Open University, and in July he was invited to take part in a huge Poetry International reading at the Queen Elizabeth Hall in London alongside a very old and inarticulate Robert Graves and Irina Ratushinskya, a Russian poet who spoke no English, in front of six hundred people. Norman commented that the audience were ready for a little light relief by the time he began to read and he was very pleased with his reception. The following February he was awarded a Civil List pension of £500 a year 'for services to literature' and shortly afterwards came an invitation to the Buckingham Palace Garden Party. Norman turned the latter down.

He was now getting regular invitations to read poetry in London, most of which he felt unable to accept. He made exceptions for ones he felt were particularly important. Invited to read at the Poetry Society in Earls Court Square – a reading timed to follow on from their Annual General Meeting – Norman accepted and then bitterly regretted it when he discovered how badly organised the whole thing was. He and Yvonne found themselves putting out chairs in the room for a small audience that eventually proved unsympathetic – 'by far the worst reception I've ever had'. He was affronted that only three of the poetry society members came to the reading after the meeting – most of the audience were members of the general public. It was another sign that the southern poetry establishment didn't value his work. Norman lamented that the Poetry Society had been taken over by 'the wild men of English poetry… the scruffiest of the pop poets and the like'. He felt angry about modern trends in poetry and complained that they 'regard anything like a capital letter or a full-stop or even a recognisable sentence as bourgeois reactionary stodge, and think that you only qualify as a truly modern poet if you write "fuck" in every other line'.[21]

Shortly after their London trip, Yvonne had a scare when a registrar found a lump in her breast at the regular check-up, and for three weeks both she and Norman feared another operation for cancer. However, her consultant decided that there was 'nothing that would merit the use of the knife' and they were both very relieved. Yvonne wrote that Norman had been unable to work and had been on the 'point of breaking down' when he thought of what might have been. They were both very critical of the registrar for giving them such a fright but, in hindsight, the registrar may have been wiser than the elderly consultant.[22]

Like most women, Yvonne feared further surgery, and it's possible that her original mastectomy in 1965 may have caused a few problems in their relationship. Many couples struggled to come to terms with the physical mutilation that mastectomy caused before breast reconstruction became routine. Afterwards, Norman was given to putting into words his admiration for women's figures in a way that suggests a fascination in excess of the attention men normally give to such things. There was an element of flirtation in Norman's relationships with other women. He wrote to his young cousin, Doreen, frequently about her charm and her captivating appearance, 'The latter ought, strictly speaking, to be irrelevant … but, somehow, however charming she might be, I feel I'd be rather less enthusiastic about a flat-chested cousin!'[23] In another letter, after seeing Doreen dressed for work, he explains that when she came to Millom she was usually wearing 'much looser or chunkier clothing, so that in your closer-fitting office jumper and skirt, you gave me a better opportunity to appreciate your basic structure. And, as you know, I'm the kind of poet who believes in form and proportion; – everything in its right place and nothing missing.'[24] This is a very revealing comment, since his wife Yvonne had one breast missing, and feared to lose another. Yvonne, who had originally been slim and blonde, had also put on a lot of weight and by 1974 was looking rather matronly. Norman confessed that he sometimes peeped at women bathing topless in the dunes near Haverigg. There are so many references in his letters to appreciation of the female form (including flat-chested Russian ballerinas and a naked Jenny Agutter in 'Walkabout') that it's difficult not to come to the conclusion that there was a degree of unrequited longing and frustration. It's also impossible not to speculate that he may have been in love with his much younger cousin.

Norman liked the company of women and when he was friendly with

CHAPTER SIXTEEN

married couples often preferred the wives to the men, however well they got on. He had met the poet David Wright in the late sixties, when David was living near Keswick with his wife Philippa. David Wright had been born in South Africa and was profoundly deaf – the result of scarlet fever when he was seven years old. Norman found his poetry difficult – he described the rhythms as 'halting' – and thought that this was a result of David's deafness, but he had a great respect for David's reputation as a critic and an editor. Norman was very fond of his wife Philippa, who had been an actress, and his letters were sometimes addressed to her rather than her husband. Norman couldn't remember how to spell her name – his spelling was never good – and so he always called her Pippa. David and Pippa gave Norman a great deal of moral support during the period when he was unable to write. Norman was very grateful that David had included him in the new *Faber Anthology of Modern Verse* and told him that 'younger readers depend almost entirely on such collections if they are to know that one exists – at least they do if one hasn't brought out any new volumes for some time.' It was a welcome comfort after Norman's experience with Philip Larkin.[25]

Norman sometimes went into schools, and often did readings for local writers' groups, appearing occasionally at the Brewery Arts Centre in Kendal, which had a thriving poetry community, and also at the Maryport Settlement where a new poetry workshop group had been set up. There were many young poets in Cumbria who were encouraged by Norman Nicholson. Among them were individuals who went on to develop a national – and in some cases international – reputation; Geoffrey Holloway, William Scammell, Neil Curry, Chris Pilling, Patricia Pogson and Janni Howker. It was through these group meetings that Norman met a local journalist called Irvine Hunt, who was also a poet, and they became quite a successful 'double act'. Norman described him for Doreen after a reading at nearby Ulverston – 'Irvine Hunt, with whom I shared the reading, is a young man – actually he's over forty, but looks much younger – who has made a considerable name locally, and in mid-Lancashire, reading his own verses, mostly with folk and pop groups and the like. It's light verse, easy to take in, often topical, full of laughs, but neatly made, for the most part, and delivered with great spirit. He goes down very well with the teenagers, but he's quite modest about his own gifts, and, at least he's never obscene! As a person, Yvonne and I like him quite a lot. Certainly, he puts over his act with such vivacity, that a more serious poet might have found it very difficult to follow him without the experience to win over the audience in a different way – which, not to be unduly modest, I've got! … we have a respect for each other.'[26] The two men, very different, became firm friends.

One of the young poets who was encouraged by Norman was Mike Smith, who attended the Kendal poetry workshops. He was occasionally in Millom and one day he plucked up the courage to knock on Norman's door. Mike was surprised to be welcomed in and asked to stay to lunch. Norman generously agreed to do an interview with him on the subject of poetry and Norman also offered to make a recording of some of his poems. It was all done with an amateur tape recorder and microphone and the sound quality wasn't of the best, but the interview is a fascinating insight into Norman's mind. He told Mike that he saw himself as an entertainer rather than a philosopher and as an observer rather than a participant. Norman regarded that 'detachment' from the community as necessary for the poetry. When asked how his poetry had changed over the years, he explained that his poems now had to be written within 'the limitations of my own breathing' which affected the length of the lines. It's clear on the tape that his breathing is husky and shallow – the effects of years of lung disease – difficult for one who regards himself as an oral poet. Even when putting words on the page, Norman is thinking about the words spoken aloud, shaping the phrases. One of the most interesting moments occurs when Mike probes Norman about the choice he made to stay in Millom and the effect it has had on his development. Did he think it important for a poet to have the society of other poets, Mike asked, and to be in touch with other poets? Norman declined to answer, stating that he didn't have anything to say on the subject.[27]

Chapter Seventeen

In September 1977 Norman had a big surprise. He received a letter from the Poet Laureate, Sir John Betjeman, informing Norman that he'd just recommended him for the Queen's Gold Medal for Poetry – one of the highest honours a poet can be given. Norman wrote back to Betjeman that 'to one who has always lived his life so much on the edge of things, this comes as a totally unexpected honour'.[1] In October the formal letter came from the Keeper of the Privy Purse at Buckingham Palace, advising Norman and his guests to be at the Palace on Wednesday 23rd November at 12.15 exactly. Norman hired a morning suit from a shop in Millom and arranged to go to London with Yvonne. They stayed with her sister in Barnes, and Yvonne's nieces, Liz and Sarah, agreed to drive Norman to the palace, in Liz's yellow mini, and they would wait while he and Yvonne went upstairs with the Keeper of the Privy Purse. When they arrived, Liz was allowed to park the car in the palace courtyard, but she and Sarah were astonished to find that they had to walk outside the gates to wait for their uncle and aunt.

Yvonne, proud and excited to be invited to the Palace, was determined to remember every moment, and wrote about it later, to preserve the occasion for posterity. John Betjeman was there, 'improperly dressed' in a crumpled lounge suit and yellow satin tie. He was shown in to the Queen first and after a few moments a buzzer sounded and Norman was 'marched in and announced in ringing tones'. Yvonne was 'delightfully entertained' by one of the Queen's ladies-in-waiting and an equerry. Inside the audience room, the Queen read a few lines of Norman's poem On the Closing of Millom Ironworks, which she had liked, presented the medal and accepted a copy of Norman's latest pamphlet, *Stitch and Stone*. Then she talked about Ted Hughes, who had received the medal the previous year. Norman thought that Ted had made an enormous impression on her. Then it was back to the Keeper of the Privy Purse for large whiskies before leaving to have lunch with John Betjeman. 'Sir John took us all to his home (including the girls) for champagne, then to his local Italian restaurant for lunch'. Yvonne was mortified that she dropped the medal in the road getting out of the car.[2]

Norman certainly got his share of publicity for this award. He was photographed outside the palace with Yvonne and the medal, and appeared on local as well as national television. Friends wrote to congratulate him and Percy Kelly's wife Chris drew a lovely cartoon of Norman with his hand cupped to his ear, asking the Queen to repeat what she'd just said.

The award of the Queen's Gold Medal gave Norman a tremendous psychological boost. In the months that followed he began to write prolifically. Yvonne felt that the award had stimulated him. They planned to visit Norway again in June 1979 – flying to Bergen this time – but it didn't prove as enjoyable as their previous trip. Neither of them was in good health. Norman spent the winter of 1977/78 sleeping on the guest bed in the sitting room, rather than his attic, because of bronchitis, and shortly afterwards he made it his permanent bedroom, leaving the attic free for guests. Yvonne was having a great deal of trouble with her back and neck and was often in great pain. The doctors prescribed traction, but it often gave only temporary relief and the specialist told her that she had some 'deterioration' in the spine. She also had dizzy spells which were attributed to the frequent stretching of her spinal column.

Norman had a great many invitations to read, following the award of the Medal, but he accepted very few. Through the first half of 1978 he did only local readings and found that not even northern audiences could be relied on to give him a good hearing. In April Norman read at the public library in Liverpool and the audience was so noisy and inattentive he refused to read the last poem and cut the evening short. Norman had less and less breath for the performance of poetry. He was impressed by the fact that David Wright would ask his wife Pippa to read for him, and so Norman began to allow Yvonne to read his poems during the second half, in order to rest his voice. In *Black Combe White*, he describes a poetry reading in terms that suggest disillusion. The poet who had once so joyfully reached out to the audience, the poet who needed to be heard, was now finding the experience tough.

> Sixty-mile drive to a reading – arriving by dark,
> The audience sparse, the room unsuitable,
> And bed in a cold hotel.

CHAPTER SEVENTEEN

Only a glimpse of Black Combe on the horizon, 'its unmistakable cleft forehead' dusted with snow, lifts his spirits. The sixty mile drive back towards Black Combe's 'dark, parental presence', is a retreat from alien territory, towards the comfort of the familiar.

> Home at last to the known tight streets,
> The hunched chapels, the long canals of smoke …[3]

During 1978, Norman was writing the poems that would eventually become *Sea to the West*, which many people thought was his finest collection. It contains some of his most famous poems, On the Dismantling of Millom Ironworks, Wall, Beck, Scafell Pike, all the Black Combe poems, the Norwegian poems, and Cornthwaite, the acknowledgement of his own Scandanavian heritage. The tone is elegiac, which is hardly surprising, since Norman was aware that this was probably his final collection. He had always written poetry slowly, working from a narrow field of material, and the seams he mined, like the Hodbarrow iron lodes, were almost worked out. There is less of Millom in the collection and more of the wider Lakeland landscape and its constantly changing character.

> Not the beck only,
> Not just the water –
> The stones flow also,
> Slow
> As continental drift …
> Wide cataracts of rock
> Pour off the fellside …
> Ingleborough and Helvellyn
> Waste daily away …
> The pull of the earth's centre –
> An irresistible momentum,
> Never to be reversed,
> Never to be halted,
> Till the tallest fell
> Runs level with the lowland …[4]

Norman commented, in the Poetry Society magazine, that since *A Local Habitation,* his poetry had become less concerned 'with the stability of a community rooted in a particular locality, than with the many and varied processes of change ... in the world of man and ... in the world of nature'. But the poems are still rooted in the north. Norman quoted Eliot: 'Home is where one starts from', and added – 'It seems to be where I finish'.[5] In his poem The Shadow of Black Combe, Norman anticipates his own death, repeating the local saying that 'everybody born/Under the shadow of Black Combe/Will come back there to die'. But Norman is not leaving anything to chance 'I'm staying here ... One death will do for me'.[6]

In 1978 the last of Norman's prose works was published by Robert Hale. *The Lake District, An Anthology*, was a kind of literary topography of the lakes, a pick-and-mix of poetry and prose, some of it in dialect, written by some of the most distinguished resident and visiting writers across four centuries of literary history. There are excerpts from Wordsworth, Charlotte Brontë, Jane Austen, Keats, Coleridge, Daniel Defoe and many others. It is witty, broad ranging, and an absolute treasure-trove of writing about the Lake District. Contemporary writers are poorly represented. Norman himself appears, with only brief contributions from Kathleen Raine, Irvine Hunt, Melvyn Bragg and David Wright. Norman had spent many hours in the Millom library reading books sent through the inter-library system, in order to compile the anthology, and many more hours at home writing letters to seek permission to use quotations still in copyright. This time the book had been typed by Yvonne, who had also acted as his research assistant.

Norman was also working on the selection of poems for a projected book of selected poems that Faber were hoping to bring out, drawn from his first three collections, but the project moved slowly. In 1980, Liverpool University conferred an Honorary Doctorate on Norman, which was deeply appreciated. There were many family jokes about 'Dr Nicholson, I presume' but he felt uncomfortable about being teased on this subject. *Sea to the West* was launched at the Poetry Society in London on the 4th June 1981. It was welcomed by Norman's friends and lovers of his poetry. The Cornish poet Charles Causley, who had kept up a regular correspondence with him, wrote to say that 'with so much awful stuff sloshing around the poetry scene, your book beams away like a lighthouse'.[7] Anne Ridler hoped that the success of *Sea to the West* would prod Faber to bring out a collected edition of Norman's poetry, though they were still dragging their feet on the Selected.

Norman's poetry was now being noticed by a younger generation. Matt Simpson, a poet born in Liverpool and published by northern press

CHAPTER SEVENTEEN

Bloodaxe, wrote in *PN Review* that although *A Local Habitation* had been 'greeted as a genial work and recommended for its colloquial modesties', *Sea to the West* had given Norman the critical attention he deserved but 'has generally been deprived of'. Ian Hamilton, poet and editor, with a reputation for being tough, began his *Sunday Times* piece on Norman in the negative tone he had come to expect: 'Norman Nicholson is one of those poets everyone rather admires but hardly anyone gets excited about. He crops up in surveys under "regional" and his small but glumly loyal following tends to have some Lake District axe to grind'. Ian Hamilton then made the surprising admission that, having read *Sea to the West*, that assessment of Norman's work was quite wrong.[8] The ecological aspect of Norman's poetry was also acknowledged. Peter Porter in *The Observer*, complimented Norman on 'some of the most attractive and vigorous writing about nature to appear for many years'.[9] Fleur Adcock, a New Zealand poet living in Britain, selected Norman as her 'Poet of the Month', though not without qualification. Like others she noticed what Norman himself called his 'knick-knack conceits', and she picked out his tendency to drift 'into slightly portentous philosophising with a fondness for paradox'. However she, too, praised the 'strong verbs and craggy nouns' he chose to represent the landscape.

Philip Gardner also entered the debate in the *Poetry Review*, describing Norman's career as 'distinguished and lonely'. Gardner commended his 'musical intricacy' and observed that *Sea to the West* 'hints at finality' and had a 'bleak, emotional power'. He was another voice calling for a collected edition of poems from Faber.[10] Robin Skelton in the magazine *Stand* wrote a thoughtful piece of literary criticism of the kind that Norman hardly ever received. It is a generous summing up of his abilities as a poet. 'Norman Nicholson is a poet of major significance. His poetry is at once intellectually rigorous and filled with deep humanity. It is a poetry of both delight and query, of both celebration and predicament. It continually asserts with zest, humour and dignity, the splendid complexity of the human creature, and the astonishing richness of the experience of being alive'.[11]

But by far the best publicity that Norman had, was to be featured on *Kaleidoscope*, where the collection was reviewed by Melvyn Bragg and the programme included readings by Norman and an interview with Melvyn. In conversation Norman states that he writes 'consonantal poetry' designed to be read aloud and listened to, adding, 'I am very much concerned with poetry as sound'. Norman read Beck, Scafell, and the programme ended with Sea to the West.[12] A week after the launch of *Sea to the West*, Norman was awarded an OBE, on the 18th June 1981. It seemed that public recognition of his work had finally arrived.

Throughout the previous nine months Yvonne had been feeling ill. She was having the usual trouble with her back and with a 'pinched nerve' in her neck. In September 1980 she had also developed 'a cough that interrupted her speech' which was at first attributed to her allergic asthma, then to bronchitis and then to a suspected hiatus hernia. A chest specialist examined her and told her that there was 'nothing organically wrong with the chest'. After Christmas she was no better and was sent to an Ear, Nose and Throat specialist who also reported that he could find nothing wrong with her. Norman told Doreen that Yvonne was 'not satisfied ... that everything is being done to help her, and our doctor is going to arrange a private consultation with the Whitehaven surgeon to make sure that nothing that can be done is being overlooked.'[13] By April Yvonne was suffering from swollen eyes and still feeling dizzy, which the specialists attributed to 'the pressure of arthritis on a nerve'. She was no longer able to drive. On the 22nd June, in the same week that Norman received news of his OBE, Yvonne discovered a cyst in her breast, where the lump had been in 1976. The consultant again told her that it was 'probably harmless', but they might take it out if it didn't disappear of its own volition. Norman, who appears to have suspected something more serious, immediately cancelled all poetry readings that had been planned for July. Yvonne was taken into hospital for tests on the 17th of that month and ten days later Norman wrote to Doreen. 'I fear I have bad news, and am writing now so that Yvonne does not have to tell you over the phone. Last week we learned that she has developed cancer of the lung'. This was, Norman told Doreen, probably linked to 'the breast-cancer of fifteen years ago'. The only possible treatment was 'some form of drugs ... and perhaps some radiation... we can only hope that we'll get at least a remission of reasonable health, which, I'm determined, she is to enjoy as much as she possibly can'.[14] Norman cancelled all his engagements for the summer and autumn, including a trip to Buckingham Palace in November to accept his OBE.

Yvonne, who was already too ill to get out of bed, was admitted to the local hospital at Whitehaven for a course of chemotherapy. In the weeks before her admission she had recruited two young women to clean the house and prepare meals while she was away. Margaret Spencer and Jean Clarke were both Millom girls and Margaret had originally been one of Yvonne's students. She confessed to being rather in awe of her former teacher. They managed the household for Norman while Yvonne was away

CHAPTER SEVENTEEN

and then cared for Yvonne when she was discharged from hospital. At the end of August Yvonne was allowed home 'comfortable and cheerful' despite the loss of her hair. The side effects of the chemotherapy had not been as severe as she had feared and she was up-beat about the future.

Norman was less hopeful about the outcome than Yvonne. He wrote to Doreen that he thought it 'unlikely that she'll ever be very active again'. He added that 'we certainly have a hard time in front of us'. Norman explained that he would be unable to talk freely to Doreen on the phone, because, when Yvonne was within earshot, he always tried to be 'as optimistic as possible. I want Yvonne to be surrounded with an atmosphere of hope as long as this can be managed . . . These anxieties', Norman stressed, 'are for your ears only.' He apologised for burdening Doreen with his worries; 'it is such a comfort to know that there is someone to whom I can speak knowing I have real sympathy and affection in return'.[15]

Throughout the winter Yvonne was in and out of hospital for courses of chemotherapy that left her exhausted. The lump in her breast was removed in November. She found it difficult to come to terms with the loss of her hair and bought a wig. In January she was told that she would have to go to Newcastle General Infirmary for radiotherapy that would probably last about four weeks. This was a long way from home. Yvonne's own family rallied round and her nieces drove up from London to take her to Newcastle and planned to visit at weekends. Norman was to stay in Millom and told Doreen that 'we both feel that it would be unwise for me to try to get over to see her ... the hazards of the train journey, at that time of the year, are too great'. Yvonne also feared that he might contract a lung infection in hospital and was resigned to going alone. It was a bleak prospect.

Yvonne wrote to Norman every day while she was in Newcastle. Her letters are optimistic, full of hope that one day their normal lives can be restored and that she will be able to take him out in the car again. Yvonne is determined to get well 'as permanently as possible ... I know what this separation means to you, my darling, and I shall do all in my power to make certain it need not occur again'. She describes being woken at 6am on a winter morning, the view from her window – a city view with a busy road – and the frustration of not being able to get the *Guardian*. Yvonne rang Norman in the evening when she could get the telephone trolley. Norman apparently sounded tense and anxious, and in the letters she tells him to keep cheerful and listen to music. Yvonne found the radiotherapy very trying and distracted herself by reading novels from the hospital library and Norman's new collection, which she had taken with her. 'What put me on the road to some sort of recovery was dipping into *Sea to the West*. It brought you very close and gave me courage to continue'. She commented on Norman's letters to her – 'your spelling … is most amusing – quite apart from the slips of the typewriter. It's just as well one of us can spell'. Norman's letters to Yvonne have not survived.

There were more side effects from the radiation than Yvonne had had from the chemotherapy. It made her feel 'languid and sleepy', her skin burned and she developed a rash on her neck and face. She was very disappointed to be told that she needed more than the sixteen treatments originally envisaged and wrote Norman a poignant letter. 'My darling, I too long for you and could howl my eyes out over the possible delay. But time passes, however slowly, and as long as it means there has to be no return here I shall put up with it… I've missed you sorely, today especially, my love to you my dearest one, your Yvonne'.[16]

Although Norman was unable to visit, Yvonne was often overwhelmed with visitors she was too tired to cope with. Rene and Sid Chaplin were among the friends who came, as well as Norman's fellow poets Jon Silkin and Michael Standen, and Doreen came over from Carlisle when she could. Yvonne's family made a big effort, despite the distances. Rosemary, Eric, Liz and Sarah drove up from the south of England and London at weekends. But, far from getting better, Yvonne's condition was deteriorating. In her last letter, Yvonne told Norman that x-rays had shown that there was 'a shadow on the pleura'. This was not good news. Yvonne was discharged from hospital at the end of February, but it was not the triumphant homecoming they had hoped for.

At the beginning of May Norman wrote to Doreen that Yvonne had taken 'a considerable turn for the worse'. Soon after her discharge from Newcastle, she had begun to experience pins and needles and numbness in her legs, which the doctors initially thought was a response to the radio or chemo-therapies. But it soon became clear that it was the disease itself. Yvonne could barely walk across the room and found stairs impossible. Tests showed that the cancer had attacked the nerves at the base of the spine which controlled her legs. Norman recorded sadly that 'Yvonne is not likely to be able to walk again except in a very limited way'. He was anxious that Yvonne shouldn't know what he feared, though he admitted to Doreen that she probably was aware of the seriousness of the position. Neither of them was being frank with the other.[17] All normal routines had been abandoned. The household was being run by Margaret and Jean, and District Nurses came in and out during the day to treat Yvonne. At the end

CHAPTER SEVENTEEN

of August she went into hospital in Whitehaven for more injections into the base of her spine to slow the spread of the tumour, but her condition quickly worsened. The cancer was galloping through her body. She drifted in and out of consciousness and, apparently, words were said that Norman believed to be hostile towards himself. The poet Matt Simpson was one of those who went to see Yvonne at the end of August and was distressed by her condition as she lay, hollow eyed and unresponsive – despairing, he thought – in the hospital bed, staring at a future she could barely comprehend. Yvonne was only sixty one.

On the 5th September Norman wrote to David Wright; 'I have to tell you that Yvonne died on Tuesday last in the West Cumberland Hospital at Whitehaven'. He had buried his newly-arrived copy of the *Selected Poems*, which had been dedicated to Yvonne, with her body, and told David, 'I'm receiving enormous help, but, after the last three months, which have seemed the most purposeful of my whole life, I now find things very bleak'.[18] Yvonne's funeral was held at St George's on Friday September 3rd 1982, and it was attended by many members of the family, friends and Yvonne's ex-pupils and colleagues. She was buried in the new part of the graveyard, facing Black Combe, and Norman chose the last three lines of Sea to the West, for what he intended to be their joint gravestone, altering the wording slightly.

Let our eyes at the last be blinded
Not by the dark
But by dazzle.[19]

Norman's niece Liz came to stay after Yvonne's death and helped Norman to sort through her possessions and dispose of them. Most of her belongings and valuables were left to Norman, but her engagement ring and the rings she had inherited from her own mother and from Rose, were left to Liz and Sarah. Norman was grateful for the presence of his nieces. He was overwhelmed by the number of people – more than two hundred – who wrote to send their condolences, all of which required a reply. The poet Charles Causley wrote to say that 'to think of Yvonne, of you, of your poetry, was quite naturally to think of all three; indissolubly ONE.'[20] Many commented on Yvonne's humour and sweetness and her importance in Norman's life. Anne Ridler told him to 'hold fast to the knowledge of all the happiness you gave her, and your care of her through this illness, to blot out the words spoken when she was no longer conscious. What courage

215

she had'. She adds a post script – 'Enrica has been in Italy, but I'm about to write to her'.[21] Percy Kelly, who was now living in Norfolk, sent one of his most beautiful illuminated letters to Norman, decorated with red roses, remembering Yvonne, and was affronted that he didn't receive a prompt response.

One of the most moving letters came from Ted Hughes, thinking of Norman's loneliness after Yvonne's death. 'I know how landscapes are changed absolutely when that happens.' He talked about 'how much value we instinctively put on real roots'. Above all, he told Norman 'I hope you keep on writing. These times when writing seems of all activities the most trivial and inadequate, are when it's most important – for oneself – I'm so sure of that'. And he signed his letter 'Love, Ted'. [22]

Chapter Eighteen

Yvonne had left a system in place for Norman so that after she died, he would be looked after. As well as the housekeepers, Jean and Margaret, various friends had been recruited to cook occasional meals and take him out. These included a younger colleague from the school, Peggy Troll, whose sister-in-law had been one of Yvonne's nurses, and Bessie Schiff (nee Satterthwaite) who had recently returned to Millom with her husband after his retirement. Bessie supplied Norman with steak pies and cakes and the occasional pizzas he had taken a liking to. Another friend brought venison casseroles for the freezer. Irvine Hunt was one of those who offered company and transport, and Doreen came down every other weekend to take him out for a pub lunch and bring him a new supply of the single malt whisky he loved to drink.

Norman wrote to Yvonne's sister in September, shortly after her death, of the lack of purpose he now felt. 'Obviously my life with Yvonne has been quite wonderful for me, and, in a strange way, in spite of all the sadness and anxieties and restrictions, the last twelve months have been among the most rewarding'.[1] Rosemary had asked Norman for his shirt collar size so that she could buy him some clothes, but he replied that he hadn't 'the slightest idea, having never, in the course of my life so far, bought a shirt for myself'.[2] He was now forced to do many things that he had never done before, including cook some of his own food, even if it was only defrosting a meal left by a friend.

Norman was distracted in March 1983 by the arrival of Melvyn Bragg, a local writer called Bill Rollinson, and a film crew to make a series of short programmes on the Lake District. Norman was filmed in a boat on Coniston water, in conversation with Melvyn about the Lake Poets, and subsequently reading Sea to the West. He enjoyed it enormously and Melvyn was very happy, observing that Norman's comments on Wordsworth 'had power' and were 'extremely well organised'.[3] He was also getting quite a lot of reviewing again 'which helps the illusion of being of some use'. He was asked to review a new publication about Charles Williams who had been 'almost forgotten' since he died in 1945. Norman had once been very familiar with Williams' work, but now found reviewing it a difficult task involving 'a lot of exploratory and revisionary reading'. He was delighted to find, among his newspaper cuttings, a long detailed article in the *TLS* 'which seemed to me to be very good and from which I thought I might quote'. Shortly afterwards he was amused to discover that he had actually written it himself in 1961.

September 1983 was the first anniversary of Yvonne's death and Doreen came down to stay with him at Norman's invitation. 'I'll need company – sympathetic company – even more than usual'.[4] Since Yvonne's death he had become much more emotionally dependent on Doreen and at one point asked her if she would come to Millom to live with him. But, although very fond of him, Doreen had just bought a house in Carlisle and had a job she loved and wasn't willing to make such a big change. Norman appears to have been worried that he had in some way harmed their relationship – after a visit to Doreen he wrote, 'I was glad, too, that we had that little talk which helped to clear up any small embarrassment I may have caused you'. He then goes on to talk about the different qualities of his various women friends in comparison to Doreen – 'You are less demonstrative than Liz and less uninhibited than Gudrun [a German girl, an acquaintance of Yvonne who came to stay occasionally], but you are closer to me in age and background and family relationship and can be a friend in a way that the others can't'.[5] Afterwards, although Doreen was still 'his dearest little cousin' there is very little in the letters that could be construed as flirtatious.

The volume of *Selected Poems*, which had been published just before Yvonne died, didn't get many reviews, perhaps because it came out so quickly after *Sea to the West*. Norman was very disappointed. He was no longer writing poetry – the flow generated by the Queen's Gold Medal had dried up and Yvonne's death had killed even the impulse to write. When Craig Raine at Faber asked Norman for a poem for an anthology, Norman told him that he hadn't written anything for two years and that his wife's death had left him numb; 'the power won't switch on, though I think the wiring is still in good order'. He drops a hint, in his letter to Craig, that a 'Collected Nicholson' would be very welcome 'before I finally sign off'.[6] Norman was now approaching sixty nine and beginning to think a lot

CHAPTER EIGHTEEN

about signing off. Professor Brian Cox, one of the editors of the *Critical Quarterly* and head of the English Department at Manchester University, had been trying for a long time to persuade Norman to leave his papers to the John Rylands Library. As Manchester had awarded him his first honorary degree it seemed to be an appropriate destination. Norman was finally persuaded and it was subsequently agreed that his manuscripts and letters would be deposited there.

Poetry had not quite finished with Norman yet, however. Oxford University Press approached him to ask whether he would contribute to an anthology of children's poetry called *The Candy Floss Tree*. Norman did in fact have some poems he had written some years ago, for a volume of children's poetry which was to have been published by the bankrupt Pergamon Press. Some of these poems – Weeds, Nicholson Suddenly, and Halley's Comet – had already appeared in his collections for adults, but there were others including Off to Outer Space Tomorrow Morning and Ten Yards High that had never found a home. He 'dug them out of the drawer', polished them up and sent them to OUP, who 'liked them very much'. The poems were dedicated to his nieces Liz and Sarah. To Norman's own surprise, there were occasional new poems. When Liz got married in 1984, she asked if he could write a poem for her. Norman found himself able to compose verses which were read out at her wedding reception. Epithalamium for a Niece, published in the *London Magazine* in July, became one of his most anthologised poems.

For her wedding present Norman sent Liz a cheque so that she could buy one of Percy Kelly's paintings, which she had always admired. Percy was currently living in Norfolk alone, since his wife Chris had divorced him in despair. He had become even more eccentric over the years and was currently living as a woman and signing his letters 'Roberta'. Although he was no longer writing to Norman, he had begun to send letters to Yvonne's sister, Liz's mother Rosemary. Liz and her new husband called to see Percy, while visiting relatives in Norfolk, but were rebuffed on the doorstep. They were saddened by his gaunt appearance and the chaos they could see through the open door behind him. Percy asked them to ring the following Friday and agreed to have some paintings for them to look at, but when they telephoned again he refused to see them. Liz had been horrified by the poverty that he was living in and ordered coal and groceries to be delivered. The following year, Percy invited Liz and her husband north to look at paintings they might want to buy. It was a long journey from Dorset, this time with a small baby. Once again, Percy refused to let them look at anything and turned them away, presenting them with a small tin of spaghetti hoops for the baby. Liz never did get her wedding present. Ironically, Percy was in desperate need of the money, and was admitted to hospital shortly afterwards suffering from malnutrition.

Norman had a bad attack of bronchitis in November 1983, which lingered long enough to spoil his plans for Christmas. 'The truth is, that while I am still coughing and wheezing and puffing and panting, I don't feel fit to be seen.' There was also depression – 'it's horrid being ill all on your own'.[7] He was still very unwell for his seventieth birthday in January 1984. His friends had planned a 'Festschrift' for him – a volume of poetry dedicated to him, edited by William Scammell to be launched at a party at the Lake District Visitor Centre at Brockhole. Ted Hughes, Seamus Heaney, Roy Fuller, George Szirtes, Anne Ridler and Craig Raine were among the contributors, and there were friends closer to home, such as Matt Simpson, Geoffrey Holloway and David Wright. Because of Norman's illness, presentation of the collection, now called *Between Comets: Norman Nicholson at 70*, was delayed until later in the year. Norman was still unwell in the spring and had another attack of bronchitis at the beginning of May, writing to Doreen that 'my breathing sounds like a saw at work and any extra movement, such as climing [sic] the stairs, leaves me panting for some minutes'. He cancelled all his engagements, including a planned holiday with Doreen to Scotland – 'I know I won't have the strength'. Norman was 'particularly anxious' to be 'in best form' for the arrival of another TV crew at the beginning of June.[8]

Back in February 1982, while Yvonne was in the Newcastle hospital, Norman had had an enquiry from Granada Television about his appearance in a television documentary, part of a series of South Bank Shows, fronted by Melvyn Bragg. This was a considerable accolade and would put Norman and his work in front of a very large national audience. After Yvonne's death, another approach was made and this time Norman was able to confirm his involvement. He always enjoyed television work and apparently TV and radio crews liked working with him because he was very professional and able to do most things in one take. The South Bank Show contract was quite lucrative – 'in the region of £1500' – including copyright payments for the poetry he was going to read in it.

Bill Rollinson, who had been involved in the Lake Poets programme, did the background research on Norman's life, his family, and the locations that might be included. The director was an award-winning art film-maker called John Read who was making his first film for the South Bank Show,

CHAPTER EIGHTEEN

and John decided that he would also like to do the interview with Norman. It was carefully explained, by Granada, that Melvyn might not have enough spare time to devote exclusively to this programme, which might mean too concentrated and tiring a period of talking for Norman. He accepted the explanation and was reassured that Melvyn 'has wanted to do this programme for years'.[9]

The interviews were done in the mornings over two weeks, John Read talking intimately to Norman in his living room, in front of the fireplace that had been there since he was a child, surrounded by his books and treasured possessions. Even though the recording sessions were strictly rationed, Norman's voice sounds gravelly and breathless by the end of each take. In the afternoons the TV crew went out to film the location shots – the streets of Millom, the brooding presence of Black Combe, the river Duddon, Scafell, and Wastwater. Norman was filmed walking, with the aid of a stick, along the sea defences at Haverigg. He looked extremely fragile.

The result was, according to John Read, 'one of the strongest and most direct shows Melvyn has up his sleeve for the coming season', and the programme was provisionally scheduled for transmission on October the twenty first.[10] It is an excellent piece of documentary filming. Melvyn's introduction describes Norman as a 'worthy successor' to Wordsworth, and the camera zooms in on Norman in his armchair, reading an excerpt from his poem The Whisperer. He stares directly at the screen with large eyes magnified by owl-like spectacles, and his personality beams at the viewer through the camera lens. The film expertly connects Norman's poetry with the landscape – word and image run in synchrony. Norman reads his most famous poems, Wall, Scafell Pike, the River Duddon – as well as the humorous ones – Norman Nicholson Suddenly and Weeds, the latter illustrating his preference for wild flowers rather than hot-house blooms. Norman re-tells the story of being Chairman of the children's concert and recites his prize-winning performance poem Big Steamers from memory, his eyes twinkling with pleasure. In response to questions about his own work, Norman explains that he could never be a Modernist, like Eliot, although he admired him and at first had tried to emulate his style; 'fragmentation' is alien to Norman's own voice, his poems naturally tell a story, or follow an image or an idea through in linear fashion.

Norman had, in fact, just sold Eliot's letters at auction in order to raise money for the Arvon Foundation, an organisation that gives new and inexperienced writers the opportunity to live and work with established authors for a week at a time. Ted Hughes was a great supporter of Arvon, leasing his own house at Lumb Bank in Yorkshire to the Foundation, and Norman knew that Arvon were trying to raise money to buy it outright. Norman had promised them a contribution. Eliot's letters, sold in September, brought in £400.

Norman was told, during the summer of 1984, that the local council was going to propose that he be made 'a Freeman of the Borough'. What followed was an amusing glimpse into local politics. Barrow-in-Furness turned him down because they didn't think he had done enough for the town. Councillors further north were still offended by his 'Windscale' poem, which also worried Millom councillors, since a good proportion of the workforce were employed at the re-named Sellafield Nuclear Plant. But in the end, after some political shuffling, the proposal was approved and Norman was duly elected a Freeman of the Borough of Copeland.

Other honours were being offered. Lancaster was the second university to confer an Honorary Doctorate on Norman, which pleased him, though it inspired a moment of regret. 'When I read the letter, my first feeling of pleasure was almost immediately followed by a sharp pang at the thought that I couldn't tell Yvonne.'[11] Another bronze head, this time by Joan Palmer, was commissioned and unveiled at a ceremony in Millom Library, and a London artist, Michael Browne, came north to paint Norman's portrait for the Poetry Society. Norman's thoughts were still on a Collected Poems as his permanent memorial and he hoped to be able to persuade Faber editor Craig Raine, whom he described as 'an immensely fashionable young poet and leader of the Martians', to sanction it.[12]

Norman was spending some of his time with Irvine Hunt and his wife at their home near Hesket Newmarket. The Schiffs had moved away from Millom to be near their son, and so were no longer able to help Norman as much as they had before. Yvonne's sister Rosemary and her husband came to stay when they could, but they too had jobs and family commitments. Norman's niece Liz was married with a young family and Sarah too was now planning her own wedding, busy with juggling her career and marriage plans. Jean and Margaret were still doing the housekeeping and there was a scattering of visitors who came armed with casseroles and bottles of the single malt whisky he had developed such a taste for. A fan posted one to Norman which broke in transit leaving only a soggy parcel of broken glass. Norman was lonely, though he never talked about it in his letters to friends, which are curiously impersonal, concerned with day to day trivia and literary engagements, sprinkled with humorous anecdotes. But he

CHAPTER EIGHTEEN

cut two uncharacteristically emotional poems, by Frances Harland, from magazines and kept them among his things in a folder marked 'Cuttings relating to personal and family matters'. One of the poems was called 'Grief' and the other 'The Sunday Garden' and they are full of the kind of sentiment that Norman usually deplored:

> This is her body, when her love has gone,
> Tree without leaves, comb without honey is;
> Grief like a wind moves between skin and bone –
> She is the form and shape of emptiness.[13]

He had begun to depend emotionally on an old friend and colleague of Yvonne's, Peggy Troll, who had taken over Yvonne's post at school when she retired. Peggy now drove Norman around to readings, took him for outings and accompanied him on a holiday in Yorkshire, though it was sometimes difficult since she was also looking after her elderly mother. Norman became very fond of Peggy and, when Halley's Comet made its return trip to earth in 1986 wrote a poem for her, Comet Come, published in *The Listener*. Norman's own father had seen Halley's Comet on its previous visit and he had waited eagerly to see the spectacular display Joe had described. But 1986 was one of its most disappointing manifestations. 'Faint phosphorescence in the sky … a barely/Distinguishable blur'. Norman wonders what the comet will look down on when it re-appears in 2061.

> A wiser world, or one unpeopled,
> Dead as the asteroidal dust
> It hoovers, on its orbit, through?[14]

Norman's work was attracting rather more critical attention as he grew older. Not all of it was good. Peter Swaab, in the *Cambridge Review*, described Norman as an 'oddity' in 20th century poetry. He wrote a retrospective of Norman's published poetry, which he believed had been too heavily influenced by T.S. Eliot. 'The influence of Eliot was profound enough, I think, to inhibit the emergence of Nicholson's own poetic voice'. Swaab pointed out Norman's weaknesses – the temptation to overload his lines with imagery, and the lack of 'self' in the poetry. *Five Rivers* and *Rock Face*, he felt, lacked direction despite the display of a 'considerable technical gift'. *The Pot Geranium* showed the poet maturing, using more Anglo Saxon language and avoiding abstraction, in a way that 'has something in common with Seamus Heaney'. In the later poetry, Swaab approves the move into more personal subject matter, observing that perhaps – 'it was Eliot's notion of impersonality ... which held him back'. Peter Swaab concluded that it was the limitations of Norman's location and his stubborn 'rootedness' that ultimately prevented him developing in new directions and 'set him apart from the mainstream of 20th century poetry'.[15]

In the same year, Norman gave an interview to his friend David Wright which was published in *PN Review*. It is a very revealing piece of journalism – David Wright knew Norman well enough to ask probing questions and Norman trusted him enough to give answers. When asked about the language he had used in the poems, Norman admitted to borrowings from the old Lallans dialect poetry which he described as 'the classical vernacular vocabulary' of Cumbria, adding defensively, 'I believe I've a right to inherit them'. Lallans is a version of Lowland Scots, which permeated the dialects of the north of the county but which is quite separate from the Norse derived dialects of the uplands and valleys of central Cumbria. Norman used them both and insisted that the sound of his poetry was of the utmost importance. He told David that he recited his poems 'over and over and over' to himself while composing – 'sort of hypnotising' himself into the poem.

Asked if he regretted not going to university Norman admitted that he did, particularly 'I regret not having been trained in the techniques of criticism'. But he added that if he had, it was possible that he might have become a teacher and not a poet at all. Norman still maintained that he didn't regret not having more intellectual stimulation. 'I wrote a lot of letters' and had 'much closer contact with the sort of people whom many poets never come in contact with at all'. Asked to sum up his legacy, Norman states that 'I do think that, looking at my poetry as a whole, I did survey and commemorate the period of the heavy industrial revolution in the North of England as seen in one particular town'.[16]

1986 was a year of deaths. Sylvia Lubelsky's husband Maurice died and she wrote to Norman about the difficulty of tackling household tasks alone. Sid Chaplin died suddenly in January at a writers' conference. In February Pippa Wright died from cancer, leaving Norman's friend David a widower. In a letter to David Norman apologised for not coming to the funeral, 'standing about in the cold is murderous for me', and wrote words of condolence. David had written a moving elegy to his wife which Norman liked very much, and he commented on it, and on their joint

CHAPTER EIGHTEEN

bereavements, in a postscript to the letter:

> 'I think it's just self-deception to say – as people said of Yvonne when I did my South Bank Show; "she'll have seen it and enjoyed it." But I think you may allow yourself to feel that Pippa would have been proud to know that she would be remembered in such a poem. Or, at the very least, you may feel that you are carrying on with your work in the way she would have hoped you would do. One cannot just go on living in memory – that is a kind of mental suicide. But the life I am living now is the life which Yvonne made possible in the years when we were together. I'm sure you will feel much the same about Pippa, and the best either of us can do is to make the most of what they have left to us.'[17]

Millom, degraded by unemployment, was no longer the same and Norman was bewildered by the changing atmosphere. His front window was vandalised and he told friends that he was often taunted by 'louts' in the street, who associated him with school and exams. Norman's eccentric physical appearance also made him a target. Though shaken, Norman bravely carried on. Peggy was now looking after him and managing 'his two girls', Jean and Margaret. He listened to music in the evenings, with a glass of malt whisky, and watched late night films, and sometimes cricket, in bed. He wrote a lot of letters, which are full of concern for his friends and their day to day lives – he chats about everything from wedding presents to their health. He sent an advert for saucepans to his niece Sarah, who was getting married in the autumn, and discussed holidays and babies. One of his carers, Jean was pregnant again and he joked about her being 'as round as humpty dumpty'.

Sarah was married in November, but Norman was not well enough to make the long, winter journey south. He sent presents and wrote that he was glad to see both Yvonne's engagement ring and Rosetta's on her fingers in the photographs. Norman was very frail. Several winters of severe bronchitis had affected his already damaged lungs. He sometimes found breathing difficult, particularly when it was cold, and described himself as 'hibernating' during the winter. He was extremely thin and it's possible that there was also a degree of osteoporosis in view of what happened next. Norman himself seemed to be aware of his declining health. At the beginning of 1987, he began to make arrangements for the disposition of his estate. He gave his lawyer power of attorney, in case he became incapable, or had to go into hospital. St George's vicarage had just been converted into a rest home for the elderly and Norman thought it might be a 'convenient spot to end up in'.

At the beginning of May, Norman went to Liverpool to stay with his friends Dr and Mrs Barnes, in order to give his annual poetry reading there. He sat on the bed to prepare for his reading and accidentally dropped the book on the floor. When he bent down to pick it up there was a piercing pain in his chest. Norman had snapped a rib. The reading was cancelled and he was taken to hospital in Liverpool. Unhappy to be so far from home, Norman arranged to be admitted to the cottage hospital in Millom. Dr and Mrs Barnes drove him half way up the motorway and Peggy Troll met them to drive Norman home. Unfortunately, his condition deteriorated in the cottage hospital; he had what was described by his doctor as a 'spontaneous pneumothorax' and he was taken to the West Cumberland Infirmary – the same hospital in which Yvonne had died – and put into intensive care. The broken rib appeared to have collapsed his one good lung, and the other was reduced to only a quarter of its capacity by tuberculosis and repeated bouts of bronchitis. It was clear that he was extremely ill.

The doctors were pessimistic, but wanted to perform a tracheotomy in order to put Norman on a ventilator to give the punctured lung a chance to heal. Around Norman's bed, some of his friends and relatives felt that Norman himself would not want any kind of intrusive surgical intervention, but others believed that his life ought to be prolonged as long as possible. In the end the doctors performed the tracheotomy. Norman was now unable to speak. He wrote on a piece of paper for Irvine Hunt when he came to visit, 'They have taken away my voice'. It was a bitter irony that recalled his time in the sanatorium. When Doreen visited, she found Norman utterly bewildered by the procedure and drew diagrams of his bronchial tubes to show him what had been done and to reassure him that once his lungs had healed and he could breathe on his own, the device would be removed and he'd be able to talk again. Norman's nieces came to visit, as well as his sister-in-law Rosemary. Norman scrawled illegible notes on pieces of paper – last messages that no one could read. After three weeks of confusion and discomfort, Norman finally lost consciousness and died in his sleep on May 30th 1987. He was seventy three.

The funeral was held at St George's Church on Friday the 5th June. It was 'family flowers only', and donations were invited to support Millom Hospital, which was threatened with closure. The church was packed with family and friends, including Enrica Garnier who came even though she

CHAPTER EIGHTEEN

had had no contact with Norman since he broke off their engagement. The congregation sang the rousing Wesleyan favourite, 'Thine be the Glory, risen conquering son', and Norman's poem Sea to the West was read. Summer traffic on the roads held up some of those who travelled across the Lake District to be there. Norman's friend William Scammell was one of them, arriving just in time for the interment in the new graveyard Norman had described in one of his poems – a field where once the dray horses had been allowed to run free on their weekends off, galloping along the wall beside the cricket pitch. In the poem, Norman had anticipated his own release:

…And when, one end-of-season day, they lead me
Up through the churchyard gate

To that same
Now consecrated green – unblinkered and at last delivered
Of a life-time's

Load of parcels – let me fling
My hooves at the boundary wall and bang them down again,
Making the thumped mud ring.[18]

Norman was laid to rest with Yvonne, facing Black Combe. But, although Norman had been silenced by death, his poetry continued on. Norman had once written about the fact that sound waves ripple out from the planet across the universe. 'I have heard it said,' he wrote, 'that sounds made by the human voice last far longer than we are aware of. They set up vibrations in the air which continue, fainter and fainter, spreading into space long after the human ear can detect them'. It's good to imagine Norman's voice whispering out into the solar system, fragments of sound, hefted from his imperfect lungs, drifting off into eternity.[19]

POSTSCRIPT

It was a great surprise to his grieving relatives that Norman, who had always been frugal and never lived in any kind of affluent style, left £214,170.00 in his will. Much of this money had been made by speculating in stocks and shares, particularly privatised utilities. Norman had developed quite a talent for this after Yvonne's death. He had left his property and belongings between three people – his sister-in-law Rosemary inherited the house and the 'chattels' it contained, Irvine Hunt and his family inherited the copyrights to Norman's work, though not the manuscripts themselves, and Peggy Troll inherited his residual estate – the bulk of the money after handsome legacies had been paid to his nieces and also to individual friends.

Norman's family were deluged with letters of condolence. Anne Ridler wrote to Rosemary that 'Norman's death leaves a sad lacuna in the English literary world, and altho' we couldn't meet often, I cherished his letters and the knowledge that he was in the world'.[1] Matt Simpson wrote to say that 'It was a privilege being a friend of Norman'. He had been 'a sort of father-figure to me'. Matt told Rosemary that he had been in touch with Faber about a 'collected' poems and re-issue in paperback of *Wednesday Early Closing*.[2] Faber and Faber had been unrepresented at the funeral – Charles Monteith was ill and Craig Raine unable to attend, but he did write to Rosemary that Norman was 'a man to whom one instantly warmed, and, of course, a writer to respect'.[3]

After Norman's death the local press floated the idea that the town should establish a suitable memorial to Millom's most famous son, but there were snags. One of the problems was that Norman wasn't universally liked or approved of in Millom. There were many, for whom status and respect were tied to their jobs, who would comment disapprovingly that he had 'Never done a day's work in his life'! Other comments were that

POSTSCRIPT

he was 'always very full of himself', or, as they put it in dialect – he 'thowt well on 'isself'. Even though it was often said with an affectionate twinkle in the eye, such an awareness of his own worth didn't go down well with certain sectors of the community. The newspapers mounted a campaign for a memorial, backed by Norman's supporters, and what followed would have made a good comedy. The town council 'pondered', in the words of the *North West Evening Mail*, 'how best to remember its favourite son'. First of all there was a proposal to name the recreation hall after him, but 'the poet was considered unsuitable by many because his interests were non-sporting'. Then it was proposed that the Millom Library should be renamed the Norman Nicholson Library. This, it was argued, was eminently suitable for a poet and writer. But the library renaming 'did not meet with the council's approval' either, since libraries were a public facility. In the end, it was decided that a blue plaque should be placed on the house in St George's Terrace.

Norman's sister-in-law, Rosemary, who had inherited the house, was very keen that it should be turned into a museum, preserving Norman's unique life. But Norman's money had been left elsewhere and Rosemary simply hadn't enough for the project. She reluctantly put the house up for sale and the contents were dispersed among friends and family. She continued to campaign for a memorial, and for a while, it seemed as though Abbot Hall in Kendal, which was an art gallery but also housed the county museum, might create a room to celebrate his life and work. There were quite a number of Abbott Hall connections. Norman had been a 'Friend' of Abbot Hall and had given some 'very enjoyable' poetry readings there. The proposed room would have been next to the rooms devoted to Arthur Ransome, and to the author of the Postman Pat books. They asked Rosemary for the original fireplace of the living room, which had been sold with the house and they felt they should also have Norman's favourite chair, given to Bessie Schiff. They already had samples of the wallpaper and curtain material, and they had the head sculpted by Josefina de Vasconcellos and the painting of Hodbarrow by Percy Kelly. But in the end, this project also fell through.

Finally, Millom Folk Museum offered to create a room dedicated to Norman's life. It was the most suitable place of all, housed in the school where Norman had studied, part of the museum he had opened. Rosemary Joyce was very pleased, and lent photographs and artefacts owned by the family for the display. There you can see Norman's typewriter, family memorabilia and manuscripts and there are bookcases filled with his books.

Millom Library, unable to re-name itself, opened a 'Norman Nicholson Reading Room'. Peggy Troll and other friends set up the Norman Nicholson Society, with Melvyn Bragg as patron. In St George's Church a new stained glass window was commissioned from Christine Boyce, featuring lines from Norman's poetry. Norman is remembered in Millom.

Meanwhile, his literary friends were campaigning for a 'Collected Poems' from Faber. Matt Simpson, who was pushing hard for it, was horrified by the letter sent to Norman's agent David Higham, saying that the Faber editors felt he was 'better served' by the *Selected Poems*. 'Not doing him the honour of a Collected', Matt wrote, 'is likely to "typecast him as a minor poet forever"! They ought to be ashamed of parading such transparently false reasoning'. He added that 'We must make sure that Faber don't let the sun set on Norman.'[4]

The battle was eventually won, and Neil Curry, a poet, academic and friend of Norman's, became the editor. He wrote to Doreen assuring her that he had loved both Norman and his work and that he would do his utmost to make the collection the best that was possible. Norman Nicholson's *Collected Poems* were published in 1994. The collection's diverse reception echoed the reviews Norman had had during his lifetime. The poet Don Paterson took particular exception to it.

His review was titled 'The Common Place' and he begins it with a definition. 'The greatest English Christian Provincial poet of the late 20th century ... is how Norman Nicholson is often quietly damned'. But Don Paterson didn't find anything in the *Collected Poems* 'to make the reader feel inclined to qualify that deeply modest assessment'. He understood the intended metonymy of Millom representing the universal, but thought that Norman 'appeared to be imaginatively confined by his geography (though of course he was only imaginatively confined by his imagination)'. Paterson criticised a technique that had never developed beyond Norman's first collection, and thought him 'incapable of sustaining an even surface tension throughout a poem'. He acknowledged that Norman had opted for a direct relationship between reader and poet – an accessible style – but 'like the string between two tin cans, the line has to be kept tight if the words are going to sing along it.' Norman Nicholson, according to Don Paterson, was 'no singer'. He singled out Scafell Pike for particular criticism, alleging that it 'could make the *People's Friend* without too much trouble ... so anodyne is its expression of the conceit'. But his most damning statement was that Norman made no distinction between 'an epiphany and a commonplace', ending 'This book is too long and life is too short'.[5]

POSTSCRIPT

Don Paterson's review caused an outcry. Matt Simpson immediately sent a letter to the *Poetry Review*. 'One of the functions of critics these days seems to be to piss on the graves of the not-long-buried ... To celebrate the regional is not at all the same as being – in Paterson's wearily pejorative word – provincial.' Others added their weight to the argument. If the epiphanies in Norman's poems are 'commonplace', then it is because the moments they celebrate are common to all, or at least most, of us. Paterson was forced to admit that, while he still stood by what he had said about the quality of Norman's work, the tone of the review had been inappropriate.

Norman's poetry, and *Sea to the West* in particular, was discussed in Terry Gifford's *Green Voices*, published in 1995. Gifford found strong elements of the Pastoral poetry tradition in this collection – Pastoral defined as the 'escape from adult experience to childhood innocence' personified by a retreat into the innocence of nature. 'Pastoral is the poetry of illusion'.[6] Terry Gifford observes that this element of wish-fulfilment in the title poem, Sea to the West, 'leaves a wistful tone that is reminiscent of Georgian verse'. He thought that Norman's poetry exemplified, 'not only Georgian notions of nature, but more recent Freudian readings of Pastoral'. There is a 'retreat into childhood' and a 'yearning for permanence'. The poet displays an 'ultimate need for a cosiness and comfort expressed with a whimsy which renders the "unshowy" as pretentiously naïve'. Terry Gifford seems to agree with a comment made by Terry Eagleton that Norman's later poetry fails to get beyond 'effective description'. Gifford criticises what he sees as Norman's avoidance of deeper issues in his exploration of urban and rural landscapes; 'the utter simplicity underlying these poems represents a comfortable complacency that is an escape from not only the town but from any sense of real complexities in relating one to the other'.[7]

Alan Hollinghurst in the *London Review of Books* had a contrasting point of view, where the apparent simplicity of the poems was a positive: '... the creative energy of the poems is channelled into description, and the wisdom of the vision, the revelatory magic, is either left latent or drawn into maxims of such simplicity that they send the reader back to the poem. The poem, like the landscape it describes, claims a self-sufficiency and recognises no obligation to be more than itself'.[8]

In the new millennium, after a long period of neglect, Norman's work has begun to be recognised again. The writer and 'Dark Mountaineer', Paul Kingsnorth, wrote a blog for the Dark Mountain network on Norman's environmental writing. Paul concluded that, although 'he's not in the same league as a Hughes or an Auden, ... he is, it seems to me, a better and more important writer than his lack of profile would suggest'. Kingsnorth examined the reasons for Norman's poetry being so overlooked and concluded that it was his provincial location and subject matter that were to blame. '"Lack of profile", after all, means lack of recognition from those who officially recognise Great Writers, by which in turn we mean critics, other writers, publishers and the gatekeepers of the academy, who are largely based in or focused upon London and its satellites. Nicholson lived a long way from London.'

What Norman does offer, in Paul Kingsnorth's opinion, is a vision of the survival of the planet, even after everything that man has done to it. He quotes Scafell Pike as an illustration of what the future might look like:

> A ruin where
> The chapel was; brown
> Rubble and scrub and cinders where
> The gasworks used to be;
> No roofs, no town,
> maybe no men;
> But yonder where a lather-rinse of cloud pours down
> The spiked wall of the sky-line, see,
> Scafell Pike
> Still there

And he goes on to say that: 'a writer who hunkers down, stays in his place, gets to know it but also comes to realise that he is just passing through it: this is surely an approach that will serve us well now. It is also, in these times, fairly unusual. For a writer in particular, there is perhaps nothing more unfashionable, or even unnatural, than staying at home. Maybe that attitude is going to have to change as the world does.'[9]

Norman is now recognised as an environmental writer of some significance. His work has been the subject of a number of studies by Dr David Cooper, most recently in *Poetry and Geography*, which 'sketches a topographical map of shared poetic terrains'.[10] Paul Farley and Michael Symmons Roberts also discussed Norman's depiction of the post-industrial fringe in *Edgelands*, and his name is likely to crop up in any conference on, or celebration of, environmental literature. Norman was 'green before the word was coined'; a chronicler of industrial and post-industrial rural areas, of man's relationship with the earth he stands on. He was aware of the

POSTSCRIPT

perilous nature of the course humanity seemed committed to and imagined its possible consequences with chilling effect.

> The living world of men
> Will take a lunar look, as dead as slag,
> And moon and earth will stare at one another
> Like the cold, yellow skulls of child and mother.[11]

Like Freya in the final scene of his futuristic drama, *Prophesy to the Wind*, Norman's writing points a finger at us all – You! And you! – he asks, 'What message do you send to the children of the future?'

© Kathleen Jones 2013

END NOTES

Abbreviations for frequently used citations

BHD – Brindley Hallam Dennis tapes. Interview given to Mike Smith by Norman Nicholson, circa 1977.
CP – Collected Poems, hardback, Faber and Faber, 1994
C&W – Cumberland and Westmorland, Robert Hale, London, 1949.
Cowper BC – William Cowper, British Council edition, 1960
DC – Doreen Cornthwaite
JRL – John Rylands Library, Manchester University
JRL, DCC – The Doreen Cornthwaite Collection, John Rylands Library, Manchester University
JRL, LL – The Lubelsky Letters, John Rylands Library, Manchester University
MFTD – A Match for the Devil, Faber and Faber, 1955
PG – Philip Gardner, Norman Nicholson, hardback, 1973.
PP – Provincial Pleasures, hardback, 1959, Bookcase reprint, 1993.
WC – William Cowper, John Lehmann, 1951.
WEC – Wednesday Early Closing, Faber Finds Edition, 2008.
WW – William Wordsworth; An Introduction and a Selection, Phoenix House, 1949.

INTRODUCTION

1. JRL LL, Box 2/1 Haywards Heath, 8th Dec. 1986
2. JB to Geoffrey Taylor, 24th Nov. 1944, *Letters*, Vol I, p.350
3. *The Sunday Times*, 11th June 1989
4. PG, Ch.1, P.21
5. PP, May, p.107
6. Rising Five, CP, p.224
7. Dr Philip Gardner, *Norman Nicholson*, Twayne Publishing, 1973 (PG)
8. The Provincial Tradition,' *Times Literary Supplement*, August 15, 1958, p.xix
9. JRL LL, Box 1/1 Linford
10. NN, *William Cowper*, Longman, Essex, 1960, p.5

CHAPTER 1.

1. WEC, p.46
2. PP, p.143
3. The Tune the Old Cow Died of, CP, p. 293
4. NN Five Rivers, CP p.11
5. NN, PP, p.20
6. NN, WEC, p10
7. NN, WEC, p.12
8. Keith Richardson, *Whitehaven News,* 14/9/72
9. NN, WEC, p.18
10. NN, WEC, p.9
11. NN, WEC, p.24
12. NN, WEC, p.29
13. NN, PP, p.80
14. NN, Comprehending It Not, CP p.363
15. NN, WEC, p.41
16. NN, WEC, p.42
17. JRL DCC, NN to DC, 9th April 1973
18. NN, WEC, p.50
19. NN, WEC, p.52
20. NN, WEC, p.62
21. NN, WEC, p.62
22. NN, Boo to a Goose, CP, p. 273
23. NN, WEC, p.67
24. NN, WEC, p.118

CHAPTER 2.

1. NN, WEC, p.171
2. NN, WEC, pp.70-71
3. NN, WEC, p.71
4. NN, WEC, p.72
5. NN, WEC, p.82
6. NN, PP, p.11
7. NN, WEC, p.82
8. Doreen Cornthwaite, interview 2012
9. NN, WEC, p.79
10. NN, WEC, p. 78
11. NN, WEC, p.84
12. NN, WEC, p.84
13. NN, WEC, p.98
14. NN, WEC, p.97
15. NN, WEC, p.88
16. NN, WEC, p.88
17. NN, WEC, p.92-3
18. NN, WEC, p.93
19. NN, WEC, p.93
20. NN, WEC, p.100

21. JRL, NCN 15/3/1, August 28th 1924
22. JRL, NCN 15/3/1, January 1st, 1923
23. NN, WEC, p.100
24. NN, PP, p.74
25. NN, WEC, p.100
26. NN, WEC, p.146
27. NN, WEC, p.105
28. NN, WEC, p.106
29. NN, WEC, p.109
30. NN, WEC, p.150
31. NN, WEC, p.151
32. NN, WEC, p.13
33. NN, PP, p.147

CHAPTER 3.

1. NN, WEC, p. 160
2. JRL, LL, 7th September, 1934
3. NN, WEC, p.172
4. NN, WEC, p.171
5. NN, WEC, p.168
6. NN, WEC, p.170
7. NN, WEC, p.165
8. NN, WEC, p.165
9. NN, WEC, p.167
10. NN, WEC, p.167
11. NN, WEC, p.168
12. NN, WEC, p.175
13. NN, WEC, p.176
14. NN, WEC, p.176
15. NN, WEC, p.179
16. NN, WEC, p.181
17. NN, WEC, p.183

CHAPTER 4.

1. Henry, Augustine, *Forests, Woods and Trees in Relation to Hygiene,* Constable, London, 19p.21
2. NN, WEC, p.185
3. NN, WEC, p.185
4. NN, WEC, p.190
5. NN, *They Became Christians*, ed. Dewi Morgan, Mowbray, London, 1966, p.101
6. NN, WEC, p.192
7. NN, WEC, p.195
8. NN, WEC, p.191
9. NN, WEC, p. 191
10. NN, WEC, p.191

11. NN, WEC, p.195
12. NN, WEC, p.199
13. JRL LL, Box 1/1 Linford
14. JRL LL, Box 1/1 Linford
15. JRL LL, Box 1/1 Linford
16. JRL LL, Box 1/1 Linford
17. Yeo, Dr Isaac Burney, *The Therapeutics of Mineral Springs and Climates,* Funk & Wagnells, New York, 1910.
18. NN, WEC, p.199
19. JRL NCN7/1/4/12, 5th Sept, 1963, *The Listener*
20. NN, WEC, pp.201-2

CHAPTER 5
1. JRL LL, Box 1/1 Linford Oct. 6th ?1932
2. JRL LL, Box 1/4 Westcliff on Sea, Whit Sunday 1933
3. JRL LL, Box 1/5 Wilmslow, Nov 3rd 1934
4. JRL LL, Box 1/5 Wilmslow, Nov 3rd 1934
5. JRL LL, Box 2/folder 1, Haywards Heath, April 20th 33
6. JRL LL, Box 2/folder 1 Linford, March 10th 1933
7. JRL LL, Box 1/4 Westclliff on Sea, Dec 9th 1934
8. JRL LL, Box 1/1 Linford, Wed Apr 19,?1933
9. JRL LL, Box 2/folder 1, Haywards Heath, April 20th 1933
10. JRL LL, Box 2/3 misc, Aug 7th
11. JRL LL, Box 1/3 Dalston, 26th May 1933
12. JRL LL, Box 1/4 Westcliff on Sea, April 3rd 1934
13. JRL LL, Box 2/folder 1, ?Haywards Heath, April 20th 33
14. JRL LL, Box 1/3 Dalston, Oct 8th 1933
15. JRL LL, Box 1/3 Dalston Sunday May 6th ? 1934
16. JRL LL, Box 1/3 Dalston, July 10th 1934
17. JRL LL, Box 1/1 Linford, Dec. 27th 1933
18. JRL LL, Box 1/1 Linford, July 21st 34
19. JRL LL, Box 1/5 Wilmslow, Nov 3rd 1934
20. JRL NCN Accession No 2002/001
21. NCN 1/2/14/1-20
22. NN, Musings on Modern Poetry, *Church Times*, 22, November, 1957
23. JRL LL, Box 1/3 Dalston, Sunday, June 13th, ?1935
24. JRL LL, Box 1/6 (Montana), Jan 21st ?1935
25. JRL LL, Box 1/3 Dalston, July 13th 1934
26. JRL LL, Box 1/3 Dalston, March 23rd?Year
27. JRL LL, Box 1/5 Wilmslow, Sunday June 30th 1935
28. JRL LL, Box 2/3 misc, Aug 7th ? Year
29. JRL LL, Box 2/3 misc, July 24th ? 1936
30. NN, Obituary, *Church Times*, 9 November 1956

CHAPTER 6
1. Sept 12th – 1937 JRL NCN Janet Martin Accession 2011/044

2. Sept 12th – 1937 JRL NCN Janet Martin Accession 2011/044
3. Letter from TS Eliot to George Every, 27 Sept. 1937, quoted in Philip Gardner, *Norman Nicholson*.
4. 11th Feb 38, NN to Mrs Hamer, NCN Janet Martin Accession 2011/044
5. JRL LL Box 2/3 misc., 10th Feb 1938
6. NN 'Memories of the WEA', mss Hunt family
7. NN *Cumberland and Westmorland*, p.212
8. NN 'Memories of the WEA', mss Hunt family
9. Five Rivers, CP, p.11-13
10. NN, Memories of the WEA, mss Hunt family
11. *PN Review* - David Wright Interview, Issue 46, 1985
12. Interview, Melvyn Bragg, 2012
13. JRL DPW1/14, 29/10/68
14. JRL LL, Box 2/3 misc, 19th December 1939
15. JRL LL, Box 2/1 Haywards Heath, 27th May 1940
16. NN to GE, March 20th, 1940
17. Clement Mullenger, 'Thoughts on Returning from Abroad'
18. JRL LL, Box 2/3 misc, 19th December 1939
19. Now That I Have Made my Decision, CP, p.406

CHAPTER 7.

1. Box 2/1 Haywards Heath, 27th May 1940
2. NN to GE, March 20th 1940, quoted in Philip Gardner, *Norman Nichol-son*
3. NN to GE, 24th February, 1938, ibid
4. NN, 'The Image in My Poetry', *Orpheus,* II, London 1949, p.121
5. Poem, CP, p.408
6. NN interview with Peter Orr, (ed.) *The Poet Speaks,* London, 1966, p.156
7. JRL, DPW1/31, 22/8/1986
8. Kathleen Raine, *Autobiographies*, p.190
9. Val Corbett, *A Rhythm, a Rite and a Ceremony*, Midnight Oil, Penrith, 1996, p.20
10. Val Corbett, *A Rhythm, a Rite and a Ceremony,* Midnight Oil, Penrith, 1996, p.10
11. Kathleen Raine, *Autobiographies*, p. 206
12. Cockley Moor, Dockray, Penrith, CP, p.27
13. Val Corbett, *A Rhythm, a Rite and a Ceremony,* Midnight Oil, Penrith, 1996, p.20
14. I am indebted to Prof. Alan Beattie's thoughts here, *Comet,* Vol 7.
15. Kathleen Raine, *Autobiographies*
16. VW, Diaries, Vol. V, Hogarth Press, 1984, p.245
17. Above Ullswater, CP, p.143
18. For a fuller discussion of this subject, see Professor Alan Beattie, Comet, Vol 7, Issues 1&2, pp. 1-5
19. Night in Martindale, copyright *Collected Poems of Kathleen Raine,* 2000
20. The Candle, CP, p.162
21. JRL NCN2/1-15, 1st March 1941
22. Carol for Holy Innocents Day, CP, p.4

23. NN, *An Anthology of Religious Verse,* Penguin, London 1942, pp.ix-x
24. Cleator Moor, CP, pp.16-17
25. Evacuees, CP, p.54
26. *John O'London's Weekly* 28th August 1942
27. *Man and Literature*, p.214

CHAPTER 8.

1. *The Presbyter,* Feb. 1944
2. TS Eliot, *After Strange Gods,* London, 1934, p.38
3. JRL NCN1/1/4 – AC to NN
4. JRL NCN1/1/4 – AC to NN
5. JRL NCN7/2/4/56
6. George Barker, *The Spectator* 4th Feb 1944
7. NN, Memories of the WEA , mss Hunt family
8. John Betjeman, *Daily Herald,* 6th May, 1944
9. *New English Writing* 31st Aug 1944
10. JRL NCN2/2/2
11. JRL NCN1/1/1, AY to NN, 31st July, 1944
12. For the Grieg Centenary, CP, p.36
13. Philip Gardner, *Norman Nicholson,* [PG] p.54
14. NN 'The Comic Prophet', *The Listener,* 6th August, 1953
15. September in Shropshire, CP, p.43-4
16. NCN1/1/3/1, AR to NN, 22nd April 1943
17. The Boathouse, CP, pp.196-7
18. JRL LL, Box 2/3 misc, 14th March 1944
19. *The Times* 23rd Sept 1944
20. *The Observer* 10th Sept 1944
21. *John O'London's Weekly,* 22nd Sept 1944
22. Askam Unvisited, CP, pp.37-38

CHAPTER 9.

1. Browne, E.M. & H., *Two in One,* Cambridge University Press, Cambridge, 1981, p.153
2. JRL NCN1/1/16/2
3. Browne, E.M. & H., *Two in One,* p.156-7
4. JRL, NCN1/1/8 Mercury Theatre, 21st Sept. 1945
5. JRL, NCN1/1/11 KR to NN 7th April, 1946
6. *The Old Man of the Mountains, Pt. I,* p.12-13
7. *The Old Man of the Mountains, Pt. I,* p.15
8. *The Old Man of the Mountains, Pt.I* p.19
9. JRL NCN7/1/3/5 *Church Times*
10. JRL, NCN1/1/13, 5th Nov. 1947
11. JRL, NCN1/1/8, 17th Feb 1946
12. Browne, E.M. & H., *Two in One,* p.158
13. Browne, E.M. & H., *Two in One,* p.160
14. JRL, NCN1/1/12-17/12 GS to NN, 19th Jan. 1947

15. JRL NCN1/1/15/1, MS to NN 20th May 1947
16. *The Spectator* 10th Oct. 1947, DS Savage
17. *The Listener,* 30th Oct 1947
18. JRL LL, Box 2/2 Hayward's Heath 17th Jan. 1948
19. *The Listener*, 22nd July, 1943
20. Philip Gardner, *Norman Nicholson*, [PG] p.58
21. PG, pp.63-64
22. Howard Sergeant, *Poetry Quarterly,* Autumn 1948, p. 105
23. Kathleen Raine, *New English Review,* Jan. 1949
24. St Luke's Summer, CP, p.132
25. Across the Estuary, CP, pp.166-9
26. Ridler, Anne, *Memoirs,* p.201-2, Perpetua Press, Oxford, 2004

CHAPTER 10.

1. JRL NCN1/1/22/1, 21st December 1949 J.C. Hobbs – NN
2. C&W, p.10
3. C&W, p.17
4. BHD tapes
5. C&W, p.72
6. C&W, p.74
7. C&W, p.231
8. C&W, p.209
9. C&W, pp.59-61
10. C&W, p.26
11. JRL NCN1/1/21/1-6, 1st Dec. 1949 Mary C. Fair to NN; 7th Jan. 1950 Mary C. Fair to RH
12. BHD Tapes
13. WW, p.ix
14. WW, p.xii
15. WW, p.xiii
16. WW, p.xiv
17. WW, p.xix-xx
18. See *The Image of the City,* Charles Williams, ed. Anne Ridler
19. JRL NCN1/1/3/1/, 1st April, 1959
20. WW, p.xxvi
21. HGW, pp.9-10
22. HGW, p.98
23. HGW, p.49
24. HGW, p.80
25. HGW, p.98
26. *On My Thirty-fifth Birthday,* CP, p.223
27. HGW, p.32
28. PG, p.125
29. HGW, p.27
30. PG, p.126
31. *Prophesy to the Wind,* p.61
32. Ibid, p.23
33. NN to GE, 7th Oct 1951, Quoted in Philip Gardner

34. Conversations with Anna Hopewell
35. JRL NCN 16/6/1
36. Alan Beattie, *Comet,* Vol.6, Issue 3, 2011, p.5

CHAPTER 11.

1. Cowper BC, p.6
2. Cowper BC, p.5
3. WC, p.82
4. Cowper BC, p.12
5. WC, p.127
6. WC, p. 19
7. Cowper, William, *The Task*, Book III
8. JRL NCN1/1/27, Mary Barklam Johnson to NN, 5th Nov 1951
9. NN *Orpheus*, II, 1949,
10. JRL NCN7/1/4/4, *The Listener*, 24th Jan 1952
11. JRL, NCN1/1/30/1&2, PH Newby to NN, 17th Jan 1952
12. MFTD, p.34
13. MFTD, p.40
14. MFTD, p.32
15. MFTD, p.75
16. NN to GE 28th Aug 1953, quoted in Philip Gardner
17. PG, p.140
18. PG, p.136
19. NCN1/1/23/ 19th June 1959
20. PG, p.133
21. PG, p.134
22. JRL NCN7/2/20
23. WW, p.xxv
24. PG, p.135
25. MFTD, p.79
26. Professor Yvonne Sherwood, *The Prostitute and the Prophet*, Sheffield Academic Press, 2004
27. Prof. Alan Beattie, *Comet*, Vol 6, Issue 3, 2011
28. *The Sunday Times,* 6th Sept 1953
29. *The Manchester Guardian,* 6th Sept 1955
30. 'The Introvert', 12th Sept 1937 JRL NCN Janet Martin Accession 2011/044

CHAPTER 12.

1. WC, p. 137
2. The Pot Geranium, CP, p.179
3. From a Boat at Coniston, CP, p.195
4. The Buzzer, CP, p.226
5. JRL, LL, Box 2/1 Hayward's heath, ? 10th May 1954
6. JRL NCN1/1/31-41, Canon Sam Taylor to NN, 15th February, 1954
7. PP, p.46

8. Kathleen Raine, *Encounter*, March 1955
9. *The Lakers,* p.213
10. Ibid, p.214
11. Ibid, p.215
12. PG, p.94
13. JRL, NCN1/1/36
14. JRL, NCN1/1 /43/3
15. JRL, NCN7/2/22
16. *The London Magazine* Aug. 1954, Vol 1, No.7, pp.86-93
17. JRL, NCN1/1/39, JL to NN, 19th July 1954
18. JRL NCN1/1/3/1, AR to NN, 27th Aug. 1954
19. JRL NCN1/1/40, SG to NN, 4th Aug. 1954
20. PP, p.114

CHAPTER 13

1. JRL, NCN1/1/34, 18th Sept 1953
2. JRL, NCN7/1/45 12th August 1954, *The Listener*, 'On Being a Provincial'
3. JRL, LL, Box 2/1 Hayward's Heath, 30th May 1956
4. Rosemary Joyce, ms Doreen Cornthwaite
5. 'Letters from Cumberland', 4th April 1974, *The Listener*
6. Windscale, CP, p. 282
7. Roger Highfield, *Daily Telegraph*, 9th Oct. 2007
8. Maryport Educational Settlement, Annual Report, 1957/58
9. Pamela Kiely to Philip Gardner, 5th Feb, 1968, PG, p.144
10. *Birth by Drowning,* p.56
11. Ibid, p.58
12. *Church Times,* 3rd June, 1960
13. *TLS* 8th July 1960
14. PG, p.151
15. JRL NCN1/1/54, 15th July 1959
16. An Anthology of Summer, *John O'London's Weekly*, 8th July 1949
17. PP, p.190
18. PP, pp.189/90
19. 'Bob', private collection
20. PG, p. 100
21. PP, p.185
22. PP, p.187
23. PP, p.80
24. PP, p.74
25. PP, p.64
26. PP, p.63
27. PP, p.68
28. PP, p.107
29. 'No Poetry in Railways' , *The Listener*, 4th Dec, 1958
30. 'Regional Poets of the Forties', *Aquarius*, No 17/18, 1987, pp.84-89
31. JRL LL, Box 2/1 Hayward's Heath, 17th Jan 1960
32. JRL NCN7/1/4/10
33. *New Statesman*, 17th October, 1959

34. *The Observer*, 11th October, 1959
35. JRL NCN7/1/4/9 *The Listener*, 26th June 1958
36. JRL NCN7/1/4/10 *TLS* 15th Aug 1958
37. Patrick Kavanagh, 'The Parish and the Universe', *Collected Prose*, MacGib-bon and Kee, Dublin, 1967
38. NN to AY, 28th Aug, 1960

CHAPTER 14.
1. 'Poets of the Fifties' BBC Home Service 25th Sept. 1956
2. Interview with David Wright, *PN Review*, Issue 46, 1985
3. *North Face*, quoted in PG, p.95
4. ms letter Hunt family
5. JRL NCN1/1/60 1st February 1960
6. 'Poets of the Fifties', BBC Home Service 25th sept. 1956
7. David Wright, *PN Review*, Issue 46, 1985
8. JRL NCN1/1/82, HS to NN
9. Rosemary Joyce, DC mss
10. Bessie Schiff to Rosemary Joyce, Private Collection
11. NCN1/1/63/1, 28th April 1961, Sheila Fell to NN
12. Anne Ridler, *Memoirs*, The Perpetua Press, Oxford, 2004
13. JRL NCN1/1/51, 3rd Sept. 1957 Norman Burkett to Norman Nicholson
14. JRL NCN7/2/27
15. DPW1/19, NN to DW, 7th Nov 71
16. Rosemary Joyce, MS Sarah and James Ross
17. NCN1/1/69/2, 26th April 1963
18. JRL NCN1/1/72, Border TV to NN, 7th Jan. 1964
19. JRL LL, Box 2/2 Haywards Heath
20. Roger Bush, April 2012, *Comet*, page 12
21. JRL LL, Box 2/2 Hayward's Heath – 13th Jan 1967
22. http://en.wikipedia.org/wiki/A._L._Rowse
23. JRL NCN1/1/113, 22nd August, 1967 A.L. Rowse to NN
24. Rene Chaplin, Mss, Sarah and James Ross
25. NCN1/1/135, RC to NN
26. 'Regional Poets of the Forties', *Aquarius*, No 17/18, 1987, pp.84-89
27. *PN Review*, Interview with David Wright
28. BHD Tapes
29. The Seventeenth of That Name, CP, pp.311-313

CHAPTER 15.
1. Glen Orchy, CP, p.358
2. On the Closing of Millom Ironworks, CP, p.297
3. Sue Dawson, *Comet*, Vol. 6, Issue 2, p.15
4. The Tune the Old Cow Died Of, CP, p.294
5. On the Dismantling of Millom Ironworks, CP, pp359-360
6. JRL DC, NN to DC, 22nd Nov. 68
7. The Cock's Nest, CP, p.310

8. Great Day, CP, p.308
9. Giorgio Melchiori, 'Norman Nicholson e altri poeti inglesi', *Lo Spettatore Italiano* VIII.
10. JRL, DC, 9th May 74
11. PG, p.153
12. PG, p.159
13. PG, pp. 159-161
14. NN to Liz Joyce, 29 Dec.1972, Private collection
15. *Comet*, Vol. 7, No1&2, p.1-6
16. *Cumbrian Brothers,* David A. Cross, Fell Foot Press, Carlisle, 2007, p. 7
17. Walney Island, CP, p.187
18. PK Letters, Chris Wadsworth
19. *Cumbrian Brothers,* David A. Cross, Fell foot Press, 2007
20. The Dumb Spirit, CP, p.265
21. The Elm Decline, CP, pp.283-5
22. JRL NCN7/2/31
23. *The Listener,* 26th Oct. 1972
24. *New Statesman* 1st Dec. 72
25. JRL NCN1/1/3/1, AR to NN, 14th Dec. 72
26. JRL NCN1/1/52, 3rd Feb. 1973
27. JRL NCN1/1/52 21st Feb. 1973

CHAPTER 16.

1. 'Letter From Cumberland', 4th June 1973 to Ted Fisher, The Listener, 4th April 1974
2. Ibid
3. 'Letter from Cumberland', 17th Jan 1973 to Liz Joyce,
4. JRL DC, 5th April, 1973
5. 'Letter from Cumberland', July 23rd, 1973, NN to JE Fisher, The Listener, 4th April 1974
6. Ibid
7. JRL NCN7/1/4/19
8. JRL DC, NN to DC, 27th July 74
9. JRL DC, NN to DC, 8th Jan 74
10. WC, p.16
11. Conversations with Dr David Cooper
12. WEC
13. Matt Simpson to Doreen Cornthwaite, 21st April 89
14. JRL NCN7/2/34
15. JRL NCN1/1/164/1-3
16. BHD Tapes
17. JRL NCN7/2/33 Stitch and Stone
18. JRL NCN1/1/135 Sid and Rene Chaplin 1970 – 1986
19. *Poetry Review,* Vol 70, No 1-2, Sept 1980
20. Hard of Hearing, CP, pp.365-6
21. JRL DCC, 29th Sept. 76
22. JRL DCC, 7th December 76
23. JRL DCC, 18th Jan. 76

24. JRL DCC, 18th Oct. 76
25. JRL DPW1/2
26. JRL DCC, 9th April 1973
27. BHD Tapes

CHAPTER 17.

1. NN to Sir John Betjeman, 28th Sept. 1977, Sarah & James Ross
2. Yvonne Nicholson, mss Sarah Ross, interview Liz Simpson
3. Black Combe White, CP, pp.327-8
4. Beck, CP, pp.319-20
5. NCN7/1/4/19 Poetry Book Society Bulletin Sea to the West
6. The Shadow of Black Combe, CP, pp.325-6
7. JRL NCN1/1/103, CC to NN
8. *The Sunday Times* 21st June, 1981
9. *The Observer*, 2nd Aug. 1981
10. *Poetry Review* vol 71, No 4
11. JRL NCN7/3/ 1, Robin Skelton, *Stand*
12. BBC Kaleidoscope, 11th June, 1984
13. JRL DCC, 30th March, 1981
14. JRL DCC, 27th July, 1981
15. JRL DCC, 24th August, 1981
16. The letters of Yvonne Nicholson, private collection
17. JRL DCC, 24th May 1982
18. JRL DPW1/26
19. Sea to the West, CP, p.339
20. JRL CC to NN, 12th Sept 1982
21. JRL NCN1/1/3/1 AR to NN – 23rd sept 1982
22. NCN1/1/221 Ted Hughes to NN

CHAPTER 18.

1. NN to Rosemary Joyce– 11th Sept 1982, private collection
2. Ibid, 26th Nov 1982
3. JRL DCC, 15th June, 1983
4. JRL DCC, 21st Aug. 1983
5. JRL DCC, 8th July 1983
6. JRL NCN1/1/220
7. JRL DCC 1st Dec. 1983
8. JRL DCC, 11th May, 1984
9. JRL DCC, 11th May, 1984
10. JRL NCN6/6/1, JR to NN
11. JRL DCC, 18th April, 1984
12. JRL DCC 12th Sept. 1984
13. Frances Harland, source unknown, see *A Shell in My Hand: Verses*, Frances Harland, Dulwich Village, Outposts Publications, 1957
14. Comet Come, CP, p.431
15. JRL NCN7/3/8, Peter Swaab, *Cambridge Review*, June 1985, vol 106,

No. 2287
16. *PN Review* – David Wright Interview, Issue 46 1985
17. JRL DPW1/31, NN to DW, 22nd Aug.1986
18. The New Graveyard, CP, p.376
19. Norman Nicholson, Talk, 1953, mss Hunt family

POSTSCIPT.

1. Private Collection, 13th June 1987
2. Private Collection, 17th June 1987
3. Private Collection, June 1987
4. MS to DC, 21st April 1989
5. *Poetry Review* Vol 84, No 4, Winter 1994/95, p.73
6. *The Pastoral Mode*, Loughrey, Bryan, ed. Macmillan, London, 1984, p.154
7. *Green Voices*, Gifford, Terry, Manchester University Press, Manchester, 1995
8. *London Review of Books*, vol 4, no3, Feb 1982
9. Paul Kingsnorth, 'Out on the Stubborn Skerry', http://dark-mountain.net/out-on-the-stubborn-skerry/
10. *Poetry and Geography*, ed. Neal Alexander and David Cooper, Liverpool University Press, Liverpool, 2013
11. Gathering Sticks on Sunday, CP, p.209

SELECT BIBLIOGRAPHY

The bulk of Norman Nicholson's papers can be found at the John Rylands Library, Manchester University, Manchester, UK. There are also papers at the following locations:-

DM1 107 Penguin Books Ltd, (restricted) University of Bristol Library
William Plomer Collection, University of Durham Library
John Bate Collection, Edinburgh,
BBC Written Archives Centre
University of Leeds, Brotherton Library
National Library of Wales
University of Reading
University College, London Library
University of Hull, Brynmor Jones Library
Bodleian Library (Anne Ridler)
Literary and Philosophical Society, Newcastle Upon Tyne
Harry Ransom Humanities Research Centre, University of Texas, Austin

Books and Pamphlets by Norman Nicholson: -
A Choice of William Cowper's Verse, Faber and Faber, London, 1951
A Local Habitation, Faber and Faber, London, 1972
A Match for the Devil, Faber and Faber, London, 1955
An Anthology of Religious Verse, Penguin, Middlesex, England,1942
Birth by Drowning, Faber and Faber, London, 1960
Candy-Floss Tree, The, with Gerda Mayer, Frank Flynn, OUP, Oxford 1984
Cloud over Black Combe, Pig Press, Durham, 1976
Collected Poems, ed. Neil Curry, Faber and Faber, London 1994
Cumberland and Westmorland, Robert Hale Ltd, London, 1949
Fire of the Lord, The, Nicholson and Watson, London, E.P. Dutton &

Co, New York, 1944
Five Rivers, Faber and Faber, London, 1944
Greater Lakeland, (re-write of *Cumberland and Westmorland*) Robert Hale Ltd, London, 1969
Green Shore, The, Nicholson and Watson, London, 1947
H.G. Wells, Arthur Barker Ltd, London, 1950
Lake District, The, An Anthology, Robert Hale Ltd, London, 1977
Lakers, The, Robert Hale Ltd, London, 1955
Lakes, The, (re-write of *Portrait of the Lakes*), Robert Hale Ltd, London,1977
Man and Literature, SCM Press, London, 1943
No Star on the Way Back, Manchester Institute of Contemporary Arts, Manchester, 1967
Old Man of the Mountains, The, Faber and Faber, London, 1945
Portrait of the Lakes, Robert Hale Ltd, London, 1963
Pot Geranium, The, Faber and Faber, London, 1954
Prophesy to the Wind, Faber and Faber, London, 1947
Provincial Pleasures, Robert Hale Ltd, London, 1959
Rock Face, Faber and Faber, London, 1948
Sea to the West, Faber and Faber, London, 1981
Selected Poems, Faber and Faber, London, 1982
Shadow of Black Combe, The, Mid Northumberland Arts Group, Ashington, 1978
Stitch and Stone, Ceolfrith Press, Sunderland, 1975
Wednesday Early Closing, Faber and Faber, London 1975
William Cowper, John Lehmann, London, 1951
William Cowper: Writers and Their Work, British Council Edition, Longman, Essex, 1960.
Wordsworth; An Introduction and a Selection, Phoenix House, London, 1949

Contributions, Articles, Lectures by Norman Nicholson quoted:-
'Letter From Cumberland', *The Listener*, April 4th 1974
'Millom Delivered', *The Listener*, Jan. 24th 1952
'Modern Verse Drama and the Folk Tradition', *Critical Quarterly*, Summer, 1960.
'Musings on Modern Poetry', *Church Times*, Nov. 22nd, 1957
'No Poetry in Railways' , *The Listener*, Dec. 4th 1958
'Notes on The Way' - 'The Affirmative Way', *Time and Tide*, July 21st

1951
'On Being a Provincial', *The Listener*, Aug. 12th 1954
PN Review – Interview with David Wright, Issue 46 1985
'Poets of the Fifties' BBC Home Service 25th Sept. 1956
'The Abandoned Muse', Theatre Arts, New York, Aug.-Sept. 1948
'The Comic Prophet', *The Listener*, Aug. 6th, 1953
'The Image in My Poetry', *Orpheus*, II, London 1949
'The Long Poem', *Stand* VIII, 3 1966-67
'The Poet Needs an Audience', *Orpheus*, I, London 1948-9
The Poet Speaks, Routledge and Kegan Paul, London, 1966, Interview with Peter Orr, (ed.)
'The Provincial Tradition,' *Times Literary Supplement*, August 15th, 1958
They Became Christians, ed. Dewi Morgan, Mowbray, London, 1966
'Where England Begins', The Listener, June 26th 1958

Other Books and Articles

Between Comets: For Norman Nicholson at 70, ed. William Scammell, Durham, Taxus, 1984

Boyd, David, 'Norman Nicholson: The Fire of the Lord and The Green Shore', http://vulpeslibris.wordpress.com/2011/07/20/norman-nicholson-the-fire-of-the-lord-and-the-green-shore/

Cooper, David, 'The Poetics of Place and Space: Wordsworth, Norman Nicholson and the Lake District', *Literature Compass*, 5 (2008): 807-21.

Cooper, David, 'The Post-Industrial Picturesque: Placing and Promoting Marginalized Millom'. *The Making of a Cultural Landscape: The English Lake District as Tourist Destination, 1750-2010*, Ashgate, London, 2013

Cooper, David and Alexander, Neal, ed. *Poetry and Geography*, Liverpool University Press, Liverpool, 2013

Corbett, Val, *A Rhythm, a Rite and a Ceremony: Helen Sutherland at Cockley Moor*, Midnight Oil, Penrith, 1996.

Cross, David A., *Cumbrian Brothers: Letters from Percy Kelly to Norman Nicholson*, Fell Foot Press, Carlisle, 2007.

Curry, Neil, *Norman Nicholson*, Northern Lights, Carlisle, 2001.

Curry, Neil, Introduction to *Collected Poems*, Faber and Faber, London 1994

Browne, E. Martin and Browne, Henzie, *Two in One*, Cambridge

University Press, Cambridge, 1981.

Farley, Paul and Roberts, Michael Symmons, *Edgelands: Journeys into England's True Wilderness.* London, Jonathan Cape, 2011.

Gardner, Philip, *Norman Nicholson,* Twayne Publishers Inc, New York, 1973.

Gifford, Terry, *Green Voices*, Critical, Cultural and Communications Press, Nottingham, 2011.

Henry, Augustine, *Forests, Woods and Trees in Relation to Hygiene*, Constable, London, 1919.

Kingsnorth, Paul, 'Out on the Stubborn Skerry', *The Dark Mountain Blog*, 16th Aug. 2010, http://dark-mountain.net/out-on-the-stubborn-skerry/

Raine, Kathleen, *Autobiographies*, Skoob Books Publishing, London, 1991.

Raine, Kathleen, *Collected Poems*, Hamish Hamilton, London, 1956.

Ridler, Anne, *Memoirs*, The Perpetua Press, Oxford, 2004

Roberts, Michael, and Ridler, Anne, *The Faber Book of Modern Verse*, Faber and Faber, London, 1951

Sergeant, Howard, 'A Northern Poet: Norman Nicholson', *Northern Review*, Aug. 1946

Skelton, Robin, 'The Poems of Norman Nicholson', *Stand*, X, 3, 1969

Stanford, Derek, *The Freedom of Poetry*, London, Falcon Press, 1947

Williams, Raymond, *Drama from Ibsen to Eliot*, London, Chatto and Windus, 1952

Yeo, Isaac Burney, *The Therapeutics of Mineral Springs and Climates*, Funk & Wagnells, New York, 1910.

INDEX

A
Anglia, 187
Auden, W.H., 63, 85, 89, 163, 232

B
Banner, Delmar, 153, 172
Barker, George, 13, 84, 86, 94, 132, 148, 240
BBC, 55, 90, 109, 128, 134-5, 146, 158, 169, 194-5, 198
Betjeman, Sir John, 13, 95, 177, 179, 207-8, 240, 246
Bragg, Sir Melvyn, 9, 12, 210, 217, 220, 230, 239
Browne, E. Martin, 102-4, 107, 135, 137, 150, 222, 240, 250
Bunting, Basil, 178-9

C
Carnelli, Joseph, 186
Causley, Charles, 12, 210, 215
Chaplin, Sid, 12, 178, 183, 202, 214, 224, 244-5
Cholmondeley Award, 187
Clarke, Jean, 10, 213
Comfort, Alex, 89, 90, 93-4
Cooper, Dr David, 9, 232, 245n
Cornthwaite, Doreen, 9, 184, 187, 189, 197, 200, 204-5, 212, 213, 214, 215, 217-8, 220, 226, 230, 235-6n, 243n, 245n
Cornthwaite, Eliza, 22, 24-7,
Cornthwaite, William, 22-3, 39
Cowper, William, 14-15, 109, 111, 125, 130-132, 142-3, 170, 199, 235n, 242n, 248-9n
Criterion, The, 70, 77
Critical Quarterly, The, 17
Curry, Neil, 9, 205, 230, 248n, 250n

D

Dennis, Brindley Hallam, (see Mike Smith)
Douglas, Keith, 91

E
Eastick, Liz (nee Joyce), 9, 189, 194-5, 207, 214-5, 218-220, 222, 244n, 245n, 246n,
Edgelands, 232, 250n
Edinburgh Festival, 138, 151,
Educational Settlement, The, 157, 178, 243n
Eliot, T.S., 60-63, 69-70, 73-76, 80, 85, 89-98, 102-3, 105-106, 110, 127, 148, 163, 170-1, 179, 188, 210, 221-4, 238n, 240n, 251n
Every, Bro. George, 63, 69, 73-6, 84-5, 92, 102, 127, 135, 138-9, 150, 153, 188, 238n

F
Faber and Faber, 73, 91, 94, 96, 106, 110, 117, 141, 147, 170, 200, 205, 210-211, 218, 222, 228, 230, 235n, 248n, 249n, 250n, 251n
Farley, Paul, 232, 250n
Fell, Sheila, 172, 244n
Fisher, John 'Ted', 39, 54, 60, 63, 67, 90, 170-1, 194, 245n
Frost, Robert, 95
Fry, Christopher, 103

G
Garnier, Enrica, 12, 63, 67-9, 73, 81, 92, 97-8, 100-1, 111, 113, 117, 128, 143, 173, 216, 227
Gardner, Philip, 82, 110, 127, 133, 136-7, 147, 158, 161, 187-9, 197, 211, 235n, 239-243n
Gardner, Yvonne, 9, 12, 149-150, 153-4, 158-9, 161, 165, 171-7, 183-7, 189-191, 193, 195-7, 201-4, 206-8, 210, 212-220, 222-3, 225-8, 246n
Gendle, Sylvia, 128-9
Gifford, Terry, 231
Green Room Club, The, Carlisle, 151

H
Hall, J.C., 91
Heaney, Seamus, 140, 187, 192, 220, 224
Heinemann Prize, 106
Horizon, 90, 133,
Hughes, Ted, 12, 39, 170, 178, 207, 216, 222, 246n
Hunt, Irvine, 205, 210, 217, 222, 226, 228

Huxley, Aldous, 62

J
Jennings, Elizabeth, 79, 171
Jones, David, 79-80, 171
Joyce, Rosemary, 149, 153-4, 172, 176, 189, 214, 217, 219, 222, 226, 228-9, 229, 243-4n, 246n
Joyce, Liz (see Eastick)
Joyce, Sarah, (see Ross)

K
Kafka, Franz, 89
Keily, Pamela, 135
Kelly, Percy, 9, 157, 167, 189-90, 208, 216, 219, 229, 250n
Kingsnorth, Paul, 231-2, 247n, 251n

L
Larkin, Philip, 13, 170, 171, 193, 205
Lawrence, D.H., 48, 85, 88-9, 92, 152
Lehmann, John, 86, 132, 148
Linford Sanatorium, 44-50, 52, 56-60, 68, 73, 103, 118, 141, 161, 235-8n
Listener, The, 17, 55, 70, 77-8, 80, 92, 94, 109, 134, 152, 192, 194, 223, 238-250n
London Club Theatre Group, 138
Lowell, Robert, 179-80
Lubelsky, Sylvia, 50-51, 53-59, 60-62, 67-8, 70, 73, 75-6, 83, 90, 92, 94, 103, 106, 109, 120, 141, 153, 173, 177, 198, 224

M
MacDiarmid, Hugh, 138
MacNeice, Louis, 63, 84, 132
Manchester Guardian, The, 92, 99, 213, 242n
Melchiori, Giorgio, 186, 244n
Millom Museum, 196, 229
Modernism, 79, 80, 171, 178, 188, 190, 221
Monteith, Charles, 170, 228

N
New English Weekly, 73, 76, 84, 105

New Verse, 70, 85
Nicholson, Ben, 79, 80, 91
Nicholson, Edith, 23
Nicholson, Harold, 23
Nicholson, Joe, 23, 26-7, 30, 35-8, 41-2, 44, 46-7, 49, 51, 55, 72, 100, 134, 144-5, 162, 185, 223
Nicholson, Maria, 20-21, 27-30, 41, 108, 180, 183, 195
Nicholson, Rosetta (nee Sobey), 26-8, 30-33, 35-9, 41-2, 44, 46-7, 55, 57-8, 67, 72, 100, 134, 144-5, 154, 161, 171-2, 177, 184-6, 189, 198-9, 215, 226

Nicholson Norman:
Birth, 21-2; Death of mother, 23; Father's remarriage, 26; TB diagnosis, 44; First publication, Prose, 55, Poetry, 60; First collection, 71; Heinemann Award, 106; Death of father, 144; Marriage, 153-4; Death of step-mother, 184; Cholmondeley Award, 187; Queen's Gold Medal for Poetry, 12, 13, 207-8; OBE, 12, 212; Hon. MA Manchester University, 186, 193, 219; Hon. MA Open University, 203; Death of Yvonne, 215, 218; Hon. Doctorate Liverpool University, 210; South Bank Show, 12, 220, 225; Death, 226.
Publications: *A Local Habitation,* 188, 191, 193, 194, 210, 211, 248n; *A Match for the Devil,* 135, 137-9, 144, 149, 151, 248n; *An Anthology of Religious Verse* (ed), 85, 87, 248n; *Birth By Drowning,* 158-9, 165, 169, 248n; *Cumberland and Westmorland,* 35, 100, 111, 117-8, 123, 133, 170, 174, 248n; *Five Rivers,* 71, 91-2, 95-7, 100-1, 106, 109-111, 132, 223, 249n; *Greater Lakeland,* 170, 249n; *H.G. Wells,* 14, 109, 123, 124-5, 249n; *Man and Literature,* 89, 91, 92-5, 249n; *Prophesy to the Wind,* 125, 127, 135, 151, 233, 249n; *Provincial Pleasures,* 147, 152, 159-163, 169, 180, 198, 249n; *Portrait of the Lakes,* 35, 170, 172, 174, 249n; *Rock Face,* 82-84, 107, 110-113, 223, 249n; *Sea to the West,* 118, 202, 209-211, 214, 215, 217-18, 227, 231, 249n; *Stitch and Stone,* 201, 207, 249n; *The Fire of the Lord,* 98, 100, 107, 248, 250n; *The Green Shore,* 107, 109, 149, 249, 250n; *The Lake District: An Anthology,* 210, 249n; *The Lakers,* 145-6, 249n; *The Old Man of the Mountains,* 100, 104-6, 109, 127, 150-1, 249n; *The Pot Geranium,* 61, 115, 141-4, 147-9, 188, 223, 249n; *The Shadow of Black Combe,* 201, 202, 210, 249n; *Wednesday Early Closing,* 24, 32, 198, 199, 200-1, 228, 249n; *William Wordsworth,* 109, 123, 249; *William Cowper,* 14, 15, 109, 111, 125, 130-2, 142-3, 170, 248-9n;

Nicholson, Winifred, 78-9

O
Observer, The, 90, 99, 127, 163, 200, 211, 240n, 246n
Orpheus, 132, 239n, 242n, 250n
Oxford Book of Twentieth Century Verse, 193

P
Paterson, Don, 230-1
Pickard, Tom and Connie, 178
Pilgrim Players, 102, 135
Poetry (Chicago), 69, 70, 84
Poetry (London), 84, 86
Poetry Review, 202, 211, 231, 245n, 246n, 247n
Pound, Ezra, 136, 171, 178

R
Raine, Craig, 170, 200, 218, 220, 222, 228
Raine, Kathleen, 9, 12, 79-84, 86, 90-92, 97, 99, 103, 110-111, 113, 118, 128, 133, 146, 171, 201, 210, 239n, 241n, 242n, 251n
Religious Drama Society, 135, 137
Ridler, Anne, 12, 73, 86, 89-91, 96-7, 102-3, 110, 113, 123, 128, 139, 148, 171-3, 176, 188, 192-3, 200, 210, 216, 220, 228, 241, 244n, 248n, 251n
Roberts, Janet, 70, 77-9, 80, 90, 97, 117,
Roberts, Michael, 69, 70, 77, 79-80, 90, 93, 118
Ross, Sarah (nee Joyce), 9, 189, 207, 214, 215, 219, 222, 225, 244n, 246n
Rowse, A.L., 13, 177-8, 244n

S
Saveri, Robert, 186
Scammell, William, 205, 220, 227, 250n
Schiff, Bessie (nee Satterthwaite), 40, 54, 69, 95, 178, 188, 217, 222, 229, 244n
Sergeant, Howard, 110, 132, 251n
Silkin, Jon, 178, 214
Simpson, Matt, 170, 200, 211, 215, 220, 228, 230-1, 245n
Skelton, Robin, 147-8, 152, 211, 246n, 251n
Smith, Mike (Brindley Hallam Dennis), 9, 206, 235n
Spencer, Margaret, 10, 212

Stand, 178, 211
Sutherland, Graham, 107-8
Sutherland, Helen, 78-80, 82-4, 87, 90, 103, 118, 153, 157, 171, 189, 190, 250n

T
Tambimuttu, M.J., 84-6, 91, 151
Taylor, Canon Samuel, 62-3, 144
Thomas, Dylan, 76, 84, 159, 170
Time and Tide, 91, 249n
Times Literary Supplement, The, (TLS), 14, 76, 92, 107, 151, 158, 164, 192, 197, 200, 218, 235, 243n, 250n
Troll, Peggy, 9, 217, 223, 226, 228, 230

V
Vasconcellos, Josefina de, 153, 172, 229

W
WEA, 71, 76, 88, 93, 95, 157, 239-40
Wells, H.G., 14, 109, 123-5, 133, 249n
Williams, Charles, 87, 91, 122-3, 133-5, 138, 153, 218, 241n
Wordsworth, William, 12, 14, 19, 80, 109, 120-123, 134, 146, 148, 175, 210, 217, 221, 235n, 249n
Wright, David, 12, 205, 208, 210, 215, 220, 224, 239n, 244n, 246n, 250n

Y
Yeats, W.B., 89
Young, Rev. Andrew, 85, 89, 95, 107, 118, 127, 135